PRAISE FOR
OVERNIGHT SUCCESS

"Morris Morrison is a beacon of light that is synonymous with a lighthouse in the harbor, at the darkest of night. Morris has annihilated excuses built by a firm foundation of hope, faith and known ledge, and Overnight Success will do the same for others. You or your organization will be forever changed through the message of this book."

~ **Janet Faulk,** Keller Williams Realty

"Overnight Success shows that true inspiration only comes from an openness to share every aspect of a struggle, while exposing the sacred, the shame, and the triumph. This book strips down the curtain and unveils the passion, love and acceptance of everything that comes in our lives - no matter what it is - and it shows the importance of the people who surround us. Morris Morrison's unyielding desire to help others stems from his own commitment to excellence in his life, and that is an inspiration to everyone because it really does come from the heart."

~ **Rodney Combs,** Microsoft

"This book shows us the importance of being intentional about focusing on what's most important our lives and in business. This book has a message that is much bigger than achieving results or success, it shows us how to get results and how to add value to the lives of everyone around us."

~ **Todd Addair,** GE Healthcare

"There is a lot to be said when a persons formidable years makes them the person that they are. This book will impact you in the same way Morris Morrison impacts our athletes because Morris's journey from New York City to West Virginia instilled in him a passion, desire, faith, & trust to fulfill his calling & dreams. You will benefit from this message by being inspired to never waiver in your calling in life."

~ **Kyle Lynn Veltri,** Womens Golf Coach, University of Notre Dame

"This is a must read for everyone because Morris Morrison is not just a motivator, he's a dreamer - and most of all, a true believer. This message will make you feel the presence of something much bigger than yourself and it will change your focus. This book is an everyday blessing for everyone who reads it!"

~ **Katie Smith,** Halliburton

"The message of Overnight Success will impact you just like Morris does from the stage as a motivational speaker. This book is a great story of what a person can do when they take responsibility for growing their talent regardless of the circumstances they face. Morris is right, success never happens Overnight, and The 7 steps that he includes in the book will help any person who is trying to find their own success. Overnight Success is also great for season leaders who want to be reminded of ways to stay on their path to success."

~ **Kevin Carr,** President of PRO2CEO, Former VP of Player Dev., The NBA

"This story is powerful and I've never had another persons focus and purpose affect me in my life like Morris has. If I had to live on an island with only a few people that I could hand pick to take with me, Morris Morrison is the first person that I would take with me along with my wife!"

~ **Bill Dixon**, 5th/3rd Bank

"Many managers today are often scared or not equipped to make the necessary changes to help them lead vs. manage. Why? Because it requires authenticity, emotional intelligence, commitment and vision. The message that Morris Morrison shares in Overnight Success will touch all levels in your organization. His simple truths will force you to reconsider, reflect and recognize the power of your role in your company. You will say, "Is this a coincidence that I am reading this message right now!"

~ **Nina Harrison,** Director of Product Education, Training & Field Merchandising Support, Electrolux Corporation

"Overnight Success will remind you that you are uniquely made with individual gifts and a purpose. The 7 steps in this book will show you how to live intentionally and they will give you a plan that you can use to grow your gifts. The message in this book will help you to defeat the pull that culture has in our lives and it will help you to transition from surviving, to thriving in everything that you do!"

~ **Jason Babicka**, Xpient Solutions

"You can't afford not to read this book because Overnight Success will force you to examine your life's goals and inspire you to be the person you were destined to be, rather you want it to or not."

~ **Rich Pekar**, Superintendent
Southeastern Greene School District

www.TheOvernightSuccessBook.com

OVERNIGHT

SUCCESS

An Inspiring Story About
Culture, Results & The American Dream

MORRIS MORRISON

WESTLAWN
publish》》ing

OVERNIGHT SUCCESS: *An Inspiring Story About Culture, Results &*
The American Dream

www.TheOvernightSuccessBook.com

The names of some characters in this book have been changed.

First paperback edition 2016.

For information about special discounts or bulk purchases, please contact
Morrison Global Brands: (704) 326-1140 or info@MorrisonGlobal.us

Designed by JH Graphics
Edited by Kristine Tippin

Manufactured and Printed in the United States of America.

ISBN: 978-0-99711582-8-1

To My Little Brother Keenan

"May your heartbeat live on forever."

To Lisa, Gummibear, Darlene, Gwendolyn, Pauline, Roberta, Weida and Aunt Dot

"A man's dreams are nothing without a woman to encourage, inspire, and bring them to life."

CONTENTS

OVERNIGHT
SUCCESS

BOOK FOREWORD

As a professional athlete and coach, I have been around many top performers. When you consistently surround yourself with people who are on top of their game, you realize a few things about their *mindset*. As a coach for one of the top college football programs in the country, my job is to make sure that we build a strong football program – and that starts with culture. The only way to build a strong culture is by building it with the right people. When we recruit players and staff into our family, we look for strong talent that will fit the culture that we are trying to build. We cannot build a successful culture of success by finding *GOOD* talent. We build our culture by finding *GREAT* talent, because it's easy to help great athletes become better. But it's not very easy to help *good* athletes become *great*... there's a BIG difference.

The players, staff, and coaches in our football family at The Ohio State University are all *GREAT* at what they do. But no matter how much talent we have, we still have to *GRIND* and work hard to get better. We are always on the lookout for any new strategy or technique that will help us get better. When we do find something that can help us get better and if we believe in it, we will use it.

We first brought Morris Morrison in to work with our team when I was a coach at the University of Notre Dame. Morris made an impact right away. Morris didn't just impact our players, he also made an impact on our staff –

especially me. I usually meet a lot of high-profile celebrities in my job, but when I first met Morris Morrison, I could tell that his mindset and approach to life were different. Once I got to know him better, I realized that he's the same person on and off stage. Morris is authentic, and you don't meet people like him every day. Morris changed the way that I saw myself as a husband, father, and coach.

As you read this book, you will have a chance to be impacted by Morris's message in the same way that I was when I first met him. Once you start reading the first chapter, you will not want to stop reading it because the storyline of this book keeps your attention, and every moment of this book was organized in a way that grabs your focus once you start reading it. When I picked my head up to take a break from reading *Overnight Success*, I couldn't believe how much time had gone by already. But even though the storyline is great, the message of this book is even better because the idea of instant gratification and *Overnight Success* is killing the chance for many people to be great, and Morris Morrison could not have written a better book at a better time. I know that this book can help any person or team do a few things that I believe are critical to success...

First - This book will help you to develop a *Laser-Like Focus* to keep you from being distracted by today's culture.

Second - Morris Morrison's highly inspirational message will inspire you to *Get Back Up* whenever life knocks you down.

Third - You will learn how to do something that all top performers do extremely well - be *Comfortable Being Uncomfortable*.

Fourth - The steps that Morris outlined in this book will give you a process that will help you to *Dominate and Compete, Consistently*.

Fifth - This book will show you how to *Grind and Work Hard* to leverage the opportunities that you have.

Sixth - This book will crush any attitudes of entitlement and remind you that *Nothing Is Ever Given to You*.

Seventh - *Overnight Success* will inspire you to *Live With Purpose* – a purpose that's focused on helping others first.

Morris Morrison has experienced moments in life that would normally cause most people to lose their focus and give up. But Morris's laser-like focus on his calling to help others is what inspired him to never give up. Whenever you interact with a person that has extreme focus and clarity like Morris does, it's inspiring to see, and that's why many companies, teams, and people around the world get to benefit from Morris's message – and right now, you will too. You are going to love this book because it won't just *inspire you*, it will also *guide you* with a process that will help you, your team, or anyone that you know take steps to get better!

Tony Alford
Associate Head Football Coach
The Ohio State University

OVERNIGHT SUCCESS

BOOK INTRODUCTION

Sometimes our lives change in the blink of an eye. Mine certainly did. I never will forget that night. As I walked into her hospital room, I knew that my life would be drastically different when I walked out. When I think about the crazy twists and turns that life can bring, I think about that night. I think about standing in the parking lot of the hospital and looking up at her hospital room for the last time. Every time I think about that night and every time I replay that memory in my head, it makes me even more amazed that I survived to make it where I am today. I mean, *what are the odds?*

I believe that our lives are most influenced by two things: *what we experience* and *who we meet*. The most critical *experience* in my life happened at that hospital. Before I finish telling you about what happened that night, I need to tell you about *someone that I met* in New York City.

INTRODUCING CLYDE RANDALL

I love traveling to New York City. Every time my flight lands in New York I get energized and excited, especially when I fly into LaGuardia Airport. Whenever I'm in LaGuardia, I always take the time to just stand there, look around, and take in the view. I love seeing all of the people coming and going from every country of the world. I love the sounds, the noises, the conversations, the hellos, the goodbyes. I love it all.

You see, I absolutely love people, and on a recent trip to New York City, I met one of the most amazing individuals that I have ever met in my life. His name was Clyde Randall. As we stood in the middle of the airport it was easy to notice Clyde. He was a tall, athletic-looking, super sharp guy. His suit was immaculate, his hair was perfect and this dude had presence – I mean, *he really stood out from the crowd*. After my conversation with Clyde, there were two things about him that stood out to me right away. First, it was clear to see that he was really good at just about everything that he did from an early age. Second, it was obvious after talking to him, was that Clyde was NOT happy with his life even though he had the type of success that many people dream of having.

Clyde was a superstar athlete and a great student when he was younger. Most things came easily to him. Yes, you know the type of person that I'm talking about – the type of person who always wins and always gets everything they want, the type of person who went to all the right schools and has the successful career. Clyde even managed to marry the girl of his dreams along the way. I mean this dude was a beast! It seemed like Clyde Randall had the perfect life. But… in the middle of our conversation, Clyde shared something with me that I did NOT expect him to say.

He looked at me and he said, "You know what Morris, everyone thinks that I have it all. And to most people, maybe I do. I mean don't get me wrong, I am very thankful for my life, but no matter what I do, no matter what I accomplish, I still feel empty."

CLYDE IS JUST LIKE ALL OF US

I have spent a lot of time in my life being around many different types of people. No matter who I'm with, I feel extremely comfortable, and I can connect with just about anyone. I have been around some of the biggest drug kingpins, some of the best stay-at-home moms, some of the most talented athletes, and some of the best fathers, pastors, CEO's, and company leaders. That's why I found it so interesting that a man like Clyde Randall who apparently had it all – money, status and success – still felt empty inside and still wanted MORE out of life. During our conversation, Clyde turned to me and said, "Morris, it seems like things are just so different today than they were back in the day when my parents and grandparents were growing up. It seems like life was just so much easier back then. When I hear them tell stories about their life, they always seemed to be so happy no matter how much money they had. But I have everything that most people dream of having and I am still empty. Morris, why do you think things are so different today?"

I said, "I agree with you Clyde. Even though I have no idea what it must have been like to live many years ago, when older people talk about the past it seems like their lives were very different from the way we live today."

MAYBE SOME THINGS REALLY HAVE CHANGED

The United States of America has experienced many changes over the years. The U.S. has experienced moments throughout history that have produced civil wars, slavery, the Great Depression, and the collapse of financial markets. But the people who survived those tough times gained something – they each developed a deeper level of *grit and determination* than they had before. If you ask me, I think that one of the biggest changes in our world today is that people have it *SO GOOD*. As a matter of fact, many people have it *TOO GOOD*. I'm talking about people just like Clyde Randall. I mean here's a guy who really seemed to have it all, the real American Dream. Yet he still wasn't happy. Why? Because he didn't have to work very hard for what he had – it all came so easily to him.

People like Clyde Randall never get to experience the true benefits of adversity. Adversity strengthens character and shows you who you really are. Clyde had no idea who he really was. People who lived many years ago were built differently. People from those generations didn't have a choice – they had to work hard.

As I think back to my conversation with Clyde Randall in the airport that day, I realized that although Clyde may have been really successful in the eyes of most people, he couldn't fool himself. *You can never fool yourself.* That's why he seemed so desperate for a boost of motivation and encouragement as we sat there in the middle of the airport in New York City. Maybe Clyde pursued the wrong dream. Maybe he pursued *someone else's dream*. Think about it. Our country and our entire world have changed drastically over the years. When things *around* us change, things *inside* of us change. Clyde achieved a version of the American Dream that has been put in our heads and our hearts since the day that we were born – but maybe he just got caught up living out the expectations and dreams of everyone around him.

ME AND THE FELLAS, BACK IN THE DAY

My conversation with Clyde Randall reminded me of many conversations that I had with my friends back in the day. When we were kids we always talked about *how to make it and become successful one day*. But we didn't just talk about how to have fame and money, we talked about *how to really be somebody*. When I think about my life today, I feel so blessed to work with some of the largest, most successful companies in the world – companies that hire only the best employees to work for them. I get a chance to see how really smart, successful people think. After being around companies like GE and Microsoft, I realized something - at the core of it all, they all have one thing in common – each of those companies are operated by everyday people. And despite their best organizational strategies or SWOT analyses, I have witnessed many instances where the people who run those organizations produced their *best results* when they faced their *biggest challenges*. Why? *Because it's amazing what a person can do, when they have to.*

I have seen it happen in my life also. After experiencing moments in my life that made me want to *GIVE UP*, I learned a secret about life: *when your options are limited, your survival instincts kick in* and you have no choice but to focus, like a laser. My life and this book were inspired by the idea that *when you find yourself in situations that push you to the limit, you realize amazing things about yourself that you never knew.* Unfortunately, most people and many organizations never get a chance to realize this because they just give up. And trust me, I completely understand why, because I almost gave up myself – many times. But I didn't, and that's why I wrote this book. This book was written to inspire someone just like YOU to stay focused on where you're going even when life distracts you, because adversity always reveals your true potential… if you let it.

THE BIGGEST CHANGE TODAY

Clyde Randall isn't the only person who feels empty inside. I work with sports teams, schools, companies, and various types of organizations, and I meet a lot of people. It amazes me just how many kids, adults, students, professionals, husbands, wives, even celebrities and superstar athletes feel just like Clyde. They feel empty inside because they don't just want to be successful, *they want to feel successful.* But what they really want, and what our world needs more people to do today – more than any other time in our history – is to live with *PURPOSE.* Why? Because one of the biggest problems in the world today is that *everyone wants more.* It doesn't matter how much we have. Instead of enjoying what we've got, many of us are focused on having it all – including me at times. Maybe it's not our fault. I guess there are many reasons why we feel this way.

When you really stop to think about it, technology has changed everything about how we live our lives. We are always connected and we never have any downtime to just focus. The worst part about technology is that it has changed how fast we get everything that we want. Okay, hold on for a minute… *maybe technology isn't a bad thing* because I love getting what I want, faster! But here's the problem – our brains are literally being *"rewired"* to not just *WANT* more, but to *EXPECT* more. *And when we don't get what we want, instantly,* we either give up or we reach for something else. Recent studies and surveys are beginning to find evidence to show us what we already know – *people are not willing to wait for the things that they want.* Today, people want what they want, and they want it now - that's the biggest reason why people can't stand it when adversity or challenges get in their way. Older generations of people may have dealt with tougher circumstances than people do today, but the major problem in our world is not that people aren't tough enough anymore. People are still just as tough today as they always were – the challenges that people face are just different.

Today, the biggest problem is that *people are just impatient,* and they don't have the *grit and determination* to stay focused long enough to get the results that they want.

JUST TAKE A LOOK AROUND

Many people want instant results, and the idea of *Overnight Success* is attractive. When people don't get what they want, when they want it, they focus their minds on coming up with *other ways to get it, faster.* I have seen drug dealers settle for *fast money* instead of using their business insight and charisma to do it the right way. I have seen kids give up in school because they didn't have the patience to sit in class and work hard. I have seen companies waste millions of dollars creating products that failed because they tried to take them to market before they were ready. Trust me, the idea of *Overnight Success* is attractive, but it's killing the real spirit that makes people great. Check out these examples, what about…

THE KIDS who quit the soccer team in the middle of the season because they *just don't like it anymore.* They may experience the immediate gratification of getting what they want (which is getting off of the team), but that's not all they get. Eventually, those kids will develop false expectations because they will develop neural pathways in their brains that reinforce those same habits. Eventually, they will start to expect to get what they want when they want it. When they don't get what they want, they'll just take their ball and leave. This is one of the biggest places where entitlement attitudes are born in today's kids. This is also the beginning stages of the *start it and quit it if I don't like it* attitude. Those type of kids will never know what they're really made of because they'll never learn how to stare adversity in the face when it shows up. Then, they'll carry that same type of *MINDSET* with them into the future and those kids can easily grow up to become…

THE STUDENTS who drop a class from their schedule in college just because they performed poorly on a test, or simply because they *just didn't like the class* . They may exercise their legal right to drop a class if they want to, but they will also exercise their right to get something else – a higher likelihood of depositing an *"F" in their MINDSET* when it comes to dealing with adversity. Why? Because they've already formed the habit of walking away from things when they don't get what they want. And *those students* can easily grow up to become…

THE EMPLOYEES who leave their jobs because they don't like their new boss or because they don't agree with their recent performance evaluation. They may find a new job that they're excited about, and it may even make them happy at first, especially if they get a higher salary. But once again, they will develop an unhealthy *MINDSET* that could lead to career stagnation from never acknowledging personal and professional blind spots. Those types of employees never really grow. They just take up space in organizations. Those types of employees also never really learn how to accept responsibility for their results or their career development. They will always blame their organizations or even worse, their managers, for their career trajectory. Instead of growing their skills, they just leave. And *those employees* can easily become…

THE SPOUSES who divorce their husbands or wives just because they simply aren't *happy anymore*. They may remarry to find happiness again (just like employees do when they leave one company to work for another), but they will soon realize that there is a reason why first marriages have a 50% divorce rate on average, and second marriages have a higher (60%) divorce rate. And those spouses can easily become, well, I think you get my point by now.

OKAY, SO THINGS HAVE CHANGED – WHAT NOW?

Can you see a pattern? The problem that we are facing is really easy to understand – the idea of instant gratification and *Overnight Success* keep many people – people just like you and me – *from experiencing our chance to be great.* We all need to stop running from our chance to be great.

I could give you hundreds of examples of how our desire to achieve more, now, is destroying our results. But I won't. My point is simple and it's easy to understand. If you don't believe me, just ask an older person. Any person over the age of 70 will shake their head side to side with a look of disbelief when they talk about *just how bad things are today*. Still don't believe me? Ask any Baby Boomer and they will have the same response.

Now that I have painted the picture for you, the question is, "What can we do to continue the legacy of our great country, a place where vision, purpose and work-ethic fueled our idea of the American Dream?" The solution is you... the answer is you.

As you prepare to read the rest of this book, you will hear the rest of the story about what happened to me that night when I stood in the parking lot of that hospital, and you will understand why that experience changed my life. But most of all, you will understand why *you must make a decision to follow your own vision* if you want to pursue *YOUR DREAM* and not someone else's.

I wrote this book because I want to share a message that will inspire you, and give you hope. And I want to give you an opportunity to hit the *RESET BUTTON* and possibly *change how you see yourself* and the impact you can make in this world.

This book has been organized around 7 specific steps that you can use to get refocused and re-energized. The *7 Steps to "C" Your Way Through* is a framework that will help you to become focused on achieving the results *THAT YOU WANT.* This book is a collection of real stories from my life, but if you read closely, you will see that this book is NOT about me. This book is about the amazing people who *changed the way I saw myself* and most importantly, my purpose. This book is about the people who inspired me to never give up – the people who surrounded me with a *CULTURE* that helped a broken kid grow up to become a man – a man who now, because of those people, *gets to fight every day* to live out the dream that he was called to live.

This book will not fill your head with tons of research just to prove that we are *addicted to instant gratification and the idea of Overnight Success.* We don't need research to tell us what we already know. What we do need is something that will make us want to say *"No"* when we're tempted to take the easy road. What we need is something that will make us want to FIGHT when life distracts our focus. And what we need now, more than any other time in our history, is something to fight for – a *PURPOSE.* And that's what this book will do - this book will help you, your company, your team, or your family take one step closer to becoming clear about *what you're fighting for.*

Once you finish reading this book, there is something else that you need to do – *read it again.* Read this book as many times as it takes until the stories become so real that you can see yourself in the story's. Read it until the ideas become *your ideas.* Whatever you do after you read this book is completely up to you. Hopefully, if this book sparks something inside of you in any way, you'll be inspired to pass the message on to someone else. Either way, *I hope you're ready... let's go.*

OVERNIGHT SUCCESS »»

Chapter

The American Dream

There is no such thing as an Overnight Success, especially with the things that matter most in life. Some people make their success look like they achieved it overnight because they make it look so easy.

I have always believed that success begins with the culture that you're surrounded in – it always does. The Bryan Family is a perfect example of how culture impacts success. Their oldest daughter Cara is an amazing athlete who broke many records. She was also the top student in her school. No one else achieved better results than her, and she made it look easy. In college, Cara did the same thing. Today, she is a highly paid, highly sought-after radiologist. This girl is a beast – *she even made medical school look easy!* If you didn't know her story, there is no way you could ever understand why she was so focused and determined. Let me tell you why.

Cara's father Robert had a crazy life as a kid. Robert lost his dad at an early age, and the absence of a father figure caused Robert's life to spiral out of control once he started making poor decisions. Then, fate stepped in. He met a girl. Robert fell in love with an amazing woman named Kim. As I think about Robert's story of success, I realize one thing about great movies and great music: there is always a girl! Women are God's greatest gift to this world, and after Robert met Kim, he knew that he wanted to marry her right away before someone else did. Kim was his angel and she's an amazing woman. She's so amazing that only she could tame the wild animal inside of

Robert, and that's exactly what she did. She helped Robert find purpose and direction in his life, and together they began to build a family of their own.

They had three girls and one boy. As they grew their family Robert and Kim held three things close to their hearts as they developed the culture and direction of the family they wanted to grow. Robert and Kim Bryan wanted their family to represent the essence of what the American Dream was all about. Their focus kind of sounded like this:

First, they wanted to honor their faith and honor God in everything they did.

Second, they wanted to always work *hard*. Work-ethic meant everything to them.

Third, they wanted to break any unhealthy generational cycles in their family by producing amazing kids that would change the world.

Kim was a school teacher and Robert was an entrepreneur who dabbled in real estate and various other successful ventures. In his heart, Robert was just a hard-working farmer. He was a big, burly guy who wore bibbed overalls everywhere he went. *Robert still wears bibbed overalls everywhere he goes today* even though he's become VERY successful and has the money to purchase the finest Gucci or Armani.

Those are the parents that Cara Bryan came from: a hard-working dad who had a farmer's heart and a school-teaching mother. That's why Cara's drive and motivation were off the charts. That's why she worked so hard that she made *medical school* look easy. From the outside looking in, no one saw her effort and determination. No one saw her grind, they just saw her gifts, and it was easy for others to think that everything came so easily to Cara. Actually, that's not entirely true. A few people did see Cara's grind, work-ethic, and determination – her younger brother and sisters witnessed the whole thing.

The next sibling in line after Cara was Christa. Christa had a big sister that modeled the way for her and showed her how it was done, so Christa was motivated too. Christa went on to break many of Cara's sports and academic records in school. And today, as she finishes up dental school, Christa Bryan is preparing to purchase her first dental practice. Wow, the legacy continues!

There was someone else watching Cara and Christa – their younger sister Caity. The funny thing about observing another person's success from a distance is that *if you do not know the person's backstory,* you will never know what really drove him or her to succeed. When we see really successful people, teams, or organizations achieve amazing results – especially if they're achieving results that we want to experience – it's easy to think that it came easily for them. Most of the time, we are never close enough to learn the plays that they are running to score those points. But when you see them running the plays right in front of you, just like Caity did, you can *learn the plays* . If you can learn the plays, you can *raise your game* and... *change the game*. And that's exactly what Caity Bryan did.

As the younger sister of Cara and Christa, Little Caity wanted to run big plays and score big points too because she was motivated. I call her *"Little"* because she was the shortest of the Bryan girls, but her heart was just as big. Little Caity went on to break most of her older sisters' athletic and academic records – what can I say, she really loved being first! That's what happens when you are the younger sister of two older successful women. She had drive in her heart and she wasn't afraid of hard work. Today, little Caity is attending optometry school at The Ohio State University.

Remember I mentioned that Robert and Kim had three girls and one boy? Well, their only son Benjamin was raised in a family where God came first and work-ethic was second. So what did the only boy in a family of all female siblings do when he was surrounded by such amazing talent and work ethic? He did what any self-respecting gentleman should do – *he raised his game* too. Today, Ben owns a very successful heavy-equipment excavating business. Not surprisingly, his company is bringing in all of the business that it can handle!

Robert and Kim Bryan were a perfect four-for-four in raising a great group of kids. As parents, Robert and Kim were more than successful in reaching their goals for their family. They certainly broke many previous generational cycles in their family and they did an amazing job creating a *CULTURE* of faith, family, and a focus on hard work. But if you looked at the success of the Bryan Family from the outside, you would never truly understand WHY they achieved the results they did. To someone who didn't know the Bryans firsthand, they might look like just another American family who went to all of the right schools and had all of the right opportunities. But to those of us who know the Bryan family personally, we're not surprised by their results. None of their achievements came as a surprise to any person in the Bryan family either. They never lost sight of their focus and they never stopped grinding and working hard.

I got a chance to witness how they operated as a family with my own eyes and *I learned their backstory.* I understood why they worked so hard, and the Bryan family helped me realize something very important. Everyone's dream begins somewhere, and it starts with *CULTURE* . The Bryan family's vision for their American Dream started in the hearts of Robert and Kim Bryan, and they used that vision to inspire the culture in their home. As a result, everyone that their family came into contact with was influenced by the culture that they created, *especially me.*

You may have met someone before that made their achievements look easy. You know, like the student who always gets straight A's, the mother who always seems to have it together as a parent, or the opponent that your team hates facing each year because they're always on top of their game. They make you think to yourself, *"How are they always that good?"* In corporate America, I love working with organizations that have multiple business units across the globe because there's plenty of competition among the different units. When a particular branch consistently outperforms others, sibling rivalries naturally occur. And what do siblings do best? They compare. They compare everything, and it's easy to make excuses for the apparent *Overnight Success* of others that you are competing with. People may say things like, *"They had more resources at their disposal than we did. Plus, they haven't had nearly the amount of changes in leadership like we have over the past 18 months."* Yeah, they can keep telling themselves that. It's easy to overlook the *real reasons* why great teams outperform everyone else. But maybe they're just *better* than everyone else. Maybe they *out-hustled* everyone else. Or maybe they just *wanted it* more than everyone else.

I have learned that the top students, the greatest parents, even the best teams that we face in sports and in business never have *Overnight Success.* Over time, they develop a *CULTURE* of success that motivates everyone to bring their best, and they just make it look easy.

THE CULTURE THAT STARTED MY AMERICAN DREAM

My American Dream started in a place which has become familiar with everyone around the world as the place where BIG dreams begin – New York City. Just seeing the words *New York City* inspires me. I love everything about New York: the sounds of the cars and taxi cabs, the loud noise of jackhammers on the pavement, and the constant chattering of voices from the people – yes, I even love the people. Most of all, I love the energy of New York City. I guess it makes sense, because the first thing that most people say when they meet me is, *"Morris Morrison, you have so much energy, where do you get all of it from?"* Who knows, maybe New York City has something to do with it, maybe it doesn't. What I do know is I love New York City. I feel like *I am... New York City.*

My American Dream began in the middle of New York City before I even came into this world. When I think about my parents and the life that they had in New York City, as I learn more about who they were and what they represented, the more I understand the backdrop and foundation that my life was created from. Trust me, my parents were NOT Robert and Kim Bryan, but they were my parents and I am glad that my mom and dad met in New York City when they did.

My father's name was Billy. He lived his whole life in New York City - Harlem, to be exact. He saw New York and Harlem go through some of the biggest changes they have ever experienced. Most of those changes were because of one plant which is grown throughout the world - the poppy seed plant. The plant has been used since the beginning of time. Early Egyptians used the poppy seed plant for the *sedative effects* it produced. This plant was also the genesis for a drug epidemic in the United States during the 1970's that changed the lives of many people forever with the introduction of a new drug: heroin.

The poppy seed plant is also responsible for producing a pretty dramatic twist at the end of this book, so pay close attention to how this whole story comes full circle.

Most people in New York City were familiar with heroin, which was one of the most popular ways to get high in the 1970's. And in Harlem, people on the streets either sold heroin or they used it to get high. Before I go on, there is something that I want you to know about me. I am a naturally highly curious person that likes to find the irony or interesting details in stories. So when I look at the word *HEROIN*, I can't help but be attracted to the root word, *HERO*. I can't help but wonder who the person was in South America (where the drug is said to have originated) that came up with the name *HEROIN*. When they realized that they needed to give this drug a name, I wonder if someone said, *"Okay, before we start to ship this new product to the United States, we need to call it something. Any ideas, anyone?"*

Someone in the room probably stepped forward and said, *"Let's think about the things that American's love the most... oh, I've got it! They absolutely love being the hero and the big brother that swoops in to save the day. Yeah, that's it, the HERO. Let's call it HEROINE. But first, let's drop the 'e' off of the end of the word."*

And there you have it. *HEROIN* was born.

At this point, you may be wondering why I'm telling you so much about a drug. Well, it's simple - heroin changed my life. When my father Billy got caught up in the drug scene in New York City, his life was altered and his legend grew.

My Uncle Donnie used to tell me stories about the times he spent in New York with my father Billy. Uncle Donnie said that he was always treated *differently* when he visited New York City just because he was the cousin of "Wild Man." Yep, you heard me. They called my father *Wild Man*. My father, Billy "Wild Man" Capers did what most people in New York City did when they sold drugs: he did *Whatever He Had To Do* to protect himself, his business, and those around him.

Uncle Donnie also told me stories about how *crazy* my father was. No... really, Uncle Donnie tried his best to describe to me just how wild my father was, and how bad his temper was. If you still can't picture my father clearly, just imagine this - a tall, good-looking, dark-skinned African American brotha with the savviness of a cheetah and the shrewdness of a honey badger. He was smooth and ruthless at the same time. Many people loved him, but more people feared him. The most interesting detail about my father wasn't how he looked or who he was though. The most interesting detail about my father was the woman by his side - my mother.

THERE'S ALWAYS A GIRL

My mother's name was Darlene "Wild Woman" Morrison. Okay, so her nickname wasn't actually *Wild Woman,* but it sure would add a touch of irony to this story if it was.

Darlene Morrison was from a small town in Grundy County, Tennessee. Grundy County, Tennessee served as the inspiration for one of country music's biggest hit songs: "The Grundy County Auction" performed by John Michael Montgomery in the 1990's. In Grundy County, there was a small town named Palmer where my mother was from. Palmer, Tennessee wasn't exactly a thriving metropolis. With a population in the 1970's of less than 1,000, the small, 5.3 square miles of the town simply did not have a stage that was big enough for my mother. My mother needed a stage that was big enough to support *HER* dreams.

My mother's journey took her 40 miles southeast to the closest big city that she could find - Chattanooga, Tennessee. But Chattanooga still wasn't big enough. By the time she was 19 years old, Darlene realized that there was only one city in the United States of America that was big enough to support her big ideas and her even bigger personality. That's right, Darlene Morrison knew exactly what she wanted and where she needed to be - it didn't matter if she had to be a model, an actress, or a dancer. She knew that she needed the big stage and the bright lights. She needed New York City.

The little girl from Grundy County, Tennessee was ready for the hustle and bustle of New York. What inspires me the most about my mother was *WHAT* she represented. In her own way, my mother represented The American Dream to the fullest. Her clarity of vision, her drive, and her fortitude to pursue what *she wanted* out of life were amazing. Her ideals were exactly what the dream of America was founded on.

The part that intrigues me the most about my mother was her race - my mother was a white female from a small town in the south. Although she had never ventured too far out of the state of Tennessee, my mother was never intimidated by the idea of going to a place as large and diverse as New York City. That absolutely amazes me, because a large portion of Americans never leave the area where they grew up. Studies show that most people who stay close to home do so because they feel like they belong there. Statistically, the group of people who are most likely to leave home are those with college degrees. Well, my mother was not afraid of leaving the place that she called home, and she definitely didn't have any degrees. I guess there is something that studies and research can't measure: the vision, purpose and desire that sit in a person's heart. The people who have the courage to go places they have never been before, or the courage to pursue their dreams...people like that are just built differently. This whole world was moved forward by individuals who saw things from a different perspective - people who were not scared to step out and walk towards what they really wanted out of life. People like that are fueled and motivated by something bigger, just like my mother was.

I was amazed by what my mother represented. When I think about my mom, I think about the millions of people who were the exact opposite of her - people who never pursued what they really wanted out of life. I think it's sad because *every person already has everything that they need to pursue what they were created to do.* When most people fail to reach their goals, it has nothing to do with talent or ability. People fail to reach their goals because they don't have the courage to take the first step. My mother wasn't scared to transition to a big place like New York City, because she knew exactly what she wanted out of life. *That* is what guided her.

FROM TENNESSEE TO NEW YORK CITY

Everyone's American Dream begins somewhere. My mother's began with the decision to leave home and what was familiar to pursue the desires of her heart. I often wonder what it was like for her when she first arrived in New York City. Obviously she wasn't intimidated! Why would she be? If she had the courage to leave a small town in the south to go to New York City, that courage gave her everything she needed to arrive in New York full of confidence.

My mother wasn't just confident, she was also very beautiful. When she walked into the room, she shifted the energy of everyone around her. You've met people like my mother before, we all have. People like her affect others. Her presence alone changed things. And when she smiled, she lit up the room. People tell me that I get a lot of my personality from her, along with her wit, her energy, her gregariousness. When I think about how full of life and how spirited she must have been, I can't help but imagine what it must be like to combine the enormous energy of a place like New York City with the big personality that my mother had. Those two added together must have been something really special - a perfect combination of nature and nurture. When you combine two powerful forces like that together, you can never predict exactly what will happen.

Ultimately, the city won. In the end, New York City was simply too much for my mom. When my mother left Tennessee and headed to New York City, her parents didn't know what to expect. After she went to New York City, my grandparents still knew very little about her life. They knew very little about who she really was while she was in New York. They didn't know much about who she really spent her time with and how she lived her life. I mean, of course they knew a few details, but only the details that a child would choose to share with his or her parents.

My mother did manage to make it back home for a few brief visits with her family in Tennessee after she moved to New York City. With each visit, my family couldn't help but notice my mother's rapidly changing appearance. Her image took on a whole new look, and I am not talking about wardrobe changes. There were many changes. From her hair to her weight, and even her overall health... everything was different. But, like most parents, they didn't question much. They let my free-spirited mother live her life. They were just happy to hear from her when she called and happy to see her when she visited.

My family in Tennessee was made of good, simple-living folks from a small southern town. They raised a daughter who had a personality that was larger than life. What do you do when God gives you a daughter that needs her own space to live her life? You give it to her. And that's what they did.

When the city of New York shipped my mother's dead body back to my grandparents in Palmer, Tennessee, my mother was only 23 years old. With very little information to draw on, my grandparents had many questions - many of which went unanswered. Even today, there are many questions surrounding what *really* happened to my mother. When the coroners removed her body from a hotel in Times Square, their initial findings pointed towards a drug overdose.

BROKEN DREAMS

My mother's American Dream did not end how she planned it. Her death left a hole in the hearts of an entire community in Palmer. As the oldest of five children, my mother's death changed the lives of her family forever.

My mother lived a very full life in her short time on this earth. She lived more life in 23 years than most people ever do. Why? Because she lived - she really lived. And she lived *HER LIFE*. She didn't care much about what other people thought because my mother was not a follower - people followed her. My mother knew exactly what she wanted in life, she dreamed *BIG* and she left it all on the table at the end of the day. Hey, I am not saying that every choice that my mother made was the right choice, but you have to keep in mind that my mother wasn't perfect (no one is), but I am proud that my mother had the courage to live *HER LIFE* and not some version of life that other people expected her to live.

It may be sad to think about a person dying so young, but what breaks my heart even more is the people in this world who die with their dreams still inside of them. We live in a country where no matter who you are - man or woman, black or white, old or young - it's never too late for you to dream, and it's never too late for you to make a decision to go after what you want in life. That is exactly what my mother did - she went for it.

I believe that at the end of many people's lives, they are buried with their dreams still inside of them. This is *the biggest tragedy in life.* In my profession, I notice that this doesn't just happen to people. I see many teams, organizations, and even relationships experience the same situation. I see teams that could have worked harder, and people in relationships who could have fought harder. So the question is, *"Why Don't They?"*

I think it all boils down to two things: culture and character. Robert and Kim Bryan created a culture for their family that helped their kids thrive. My father Billy participated in a drug culture that was an easy choice for black men in Harlem at the time. My mother left the culture she was *raised in* to pursue the culture she was *drawn to.* And that is where character comes in. It takes a strong person to overcome the power of the crowd. That's what culture ultimately is. It's the crowd, and eventually the voice in our heads. Culture becomes a powerful part of our subconscious mind that guides how we make decisions, even when we don't realize it.

In my opinion, the word character is a BIG word because character describes the complete essence of who a person is - the complete package. Character includes a person's strengths, their weaknesses, how they think, how they act, what drives them, and ultimately, what they respond to.

I believe that a big reason why most people can go through their entire lives and never become the person that they were truly created to be is because of either culture or character, and sometimes both. But culture can be a funny thing. Culture can *INSPIRE* people to be their best, just like in the Bryan Family. But culture can also *KEEP* people from being their best, just like the heroin culture in Harlem that my father chose to participate in. With my mother, culture was not the reason why she lost her life. Culture didn't do that to her. And culture also wasn't the reason why my father choose to sell drugs - *we can't blame everything on culture.* That's where character comes in. Culture may exist around us, but ultimately we choose what we respond to and how we make choices, that's on us.

Right now, you are probably thinking about my mother - a woman who lived BIG and went after what she wanted in life - and there is one more tiny little detail that you may be wondering about. You are probably wondering about me, the author of this story. What happened to the little boy who was the son of Billy "Wild Man" Capers and Darlene Morrison - two people whose love story began in New York City? Well, that part's next…

OVERNIGHT SUCCESS »

Chapter

New York City Angel

There are many details that I do not know about my life, especially from the early days in New York City. But there is something that I know for sure: when I found myself standing in the doorway of her hospital room, part of me was frozen. I did not want to go into her room because one feeling overcame my entire body – I did not want to say goodbye to her. I didn't want to say goodbye to my *Angel*.

Gwendolyn Sanders was my angel, she was my hero, she was my everything - she was the lady who adopted me after I lost my parents in New York City. Eventually, I lost her also - the night that I was forced to say goodbye to my foster parent Gwendolyn Sanders, the lady that I called *Grandma*, broke my heart. The events leading up to that night were just as dramatic as the early days of my life in New York City.

FROM NEW YORK CITY TO WEST VIRGINIA

Gwendolyn had many children – biological children that she gave birth to and many surrogate children that found their way into her home. When Gwendolyn officially adopted me when I first came to West Virginia from

New York City, I was a young child. One of Gwendolyn's sons named Chuck instantly took an interest in me and he became the father figure that I never had. I called Gwendolyn *Grandma*, and I called Chuck *Dad*.

My relationship with Chuck grew over the years. Our relationship became especially strong when Gwendolyn was forced to have her leg amputated due to diabetes complications when I was five years old. Gwendolyn was all I had, and many people wondered what would happen to me if something ever happened to her. After my grandma's surgery, Chucky did something brave - he said, "Give him to me, I will take him in. I will take care of Morris until Gwendolyn gets better."

The amazing part about Chuck was not the fact that he stepped up to be a father to the fatherless, and it wasn't his ability to instantly be a phenomenal father to me. The amazing part about Chuck was how much he truly loved me. We were close, very close. And the most remarkable part about it, a detail in the story that still baffles the minds of many people today, is how much Chuck and I really do look like father and son. We are both light-skinned, African American men who have curly hair.

One of my favorite early memories with Chuck is when he took me to see Santa Claus for the first time as a child. We took one of our first photos together – a father and his son with Santa Claus. I loved that photo. I cherished that photo.

When Gwendolyn was taken to Johns Hopkins Medical Center in Baltimore, Maryland, to have her leg amputated, it was the beginning of a long road to recovery for her – a road that would last almost two years.

During that time, Chuck and his girlfriend, Sue, raised me. Sue also had a son named Josh from a previous relationship. Josh and I were the same age and we instantly connected, we were *brothers from a different mother!* When Chuck and Sue enrolled us in kindergarten together, the teachers had no idea what they were facing. We were a team, a dynamic duo, Starsky and Hutch, Frick and Frack, Batman and Robin. Oh, there is one more thing: we were BAD! No, I really mean it. Our conduct was horrible – it was off the charts. We got in trouble together every day. And whenever there wasn't trouble, we made some. Did I mention that we were really, really bad?

When Barnes Elementary School purchased a new Disneyland carpet for our classroom, Josh and I decided that the creators of the carpet did not make a product worthy of the Disney name. So we improved it by drawing our own Disney masterpieces onto the rug, you know, to give it a more *personal* touch. Now that I think about it, that Disney carpet that we "improved" together showed my early genius: the marketing and brand management skills that I would later discover!

Those early years with Chuck and our little family with Sue and Josh were the best. We didn't have much but we had a lot of love. When Gwendolyn came back home after her rehabilitation process was complete, she continued to raise me in her home at 110 Westlawn Street, in Fairmont, West Virginia, all on her own. Once she got her health completely up and running again, Gwendolyn's son Chuck left. Chuck still lived in the same town as me, but I barely saw him anymore. There was a huge hole in my heart, because I was just a kid who missed his dad. I missed him a lot.

Instead of appreciating the fact that a guy like Chuck stepped up to take care of me at a time when I could have been placed back into the foster care system, I was hurt. I had no idea at the time that he was *NOT* my real father. Why would I think that? I mean, he *looked* like he was my dad. He *acted* like he was my dad. He *loved* me like he was my dad.

I was hurting because I missed him. Yes, I know he wasn't my real father, but it didn't matter. I had grown to love Chuck and he loved me. As far as I was concerned, he *was* my dad. As a child, I wasn't emotionally advanced enough to understand what it meant to have gratitude. I didn't know how to express thanks to a man who stepped up to help me. Instead, I slowly developed what many refer to as a father wound.

Chuck was in his early twenties and he had his own life to live, so when Gwendolyn returned back home from Johns Hopkins in Baltimore, Chuck did what most people in their twenties would do: he lived his life and I didn't see him very much any more. Every time I heard the sound of a motorcycle, I would run to the window to see if my dad was coming down Spring Street on his gold Suzuki 650 to see his little boy. Every time I heard the sound of a motorcycle, it made me cry.

Gwendolyn did the best she could to raise me. After losing her husband, Mr. Oscar Sanders, just a few years earlier, Gwendolyn was on her own, and I was not the only mouth that she had to feed. She had other kids that she was raising. During that time, I became all too familiar with our country's welfare system. We received free government cheese and peanut butter in large containers. I had a medical card that entitled me to free health care. We received food stamps to purchase groceries with. We did whatever we had to do to make it. I remember going to garage sales on weekends and shopping at the local Union Mission for clothes to wear.

One day, when we were shopping at the Union Mission, two kids that I knew from school walked past the front door outside. As soon as I recognized them, I tried to hide. But it was too late. They saw me.

"Look at Morris Morrison," they said as they pointed into the door. "He gets his clothes from the Mission, no wonder he dresses so funny!"

I was embarrassed and I hated the way I felt about myself. Once again, rather than being thankful for the life that I had and for not being left to fend for myself on the streets of New York City, instead of realizing how bad my life could have been if I were raised in the city's foster care system, instead of reminding myself of all of that, I was embarrassed and angry. And I showed it. There were plenty of times when I got in trouble for arguing and being disrespectful towards my grandmother Gwendolyn.

With a screaming voice, she would often yell back at me, "I don't know who you think you are. Your little black butt needs to be thankful for what you got and stop being so damn ungrateful all the time." Other times she would say things like, "No one owes you a damn thing. You have no idea the sacrifices that were made just so you can have the life you've got. You need to stop complaining all of the time!"

SAYING "THANK YOU" ISN'T ALWAYS EASY

It was hard for me to be grateful for the life that I had, especially since I didn't know the truth about who I really was or where I came from. I really thought that Chuck was my father. Even worse, I thought that he had left me all alone.

As a kid, I knew that my mother's name was Darlene and that she died in New York City. That's all people ever told me. They would never give me any more details than that. Even when I asked questions, everything was always hush-hush. Chuck knew that he wasn't my real father, so anytime I asked him questions about *what happened to my mommy*, he avoided those questions whenever he could.

I was hurting as a kid because I had a dead mother that I never knew, and a dad who I thought was the coolest guy in the world all because he drove a motorcycle, but he never wanted to see me anymore. I slowly began to see him the same way that all the other kids around me saw their dads – *just a man who skipped out on his kid* - just another absent father. I felt like no one wanted me and like my life didn't matter to anyone. At times, I felt like Gwendolyn didn't even want me around. Even though that wasn't true, and even though that woman loved me more than anything in the world, I still felt like a burden to her. And that's what I constantly told myself.

Remember when I said that there are two things that largely influence our lives: culture and character? Well, the biggest part of anyone's character is something that other people never really see – *the little voice inside of their heads* - that little voice controls so much of how we think and act. That little voice inside my head started to dominate my life. I saw myself as a young, poor, black kid that no one loved and no one really wanted. I felt like I was just a burden on everyone.

When the kids made fun of me for shopping at the local Union Mission that day, I had had enough. That was the last straw. I vividly remember them standing outside of the door, pointing at me on the inside and saying, "Look at Morris Morrison, look at Morris Morrison. He gets his clothes from the Mission because he's poor." It sparked a fire inside of me. Not because I felt poor. Not because I felt embarrassed by the lack of money or material possessions in my life. There was something else that ignited inside of me.

I started to dismiss everything that I saw around me. For some reason I began to feel like everything that I saw around me was NOT what I saw inside of me. My family may have shopped at the Union Mission, but I didn't feel like that was who I was. I began to feel something growing inside of me – something bigger that needed to be let out. When I say bigger, I don't mean better. I simply mean different.

Even as a young child, I felt completely conflicted with the life I was experiencing. Later, as I grew older, I learned the truth about who my mother Darlene Morrison really was. I learned that she felt the same way when she was younger before she moved away from her small, southern hometown. Her *vision for more* is what motivated her to pursue her life and her dreams. It's what led her to New York City. When you want to pursue something different from others around you, it can feel like a curse at times, especially if you do not have the freedom to pursue it. But the best part about wanting more out of life is that having a strong desire to pursue something can also be the most powerful fuel to motivate you if, and only if, you use it the right way.

BORN THIS WAY

I've always had a lot of energy and I have always been pretty motivated, even as a kid. I wanted more. More of everything. Not just material possessions either, I wanted MORE out of life. At an early age I began to take many things into my own hands. First on my list was clothing. I had to get some new gear. Many people could leave their home every day without giving a second thought to how they were dressed, but not me. Presenting myself as a well-dressed young man was just about all I had to change my image. I started out by making my own clothes to wear. I learned how to sew material so that I could create and fix my clothes. I made a decision that I would never be teased by kids again because of the way that I dressed.

Next up was my hair. My grandmother trusted a lot of people to cut my hair, but most of them had no idea what they were doing. Of course, cutting my hair wasn't easy. My head full of afro-like curly hair was a tall order for any barber. There were only two guys who could cut my hair: Little Jay and Chris Walker. When they both moved away, I was left with few options. So what did I do? You know what I did. I found an old pair of clippers to cut my own hair - yeah, I messed my hair up at first, and I messed it up a lot, but I had a full-time resident flunky to practice on: my cousin Bam Bam. His real name was Demetrius but we called him Bam Bam and I was glad that he didn't care very much about what his hair looked like, because he let me practice my barber skills on him all the time. Between his hair and mine, I had enough practice to become good. I'm glad that I did too, because being able to cut my hair was an important step if I wanted to manage my own personal brand. Between the clothes that I began to create on my own and the personal haircuts, I started to feel much, much better about myself.

I was off to a good start, but I realized right away that you need to have money in this world, especially if you have a bigger vision for what you want out of life. Fortunately, by the age of 14, I was so good at cutting my own hair that other people actually began to pay me to cut theirs too. I couldn't believe that people were willing to pay me for a skill that I had. When you think about it though, it makes sense. I had a head full of curly hair, which is the hardest type of hair to cut. After I mastered cutting my own hair, cutting everyone else's was a breeze. I got five bucks per head, and once I had the courage to diversify my client base, that's when the money really started coming in. One of the ladies at my church, Mrs. Mary Bell, actually began to pay me 25 to 30 dollars just to trim the back of her hair!

I'm not going to lie. At first, I wasn't excited about the idea of cutting a woman's hair, because in my mind, only females cut other women's hair. When Mrs. Mary Bell approached me and said, "Hey Morris, I heard that you do hair. Will you do my hair too?" I said, "First of all Mrs. Mary Bell, I don't 'do' hair. Only women 'do' hair. I cut hair. And I am sorry to tell you Mrs. Mary Bell, but I will not be 'doing' your hair. You're going to have to find someone else."

She responded, "What if you come to my house and do it? No one else will know."

I said, "Mrs. Mary Bell, I am sorry. I'm still not going to do it. I do not 'do' hair."

She said, "But I just need you to trim the back of my hair up along my neck."

"I am sorry Mrs. Mary Bell, I still can't do it."

She said, "That's too bad. I normally pay 25 dollars to get my hair did, and that's not including the tip."

I quickly replied, "What did you say? How much?"

"You heard me."

"Guess what, Mrs. Mary Bell. I now officially 'do' hair. I'll see you at your place at six o'clock."

By age 15, I started making really good money cutting and "doing" hair. As a matter of fact, if the IRS knew how much money I made cutting hair from age 13 up until I finished grad school, I would be in a bunch of trouble!

I had other ways of making money also – those instincts were always inside of me. No matter what, I could make money. I guess the entrepreneurial spirit was always a part of who I was. My business skills were given to me the day I was born. When my great-grandmother Hattie Stanley came to West Virginia from Bessemer, Alabama, she wasn't pursuing a greater life like my mother was when she went to New York. My great-grandmother Mama Hattie was running *from something*. After shooting her husband in the head with a shotgun, the local sheriff knew that Mama Hattie was simply defending herself from a man who was physically abusing her. Instead of arresting her, the local sheriff had enough empathy and compassion to help Mama Hattie out. By giving her 24 hours to get out of town, the Sheriff gave her a pass.

Mama Hattie jumped onto the next train smoking, and off to West Virginia she went – off to a place in the North where other people that she knew in Alabama had migrated to. When Mama Hattie arrived in West Virginia, she needed money and she needed work. Skilled in the art of preparing authentic, southern food, she opened up a barbecue joint. Mama Hattie's business provided a service as well. As a matter of fact, she probably had the only barbecue joint in town where the best seller was NOT the food, which says a lot because Mama Hattie cooked some amazing soul food. She owned one of the only places in town where you could purchase both barbecue and companionship all in the same night. That's right, Mama Hattie owned her very own brothel.

Ohhhh, you've got to love Mama Hattie! The truth is, I wouldn't even be here if it weren't for her. Mama Hattie wasn't the only one with natural business instincts. People in my family have always come up with innovative ways to capitalize on the wants, needs, and desires of others. For many of my family members, they chose the drug trade just like my father in New York City. Mama Hattie passed her entrepreneurial skills down to my father through his mother, Katherine. My grandmother Katherine lived in New York City, but she was born in West Virginia. She was the oldest of Mama Hattie's children. The most interesting thing about my grandmother Katherine is that at the age of 18, she too had a much larger vision for what she wanted out of life.

Grandma Katherine felt like West Virginia was too small for her ambitions. So off to New York City she went, to the neighborhood of Harlem. Years later, Katherine's only son Billy – a strong, dark-skinned brotha – met a southern white woman named Darlene on the streets of New York. Of course they hit it off right away, because Darlene reminded Billy of his mother Katherine. Both Darlene and Katherine arrived in New York with similar ambitions. They both wanted MORE out of life.

CONNECTING IT ALL

If you are tracking this story correctly, you now have a vision of my mother Darlene Morrison – a young lady who left Tennessee to pursue a better life in New York City – and my biological father, Billy, who came from a family of enterprising, resourceful brothas and sistas from Bessemer, Alabama, and Fairmont, West Virginia, who eventually ended up in New York City.

Although Billy's mother Katherine never made the effort to leave Harlem to go back to visit her family in West Virginia, he made the trip frequently. It wasn't just the love of family that inspired my father to make those trips back to Fairmont. It was also the drugs. He developed a small distribution system that made his trips to West Virginia worth it. My biological father was a drug dealer. It may not have been the most noble of professions, but even the drug business required him to be focused like a laser and shrewd as a honey badger if he wanted to survive in the streets of New York. I guess my father passed his focus and resourcefulness down to me along with his entrepreneurial skill set. I received a strong business acumen from my father's side of the family as well as the drive and determination to go after it and make it happen.

Business was good for me too. I made sizable money cutting hair, but I also did landscaping when the weather was warm, and shoveled snow when it was cold. No matter what, I was always hustling, and I was always on the move. I was never lazy. While other kids sat inside playing Tecmo Bowl and Mike Tyson's Punch Out on the Nintendo, I was working. Don't get me wrong, I played video games every now and then. I enjoyed those games too, but not as much as I enjoyed working. It wasn't just about the money either. The money was a byproduct of the work because what I enjoyed the most, was the *grind & the hustle* of making things happen.

As a teenager, I had something to show for my efforts. In school, I took the hardest classes that my counselors would let me take, and I got A's and B's. Outside of school, business was good, and I didn't have to get money by selling drugs like a lot of people around me. I had enough money to purchase my own clothes, pay for my own field trips at school, and basically take care of any financial needs that I had as a youth. The most important thing that I learned from not sitting on my butt and being lazy was the value of a dollar and the importance of having a strong work ethic. I realized early on that even though people around me in my family were using drugs, selling drugs, and having a lot of recreational fun, *I could create the life that I wanted to have without depending on anyone else to give it to me.* Wait a minute, I guess that's not entirely true, I did depend on someone else.

WHO GRANDMA INTRODUCED ME TO

I never knew my real mother and father, Darlene and Billy. The only two parents that I ever knew were my grandmother Gwendolyn who raised me in Fairmont, WV, and her son Chuck. My grandmother Gwendolyn didn't have much, but she gave me all that she had and loved me more than anything. I had to work my fingers to the bone shoveling snow, mowing grass, and cutting hair to have the resources that I needed to live my life. But there were a few things that Gwendolyn did for me that made her great in her own right. She saved me from the streets of New York, she put a roof over my head, and she kept God in my life. So when I say that I didn't depend on anyone else, that's not totally accurate. I depended on God to help me. I always have. I always will.

Developing my faith didn't hit me *Overnight* at first. I was young at the time and highly impressionable. But my grandmother always made sure that we made it to church. The best part about being young is that your mind is constantly in learning mode. (This is one of the distinct benefits of being young. Adults can continue learning as well, but the busyness of life just kind of gets in the way of the learning process.) I was learning a lot as a kid. My mind bounced between school, sports, church, and working to make money. Somewhere in between all of that, the idea of having faith in God just clicked with me.

"How can a person not believe in God?" I would say to myself. "I mean, even the Declaration of Independence which explains *why* we exist as a nation, talks about God as our creator!" It was a no-brainer to me. If 50 out of 52 Founding Fathers of The United States of America were churchgoing, God-fearing men, maybe they were onto something. Maybe faith was kind of a big deal. It was even printed on our money! Even our dollar bills said, "In God we trust!" And I was always hustling and trying to make money when I was a kid, so if God was a part of our money, I had to make a part of who I was too.

As I mentioned before, my grandmother also raised other children in our home. Sheena, Bam Bam, and Talayia were other kids that lived with us from time to time while Gwendolyn raised me. In her short 60 years on this earth, Gwendolyn raised many, many children. And she always made sure they went to church.

Our neighbors, Eddie and Francis White (Uncle Eddie and Aunt Francis as we called them), were committed to keeping the local Church Of

God on Maple Avenue open for a few of us kids even after its membership base fell off. Using their own resources, they held Sunday school and church every Sunday for me, Sheena, Bam Bam, Talayia, John, Shayla, Dwight, John-John, Tonisha, Devon, Ronnie, Julie and many other kids throughout the hood. As a teenager, after Francis and Eddie were forced to close the doors of the old, dilapidated church, I still visited other churches. Why? Because my grandmother showed me why faith in God is important, and how even America – the greatest country in the world, in my opinion – was created, founded, and based on God's principles. If it was good enough for my grandmother, and if it was good enough to base the founding principles of our country on, then faith in God was good enough for me.

Today, my faith is one of the biggest reasons why I get so much satisfaction out of helping others achieve THEIR goals. Many people often ask me why my faith is so important to me. I am very direct when I tell them, "To me, it's simple: everyone has challenges in life, everyone. And the biggest difference in how you respond to challenges and opportunities in your life will depend on your mindset, your attitude, and what you believe. My faith gives me a mental advantage and the ability to be optimistic and positive *in all things and in all situations*, no matter what. Even when I lose, even when I fall down, even when things do not go my way, my faith tells me that I still win, no matter what!"

I wasn't raised by Robert and Kim Bryan, the family that I introduced you to in chapter 1. I was raised by Gwendolyn Sanders - and the one thing that the Bryan and the Sanders families had in common, the one thing that drove the culture that they created in their homes more than anything else, was their faith in God. Gwendolyn did a lot of things for me, but introducing me to my faith was the greatest.

I was glad that I had God in my life, because things were about to change for me... quickly. My life was about to take a dramatic turn for the worse when my father Chuck was falsely accused of a crime that he did not commit. His imprisonment crushed me at the age of 15, and it broke the heart of his mother Gwendolyn, causing us to lose the biggest *ANGEL* that many of us has ever know.

OVERNIGHT SUCCESS »

Chapter

Where Dreams Begin

Some days are always better than others. For instance, birthdays usually provide great moments that serve as a cause for celebration. Other days, such as those when we have to say goodbye, are never really easy no matter how much practice you get. When you add them both together, they can produce a confusing effect.

My birthday is December 4th. Remember when I told you that I loved irony? Well, on December 4th, 1994, the only father figure that I've known, Charles Raymond Sanders – who we call Chuck – was falsely accused of shooting another man in the hand, in what the newspapers described as, "A drug deal gone bad." My dad admitted to hanging out and partying with friends on the night in question. He also admitted to experimenting with drugs and alcohol. But shooting someone? My dad would *never* shoot someone...would he?

So the story goes like this. My dad and his friends went to party and hang out one night. In the midst of their partying, they went to visit the gentleman that they usually purchased the *party drugs* from. On this particular night, instead of exchanging the money for the drugs, the dealer, who we'll call "Bobby," pulled a gun on my dad and one of his friends. On this night, the drug dealer wasn't giving them anything – he was taking something. He demanded that they give him all of their money, and a struggle ensued.

Now here's one of the interesting things about my dad: Chuck was a good-looking, laid-back, very pleasantly-mannered person. If you didn't know his background, you wouldn't know his physical capabilities – they were easily overlooked. You also wouldn't know that he was a champion wrestler, especially because of his small size. As soon as my dad saw the handgun being drawn, his instincts kicked in and they began to fight over the gun. During the struggle, the gun fired and Bobby shot himself in his hand with his own gun.

Because it was 3:30 in the morning, Bobby had no choice but to walk into the emergency room with an entry wound and an exit wound in his hand. When the police came to investigate the incident, he told them that he was, "Just walking down the street, minding my own business, when two black men tried to rob me." An interesting detail about this story is that Bobby was also black. But when he spoke with the police officers that night, he made sure to mention that my father and another gentleman were the two *black men* who shot him as they tried to rob him. Clearly, Bobby wanted his racial description to motivate the police to find my father.

Once Chuck was arrested, a very interesting court case ensued.

I will spare you the boring details. All you need to know is this: Chuck was sentenced to almost 100 years in prison for a gunshot wound to the hand.

Forget about the fact that Chuck didn't even shoot the guy, but for arguments sake, lets say that Chuck really did shoot Bobby in the hand. 100 years? 100 years in prison for a gunshot wound to the hand. People who are convicted of rape and murder are given less time that that. 100 years?

I will not try to argue my father's innocence. I will just tell you that, on my birthday, December 4th, he was falsely accused of a crime that he did not commit and he was taken out of my life. The very next day after his trial, his mother, the lady that I called grandma, the lady who was my *Angel*, Gwendolyn Sanders, went to the hospital.

My grandmother had been a diabetic for a long time, and her health had always been bad. But most people say that it was my father's sentence that ultimately killed her. Just weeks later, after saying goodbye to my dad, I found myself walking into Ruby Memorial Hospital in Morgantown, West Virginia to say goodbye to the lady who took me in and rescued me. I remember when we got the phone call that Grandma wasn't going to make it through the night. My cousin Bam Bam and I were at the house. We just stared at each other.

"Could this really be happening?" I looked at Bam and said. Bam Bam just shrugged his shoulders in disbelief. He said, "I guess we better get to the hospital." But there was a problem. Our family didn't have a car and we had no transportation to get from Fairmont to Morgantown, which was about 30 minutes away. Bam Bam and I immediately headed to the bus station to catch a ride to Morgantown. During the bus ride, Bam Bam and I just looked at each other. We knew what was waiting for us when we got to Morgantown.

THE DOCTOR WHO CHANGED MY LIFE

When we got to the hospital, I remember the strong desire that I had to talk to my grandmother and say goodbye to her, alone - I just wanted to thank her for everything that she did for me. Prior to walking into my grandmother's room, her doctor grabbed me, looked down at me, and said, "Son, your grandmother is in a coma. But we have no idea if she can hear you or not. Son, do you understand what I am saying to you?"

With uncertainty, I looked at him and I said, "I... I think so... maybe. I'm not sure." He continued, "Son, you should talk to your grandmother. Talk to her. We never really know what happens to a person when they are in a coma. Who knows, she just might be able to hear you. Even though she can't respond, I still want you to talk to your grandmother, make sure you talk to her."

I remember looking up at the doctor, then glancing at the doorway as I looked into her room, then back at the doctor again, then back at the doorway. I repeated this several times. I did not want to walk in. I guess there was a larger part of me that knew if I walked in, my sheer presence inside of her room would confirm the gravity of the moment I was in. As I began to cross the threshold into her hospital room, I thought of my dad, Chuck. I thought about the fact that just a few days before, I lost him forever.

And now, I had to walk into his mother's room and say goodbye to the lady who was my everything.

As I entered her room, I immediately began to focus on the beeps and sounds of all the machines that were attached to her and the bags beside her bed that were collecting fluid and keeping her body alive. She was experiencing kidney failure, and her body began to swell. She was almost unrecognizable. I was used to seeing the machines hooked up to her. I mean, we watched her go through a dialysis regimen for years leading up to her death. I'm not sure if you've ever experienced a loved one or family member who had to have dialysis treatment on a weekly basis, but it isn't pretty. Diabetes and kidney failure had taken over the lives of many people in my family, and the scene was all too familiar. At the young age of 56 years old, my grandmother was far too young to be leaving so soon.

As I stood beside her bed, I remember not having enough courage to look at her, to look into her eyes. As I stood there and held her hand, I turned my shoulders and head away from her. Who did I see staring in the doorway? The doctor. As we made eye contact, the doctor motioned to me. "Son, it's okay, go ahead. Talk to your grandmother. Say whatever is in your heart."

I didn't know what to say or what to do. With the encouragement of the doctor, I slowly turned towards my grandmother. As I began to try to find the right thing to say, the first words that I attempted came out in the form of a cry, and I lost it. Immediately, all I could think to do in the moment was exactly what most people would have done – I began to beg her not to leave me.

It may sound selfish, but self-preservation takes over our minds and hearts in moments like that. I knew that if I lost her, I was going to lose the only parental figure that I had left in my life. I knew that with the loss of my father Chuck to a lifelong prison sentence, losing my grandmother too would mean I was going to have to adjust to loosing the second set of parents in my life. The longer I cried and the longer I begged her not to leave me, the more hopeless I started to become in that moment.

I finally had the courage to turn and look into my grandmother's face, and that's when I saw it. I saw it when it happened. As I looked at her, I noticed that she had a tear coming from her eye going down her right cheek. As I stared at her face, I instantly looked back at the doctor. Was he right when he told me that she might be able to hear me even though she was in a coma? I couldn't believe my eyes. I couldn't believe what I *thought* I was seeing. As I saw the tear roll down her right cheek, I stared very intently at her face. For a brief moment, I thought that I saw her lip quiver very faintly, as if she was trying to say something.

It was the only sign I needed to see. In my heart, I knew that she could hear me. I *believed* that she could hear me. In that moment, I knew that my grandmother could hear every single word I was saying, but she couldn't respond. Right away, the energy in that room changed.

I've never experienced a moment like that in my life – I knew it was the last time I was going to talk to my grandmother, and the fact that she just might be able to hear every word that I was saying, but she couldn't respond - was powerful. It was the type of moment that Hollywood pays writers a lot of money to capture in a script – a moment packed with emotion and intensity. It was the moment in every story where the music starts to fade in really slowly, and a character must make a decision to do something. You know exactly the type of moment I am talking about.

As I looked over at the doctor, he motioned again, "Go ahead, go ahead, talk to your grandmother." As I held her hand tightly and began to speak to her, the only thing that could come out of my heart and my mouth was gratitude. I began to thank her for everything that she'd done for me. I said, "Thank you for giving me a chance, thank you for taking me off the streets of New York. Thank you for loving me. Thank you for taking me in, thank you for feeding me, thank you for giving me clothes, thank you for putting a roof over my head. Thank you for making me go to church, thank you for everything."

Right away, my gratitude turned into promises. Knowing that this was the last time I would ever talk to her before she died, the only thing that I could do was make promises to her about what I was going to do with the rest of the life she built for me. I began to say things like, "I promise I'm gonna graduate from high school, I promise I'm gonna go to college. I promise I'm not gonna use drugs, I promise I'm not gonna sell drugs. I promise I'm gonna make you *proud* of me, I promise I'm gonna be a good husband one day, I promise I'm gonna be a good father one day. I am going to do something with what you gave me. I promise you I'm not gonna let you down. I'm gonna be successful."

As I let go of her hand, I slowly began to back away from her bed, and there was a large part of me that did not want to leave. I knew that once I left, a new chapter in my life would begin – a chapter that was all too familiar, one that would leave me feeling all alone, once again. As I slowly began to walk out of her room, I kept stopping and pausing, because I did not want to leave her there by herself. I didn't want her to be alone, and I didn't want her to die alone. Those five to ten steps that I took leaving her room were some of the longest steps of my entire life. As I got to the door, a familiar face greeted me. It was the doctor. He could tell how upset I was. Offering me a sense of comfort and a shoulder to lean on, he gave me a small hug.

WORDS REALLY CAN CHANGE YOUR LIFE

Many of us have had interactions with medical professionals in our lives. Most of us, including you, have experienced a variety of reactions from them. Some doctors may appear to be caring, while others may appear to be factual, cold and distant. Some doctors just sound like flat-out robots when they talk to grieving families. But this doctor was different. There was something unique about the way he interacted with me, something that went beyond what most medical professionals are trained to do. It actually seemed like he cared. He actually seemed to be right there in that moment with me.

I know that medical professionals are trained on how to provide caregiver support and how to have proper bedside manner. But there was something different about this guy. I mean, if you think about it, medical professionals experience a variety of things on a daily basis. Think about the doctor who has to go into the room of the four-year-old boy who was just involved in an auto accident with his parents. His parents may not have survived their injuries, or the attempt at emergency surgery to save their lives could have failed. As his parents are transferred to the morgue and prepared for the medical examiner, what happens to him? What happens to the little boy who's laying in his room with cuts and bruises and asking where his mommy and daddy are? Trust me, doctors have seen that type of situation before – more than you realize.

But something deep inside of me could tell that this doctor actually cared about me that night. He didn't give me the standard, "It's okay son, relax, everything is going to be alright," type of speech. And I knew he didn't say anything that he didn't mean. He simply looked at me and said, "I'm sorry, I'm so sorry." And he hugged me. As the doctor hugged me, he noticed me staring back into my grandmother's room, and he could tell that I did not want to leave.

He looked at me and said, "Young man, I know this situation is tough, and I know this isn't easy for you. It sounds like you have lost parents before, am I right?"

I remember looking at him and wondering how he knew that, but then I realized that this was the same doctor who did not leave the doorway as I sat there talking to my grandmother. He was familiar with my story. He knew what dynamics I faced in my life and the gravity of what I was about to walk into when I left that hospital.

He put his hand on my shoulder and he said, "Young man, I wish there was some medicine that I could give you to help you through this situation. I wish there was some medicine that I could give you to make you feel better right now, but there isn't."

I remember thinking to myself, "What! Why would you say something like that? Why would you point out the obvious when you have no way to help me?" I guess he could tell that I had a disappointed look on my face based on what he said.

I can't really remember everything that doctor said that day, but I do remember this – he looked at me and he said, "Son, I do not have medicine to help you feel better right now, but if you allow me to, I have something else that may help you. Can I share it with you?"

I looked up at him through squinted eyes in an unsure way. Judging by the expression on my face, he looked back down at me and he said, "As a matter of fact, what I have to share with you... it can help you through this situation, but it can also help you through the rest of your life if you'll listen. Can I share it with you?"

With all the energy I had, I said, "Yes, sir." He turned and he squared his shoulders towards me. He looked me in my eyes and leaned in towards me. In a very serious, direct tone he said, "Young man, don't you EVER forget where you are from."

I said, "Excuse me?"

He said, "Don't you EVER forget, where you are from. I heard you make all of those promises to your grandmother. Do you want to make good on the promises you made her one day?"

"Yes sir", I said.

"If you really want to do something with your life young man, don't you ever forget where you're from. Son, you live in America. America! Don't you realize that you live in a country where brave men and women fight for your freedom every single day?"

"Yes sir."

"No matter who you are, no matter what you go through, you always have a chance in this country." I don't think I had ever met a more passionate patriot in my life.

He went on to say, "Son, I know this situation is tough, and I have no idea what you're gonna be facing when you go home. But no matter what you go through, don't ever forget that you live in the greatest country in the world."

As I looked at the doctor, he had a serious look in his eye. It was a look that made me actually believe that what he was saying to me came from a place deep inside his heart.

How he connected with me in that moment reminds me of a certain aspect of communication that you will read about a few chapters from now. His words came out with passion, and he was convicted in what he was saying to me.

He looked at me and he said, "Son, if you wanna be an All-American and if you want to have your own American Dream..." and then he just stopped. He was a smart man. I guess he realized he was making a big assumption even though he heard me make all those promises to my grandmother.

He said, "Son, do you wanna be successful?"

I replied, "Excuse me?"

"Do you really want to succeed in this country? Do you want your own American Dream one day?"

I said, "Yes, sir."

He said, "If you wanna be an All-American and if you want to have your own American Dream, never ever blame anyone else for your mistakes. Never blame *anyone* for *your* mistakes. Don't ever be a victim in life. Take responsibility for your own life, no matter what."

"Yes sir."

"And don't ever expect anyone to give you anything. There are no free rides. Son, you live in a country where people die on homemade boats and rafts just trying to cross the ocean to get to America to pursue their dreams. If you want your own American Dream, don't you ever blame anyone else or be a victim. Take responsibility for your life, and don't ever expect any free handouts. If you do that, you can have anything you want in this country."

I just sat there staring at him. I looked him right in his eyes. You may be wondering how I could remember in such vivid detail his words and what he shared. Trust me, if you were me, you would realize there is no way that I could *ever* forget what he said.

I have played that night and those words over and over in my mind for years and years. As he looked into my eyes, my heart was beating out of my chest and I didn't know why. My blood was pumping fast and everything was moving. With all the energy that I could gather, shaking my head up and down as if I was saying, "Yes, Yes." I just looked at him and said, "Yes sir. Yes sir. Thank you." And with that, the doctor hugged me once more and he began to walk away.

STANDING IN THE PARKING LOT

As I walked out of the hospital that night across the parking lot, my Aunt Francis was waiting in her car to give my cousin and me a ride home. I remember walking across the parking lot as I felt the blistering wind from that cold January night. Just before we got into her car, I stopped and I turned around to look up at my grandmother's hospital room one last time. That's when I saw it. That's when it happened. I actually saw it when it happened.

As I looked up at my grandmother's room on the 8th floor, the last room on the right hand side, I saw them cut the light out in her room.

With the flip of a switch, a switch was flipped inside me. In my heart, I felt like she was already gone. I stood there frozen, looking at her room. There were a million thoughts racing through my mind. I thought about the tear that came down her face. I thought about holding her hand one last time. I thought about all of the promises that I had made her before I walked out. I thought about everything the doctor said to me to inspire my own American Dream. I thought about everything. All of it was running through my head.

I had this overwhelming feeling as I stood there. I couldn't really describe it. I don't know if I was motivated, inspired, nervous or just anxious. I just stood there rocking side to side, staring up at her room. I felt like I wanted to do something. I felt like I *needed* to do something. Maybe I was simply having an emotional reaction to the situation that I was in. It felt like a combination of all of my emotions at once.

Either way, on that night, in that moment, I realized the value that emotional capital has in our lives. Emotional capital? You may be asking yourself, "What is that?" Emotional capital is something that I believe is more powerful than money. Emotional capital is something that only big moments can produce. It's something that money just can't buy.

As I sat there in that parking lot, I felt like I could run through a brick wall. Even to this day, any time I'm in that parking lot, any time I go back to West Virginia, whenever I get anywhere close to Ruby Memorial Hospital, those emotions come back, *instantly*.

West Virginia University's football stadium is directly across the parking lot from Ruby Memorial Hospital. The parking lot that I stood in when I saw them cut the light out in my grandmother's room is called the blue lot during WVU football games. As a WVU Alumni, any time I go back for a football game, and any time I step into the blue lot, the memories return. In a sea of blue and gold WVU jerseys and paraphernalia, it's easy to spot me staring off with a wondering look, up at the 8th floor – the last room on the right hand side. And with one look, just one glance, it takes me right back to that night.

That was the night when I stood there feeling like I wanted to conquer the world – I felt... the *emotional capital* of the situation. In that moment, for the first time, I felt like I had a purpose. I felt like I had a cause. I made a promise to a woman that night, a woman who was my Angel. I promised not to squander everything that she had sacrificed for me. That was also the evening that a kind, passionate doctor gave me the blueprint for a way to make good on every promise that I made her.

Although I felt focused and ambitious to fulfill a promise, once I left the hospital that night, I never felt more alone in my entire life.

The days that followed would prove to be equally as tough. The State Department of Corrections denied my father's request to attend his own mother's funeral. That crushed me even more. At the funeral home, during my grandmother's wake service the night before the funeral, they allowed my father to make a brief visit to say goodbye to his mother, but they still did not allow him to attend the funeral.

At her wake service, I just sat there feeling miserable. I remember them bringing my father through the doors in an orange jumpsuit with shackles on his feet, handcuffs on his hands, and a chain connecting the two. I remember standing off in the corner, feeling like a *lost little boy who wanted to run over and free his dad so they could ride off together and never return.*

In some strange way, I wanted my dad to save me and protect me again. I wanted him to take me under his wing the same way he did ten years prior when my grandmother was taken into surgery at Johns Hopkins. I don't know what broke my heart more that evening at the funeral home – watching my father walk inside the funeral home in orange prison gear, or knowing that he wasn't going home with me. Either way, I was heartbroken. The toughest part was seeing my father be denied the privilege of hugging and kissing his own mother. As I said goodbye to my grandmother, I knew I was saying goodbye to my father also.

The very next day as we entered the church at my grandmother's funeral, everyone began to take their seats. I joined the funeral procession with my family as we walked in to sit. That small Church of God on Maple Avenue was not a very large church. My grandmother had a very large heart and many people loved her. There was standing room only, with many people standing outside. When I noticed the funeral directors beginning to take the flowers off of my grandmother's casket to close it for eternity, I could not resist the urge to walk back up and hug her one last time. As I began to hug her, it became clear to others standing around that I was not prepared to leave my grandmother's side.

At most funerals, they close the casket before they start the service. But on this day, they had no choice but to wait. I sat there as I hugged her for what seemed like forever, not wanting to let her go.

Once we got to the graveside service on that blistery cold January day, when the service was completed and everyone walked back to their cars, I stayed behind with my grandmother's casket. I couldn't believe that everyone else just walked away and left her there, all by herself. I just sat there with her, keeping her company and talking to her. I was emotional, and I was not thinking straight. When I finally had the energy to leave the graveyard that day, a major chapter in my life came to a close.

OVERNIGHT SUCCESS

Chapter

4

The Real Heroes

Today much of how I live my life can be traced back to December 4th, 1994, when I lost my second father, Chuck. His arrest set off a chain of events in my life —including losing my grandmother – that would permanently influence the person that I would grow to be.

Today, I am lucky enough to work with some of the top companies in the world as I use my passion to help them answer one question: Why is it that some people and organizations – no matter who they are and no matter where they're from – are more successful than others?" The real question that I often ask myself is, "How did I get here?"

When you consider how my story began in New York City and the unfortunate events that surrounded my life - if you were a gambler, you probably would have bet your money on the fact that I was most likely going to end up just like many other young black kids in the streets -- just another statistic. I mean think about it, the outcome typically does not look promising for a young, black teenager on his own without the guidance of parents, especially without a dad. Children without fathers are ten times more likely to abuse substances and nine times more likely to drop out of school.

With regards to mental health, 80 percent of the kids in psychiatric facilities are fatherless. Even worse, adolescents without dads are twice as likely to commit suicide and an astonishing 20 times more likely to be incarcerated.

I think the only reason why I beat the odds and am where I am today is because I found a purpose that drives me. When I sat in the parking lot and I watched them cut the light out in my grandmother's room, I remember the emotional capital of that moment when I said goodbye to her and the emotional aspect of what the doctor shared with me about pursuing my own American Dream. Those two factors combined produced a reaction inside of me that changed my focus and changed my life, because it changed my MINDSET.

I have met many people who were already familiar with my story before they ever saw me in person. When they do finally get a chance to meet me, many of them say the same thing: "Morris I am so sorry that you went through everything you did. That must have been so tough for you!"

The only problem when someone says that to me is that I can't keep myself from smiling. Why do I smile? Well, the truth is, they couldn't be more wrong, because I have an amazing life today, and none of it would be possible without the events that occurred when I was young. Plus, remember when I told you that faith gives me an advantage over my competition? Well like I said, no matter what I go through, I know that I can still win *in all things*, no matter what. And I want to spend the rest of my life inspiring people throughout the entire world to tap into that same mindset.

Many people live by the notion that everything happens for a reason, but I don't. I believe that you are in control of what the reason is. I believe that most people have the cognitive ability to control how they respond in most situations. Don't get me wrong, I acknowledge that there are some people who are faced with challenges and have limitations with regards to their ability to function at full mental capacity. But I also believe that *if you have the mental ability to COMPLAIN about a situation, you have the mental ability to CHANGE the situation* - it's your choice.

TRANSITIONS ARE NEVER EASY

The days and months that followed my grandmother's death were really rough. Thankfully, I was surrounded by many adults, coaches, teachers, and mentors who saw something greater in me. They constantly encouraged me. I'm glad they did, because they had no idea how desperate I was. They had no idea that I began to plan my own suicide. I contemplated the fastest ways that I could kill myself with as little pain as possible. My mindset shifted towards ending my own life simply because I felt so alone. I felt like my life didn't matter to anyone at all.

Ultimately, it's the relationships surrounding us that determine how we choose to view our circumstances. If it weren't for a few critical people in my life during that time, there is a big chance that I would not be here today. Get ready for the best part about my story, because you're about to meet some of those people right now.

EDDIE WHITE

Eddie White was our next-door neighbor when I was growing up. Everyone called him *Uncle Eddie*. He was a full-time West Virginia coal miner for his entire life, and he also ran a local convenience store that he had opened up in the hood. In between his shifts, he and I would sit at his kitchen table and talk about everything from success principles to the Bible. We also had very big discussions about my future and the potential that he thought that I had.

One day when I was in the 8th grade, I was sitting in his store near some of his arcade machines when a couple of brothas from the neighborhood came in. They noticed that I was doing homework. Right away, they started making comments to me, poking fun at the fact that I was trying to get my work done.

"Look at him over there studying, look at him over there acting like a sellout and acting like a little white boy", they said. Now I'm not going to lie to you, these brothas happened to be older than me, and I was scared of them. Eddie walked over to them and just stood there. Finally, a smile showed on his face as he looked at them and began to laugh right in their faces. He pointed over to me as he looked at them, and he said, "You see that guy right there? Can I tell you the difference between you guys and Morris? Y'all are making fun of him for hustling and doing his homework, but you better laugh right now as much as you can. Go ahead, keep laughing. Get it all out. Because one day, if you are lucky, you are going to end up working for him."

Uncle Eddie came to my rescue that day. More importantly, he deposited something into my heart - he created the expectation for me to do something with my life. I learned that expectation, or anticipation of what's to come, will either produce focus or frustration in a person. For me, Uncle Eddie helped me look forward to the rest of my life.

ALLEN "BIG JAY" SCOTT

His name was Allen Jay Scott, but everyone called him "Big Jay." Yep, B-I-G. That's because he weighed between 400 and 500 pounds at any given time. When I tell you that he was big, trust me, he was BIIIIIG! To make things even more interesting, Big Jay had a twin brother called "Little Jay".

For twins, they could not have been any more opposite. As an adult male in his 30's, Big Jay was 4 times the size of other men his age. His twin brother Little Jay was about 5 foot 6 inches tall, and he was the size of a 12-year-old kid that hadn't gone through puberty yet. Little Jay on a good day weighed about 125 pounds soaking wet.

The Scott family lived on Monroe Street next to my dad Chuck. When I was old enough, I would frequently walk to my dad's house to see him. He wasn't home very often, so I eventually began to visit with the Scotts next door.

Big Jay's father, Mr. Allen Scott, was a tough old WV coal miner who refused to retire, even in his old age. I never really thought he liked me much when I was a kid, and I had absolutely no idea why. Okay, maybe I did. I used to go straight to the refrigerator whenever I entered their house just to eat up all of his favorite snacks. I used to eat all of his Werther's Original candy out of the nightstand beside his bed. He would just grunt and make funny noises when he walked past me. Eventually, the old man just got used to seeing me around.

I spent a lot of time at the Scott's residence. I don't know why I spent so much time there in the beginning – maybe it was the food, maybe it was the Werther's Original candies. When I first started hanging around their house, Big Jay used to scare me because he was so huge and I was just a little kid. I had never seen a human being *that large* before in person!

Whenever he wasn't away at work, Big Jay seemed to be at home, chillin'. I stopped over pretty regularly to get my fill of candy or food, and occasionally Big Jay and I would play a couple of video games. Eventually, as I started to progress to different grade levels in school, Big Jay was there to help me with my homework. As my life began to get more complex, he was there to listen to my problems, and he always gave the best advice. Big Jay was the big brother that I never had. It didn't matter what I needed; I always knew that Big Jay or anyone else in his family was there to help me.

When Big Jay went to purchase a new car when I was 16 years old, he actually chose one that had a manual transmission even though he could not drive a stick shift. Why? Because it was the car that I liked. After he signed all of the paperwork, he couldn't even drive the car home. He had to bring me to the dealership afterwards to drive the car home for him because *of course* I knew how to drive a stick shift!

There isn't enough room to tell you all the things that Big Jay did for me. And I could never fully express the amount of gratitude that I have for him and the entire Scott family. I will say this: when someone is willing to invest their time, energy, and resources in you, it matters, it means everything.

During the transition period after I lost my grandmother and my dad Chuck, Big Jay and his family made a big difference in my life. They didn't just *HELP* me either, they *PUSHED* me. They had high hopes for me and they wanted to see me do something with my life. When things were at their lowest point for me, even when I contemplated ending my life, I didn't just think about how much it would hurt my dad Chuck if he received that type of news while he was in prison, I also thought about how much it would hurt Big Jay and the entire Scott family. I was a permanent fixture at the Scott residence. Boy, did I love them, and I never wanted to cause any hurt or pain for people who had nothing but love for me.

JERRY AND DEBBIE JOHNSON

Andy Johnson was my best friend while growing up, and he still is today. AJ's parents were named Debbie and Jerry, and they were important people in our town. They seemed to know and hang out with all of the right people in our community - at least that's how I saw it. My friendship with AJ and the Johnson family was one of the most significant relationships in my early life. I really felt like I was somebody when I was with their family.

AJ and I played basketball together since we were ten years old. AJ was also one of the most intelligent people that I knew. He took all the gifted classes, his family had money, and he lived in one of the good neighborhoods on the other side of town. It seemed like AJ was living *the good life* , at least from my perspective.

AJ and I spent a lot of time with each other because we played sports together. Eventually, we wanted to have as much fun together as possible, so we signed up for many of the same classes. Over time, I also got a chance to experience what AJ's home life was like. At first, I hated spending time with the Johnson family at their house. I only hated it because I never wanted to leave once I was there. There was a part of me that secretly hoped they would ask me to live with them. Every time they took me back to my house after I visited with them, they had no idea how I really felt - it was always the longest car ride ever.

Every time I would go to AJ's house, I felt special just for being there. I had no idea why I felt that way at the time, but today I understand it clearly. Being around AJ and his family gave me a chance to be exposed to another culture. It opened my mind. *Could you imagine how much healthier our country would be if everyone in America would spend some time hanging out with and learning from people on the other side of the tracks?* It wasn't just AJ and his parents that I got to be around. He also had two popular older sisters named Jennifer and Marcie. He had an amazing set of grandparents and aunts and uncles who lived close by too.

I didn't have to be around AJ and his family very long before I recognized some pretty large differences between his lifestyle and mine. First of all, AJ had two parents that were actively involved in his education. They talked about his school assignments and they actually asked him how his day was? That absolutely blew my mind! It was such a culture shock for me. I couldn't imagine what it would be like if someone in my house talked to me every day about anything, especially my schoolwork. That was something that I just didn't have.

AJ's father, Jerry, was a blue-collar, hard-working guy who worked for a local electric company. He was one of the smartest men that I ever met; it seemed like Jerry knew everything. It seemed like he always had all of the answers.

His mother, Debbie, was a loyal, dedicated school teacher. Academics were always a focus in the Johnson home because of her. Debbie was always "mothering" AJ. At times I thought that it got on his nerves just a little bit, and it probably did considering he was a teenage boy going through puberty. But most of the time, I watched her "mother" AJ from afar, and I envied him. I wanted a mom just like her.

AJ's older sister Jennifer was an extremely talented student and a phenomenal athlete. When she received her acceptance letter into pharmacy school, I remember thinking to myself, "Pharmacy school... what is that? Well, whatever it is, it must be something super important if Jennifer is a part of it." Jennifer could do anything. She had so many awards and trophies that her room could barely hold them all. AJ's other sister, Marcie, was one of the brightest, most talented people that I have ever met in my entire life and socially, she knew everyone, and everyone knew her. Anything that Marcie touched with her hands turned into magic right before your eyes because her artistic talent and ability was second to none. I guess it's no surprise that today she is one of the most in-demand photographers that I know.

What AJ's family did for me was truly remarkable. They invited me into their home to spend precious time with them. *Everybody in this world – even you – is limited by what they see and experience.* That's why what they did for me was just as impactful as inviting a starving person to eat at their table. I wasn't starving for food, but I was hungry for perspective. The Johnson family forever changed the idea of what *could be* in my life by exposing me to a different culture and sharing new experiences with me.

COACH JOE GERARDE

Coach Gerarde was my freshman basketball coach. When he came to "scout" me during my 8th grade season, it made me feel good. Okay, maybe he was there to watch everybody else play too, but when he talked to me that day, he told me that the sky was the limit for me as long as I continued to work hard.

Coach Gerarde really had a gift for connecting with people. To this day he still ranks as one of the best communicators that I have ever met. He always looked you directly in your eyes when he talked to you, he always had something positive to say, and he always had so much energy and enthusiasm when he told stories. He was also one of the best storytellers that I ever met. He used all of his communication skills when he spoke to you, even when he disciplined you for something!

Coach Gerarde was a very believable guy. He was a real players' coach, and he still is today. You never second guessed whether or not he had your best interest at heart. He knew that my family didn't have a car, so he always offered me rides back and forth to practice. When we were in his car together, my focus was always on basketball. His focus was always on something else, like shaving - he always had his electric razor with him! I still think about Coach Gerarde whenever I shave my face, because the truth is, Coach Gerarde taught me how to shave right there in his car.

Coach was always direct and real with me. I still remember the day he gave me a ride to practice after he had just found out that the woman he was going to marry cheated on him. "Well, that's how life is sometimes, some people are only meant to be in your life for a short time", he said. Coach Gerarde was used to experiencing loss. His mother died in a terrible car accident when he was in middle school. Raised by his father and his extended family, he understood how to beat adversity and not let it kill his spirit.

I guess that's one of the reasons why we clicked so well. I guess that's why we never really talked much about basketball during those car rides. We talked about *other stuff* – life stuff. And we always talked about my Plan B, *my life outside of basketball*. He would say, "Morris, you are different than a lot of the other black players that I have coached. You've got a real shot kid and you don't need sports. You've got a ticket to really go somewhere one day, so don't screw it up by only focusing on basketball. Life is bigger than basketball."

I thought that the only reason why he would say those things to me was because I wasn't a good basketball player. But that wasn't it, because I wasn't the only person he said that about. "Morris, I believe that you and Rashod Kent both have a special gift that will take you far in life - you both have great heads on your shoulders. Rashod will definitely play D1 college basketball somewhere one day, and you, well… you probably won't."

I said, "Geez Coach, what are you trying to say about my hooping skills?"

He said, "Morris, you are a good player, but basketball is not your real gift. So enjoy the game while you can, but don't over-focus on it because you have a much bigger life ahead of you!" It hurt to hear that, especially because basketball meant so much to me. But I needed to hear that. I needed someone to be honest with me, and, I needed someone to give me encouragement and hope. Coach Gerarde did a great job of casting a vision for my future and creating an expectation for me to make good choices and decisions with my life, and I never wanted to disappoint him.

MAMA ROSE JOHNSON

Mama Rose Johnson was the mother of my other best friend, Germaine Johnson. Yep, that's right. I have two best friends and they both have the last name Johnson. The difference is that Andy Johnson is white and Germaine Johnson is black. I call them "The Chocolate and Vanilla Johnson's."

Germaine lived down the street from me. He and I had a vastly different upbringing than Andy did on the other side of town. Germaine lived dead-smack in the middle of the hood on Maple Avenue. Maple Avenue was called "Crack Alley" by the local newspapers and law enforcement. When we were kids, a stroll down Maple Avenue was no walk in the park for most people. But it never bothered me because I knew all of the drug dealers. Heck, most of my uncles *were* the drug dealers. It never bothered Germaine much either – he was used to it. He lived right near "The Corner," where more drugs were sold in our small town than anywhere else. We didn't exactly live in Harlem or The Bronx, but it was typical to see someone get shot, and die right there on Maple Avenue.

Germaine's mother Rose gave us all a place to go if we needed it. Her home was a retreat for many people. It didn't matter who you were. If you needed anything, anything at all, she was there for you. And she always had a warm plate of food for you. There were times when I didn't have a place to live at all, and Mama Rose welcomed me into her home. She didn't have much space available, but she made room, because that's just who she was.

When I think about the movie that Sarah Jessica Parker starred in called *I Don't Know How She Does It,* I think of women like Rose Johnson. I still don't know how she managed to do it all. Rose was a single mother with three kids, and she didn't have the support of a man in her life. Still, when we were young, her children had all of their needs met, and most of their *wants* too. Rose treated us all like we were her kids – me, Kevin Lampkin, Rashod Kent, Ronnie White, and Devon Miller – she loved us all.

Although Rose didn't have much to give, *she still managed to give everything she had to everyone.* She taught me the importance of mastering the skill of resourcefulness and the importance of fighting for what you want. Her selflessness and generosity have always inspired me. I have always enjoyed making her proud and seeing the look that she gets on her face when any of her "kids" achieve something. And to think, some people wonder why I am so driven and motivated. One of the many reasons is because I love seeing that woman happy.

MRS. LINDA MORGAN

I have never met a more dynamic educator in my entire life. Linda Morgan was the AP English teacher in my high school.

Her reputation preceded her. For years, before I even entered high school, people talked about *The Legend of Linda Morgan*. People would say, "Uh-ohhh, you are about to graduate from the 7th grade to the 8th grade. You know what that means don't you? Only a few more years until you have Linda Morgan as your teacher!"

I had no idea what all of the fuss was about. I mean, she was *just a teacher*, right? Nope. Linda Morgan transformed how students saw the entire education process. She showed up in my AP English class on the last day of school during my junior year.

"How many of you are planning on taking my AP English class in the fall?" she asked. Reluctantly, many of us began to raise our hands. It was bad enough that she imposed fear on us since junior high school, but now she was showing up during the last week of school before summer break? She handed a sheet of paper to those of us who raised our hands. "Here is your summer reading assignment. I expect you to be prepared to discuss this in the fall and you will be tested on the material. What? We all had a confused look on our faces. What is this? What is she doing? Is she even allowed to do this? I was thinking to myself, "This white lady must be crazy!" She wasn't crazy. She was just *that* good. She was establishing an expectation for our performance in the fall. I have never met another teacher like Linda Morgan.

We noticed a difference in her as soon as we crossed the threshold from the hallway into her classroom. Her room even looked different from the rest of the school. She had bright paint colors on the walls, there were nice, live plants hanging, and she had images of fine art work from leading scholars. I had never seen any classroom like hers.

To complete the effect, she would often have classical music playing in the background. Her room even smelled different than other rooms. And she smelled different too. She wore expensive perfume. I know it was expensive, it had to be! I just remember thinking to myself, "That must be *exactly* what Heaven smells like!"

Linda Morgan even dressed differently. Even though she was in her late 40's, she still looked like a younger woman who stepped right out of a magazine. She was a class act – one of the classiest women that I had ever been around in my entire life. She wore very trendy, contemporary clothes and accessories, and her glasses completed her distinguished look perfectly. This lady was a beast! Trust me, when I say that about someone, it's the biggest compliment I can give. She took everything that she did, even the appearance of her classroom and how she presented herself, seriously. In turn, every time we walked into her room we knew what time it was: it was time to work. Although she pushed us hard, to this day I have never performed so well in another teacher's classroom. I didn't even get an "A" in her class. I got a "B". Even still, I never worked so hard in my life, and I never got as much out of a class as I did hers. A "B" in her class felt like a 110% in any other class.

If you were to take a poll of any group of students who were fortunate enough to have Linda Morgan as their teacher during her 40 year career, a large percentage of those former students will name Linda Morgan as their all-time *favorite* teacher.

If you took another poll with the same group of students and ask them who their *toughest* teacher was, a large majority of them will also say Linda Morgan. By forcing us to bring our best effort to her classroom, she unknowingly allowed me to forget about anything that I had going on at home.

I once heard someone say, *"It would be a shame to go through my entire life and never truly meet the real me."* Well, at a very critical time in my life when I was searching for meaning and purpose and trying to figure out who I was, Linda Morgan helped introduced me to my potential self. She forced me to reconcile *who I thought I was,* with the real person staring back at me in the mirror. How did she do this? She did it the same way all great teachers, coaches, and leaders do – by setting standards for what she expected and giving me the chance to increase my ability by giving my best effort.

After my experience in Linda Morgan's classroom, I felt like I could do anything. She was a large catalyst for helping me achieve the only type of *Overnight Success* possible: the instant feeling that you get *when you change how you see yourself.* And it couldn't have happened at a better time.

MY DRIVERS ED TEACHER

My driver's ed teacher, Mr. Joe Cavalier, asked me to stick around after class one day because he needed to speak with me. When he approached me, he explained, "I have to nominate one student to send to a leadership conference here in the state of West Virginia. And for some reason, I feel like I am supposed to choose you."

"Say what?" I responded.

"This experience would be perfect for someone like you."

"Someone like me... someone like me. What do you mean by that?"

He said, "Trust me, this is a great opportunity to meet other talented students who are also future leaders, just like you. Don't worry, you will have a great time."

I responded, "Umm, sorry, I wish I could go but I can't. I have basketball."

He said, "Don't worry, I already talked to your coach, you're going."

I said, "What?"

"Don't worry about it, you are going."

Obviously I was in a situation where I had little choice. So I packed up and I prepared to go to the *stupid leadership conference* (sorry, but that was how I felt about it at the time).

As soon as I arrived, I noticed that there were quite a few cute girls there. I thought to myself, "Yep, this is my type of place. I was meant to be here!"

The conference taught us the importance of having strong leadership skills and integrity, and the importance of living drug and alcohol free.

It was amazing being in the same place with so many other young teenagers who were focused on making good choices and decisions in life. When you surround yourself with other people who have a strong vision for their lives, their determination is contagious. They inspire you.

I have no idea why Joe Cavalier chose me that day, but I am glad that he did because that student leadership conference made a big difference in my life. I had a great time the first year that I attended the conference. But the real benefits didn't hit me until my senior year in high school when I was invited back to attend the same conference as a mentor leader. I was one of approximately 50 other students who were invited to arrive two days early before the conference began.

Towards the end of the second day, the day before the rest of the juniors and sophomores were supposed to show up for the conference, something happened that changed my life.

Our conference leader and advisor, Greg Knight, asked us to vote for one person from the group that we would like to see on stage as the emcee and speaker for the three-day event.

"There is no way," I thought to myself. "I am not going on stage. I am not speaking in front of hundreds of my peers for three days!"

My fears made perfect sense. Public speaking always has been, and probably always will be a nightmare for many people. Public speaking has consistently been rated as the top phobia of many people. The fear of public speaking ranks above the fear of heights, clowns, bugs, snakes and death (not in that order). So, you could understand why I was willing to do everything that I could to make sure that I wasn't selected.

When the hat came around to me, I looked over at the girl beside me and asked, "What's your name again?"

"Jennifer," she responded.

I looked down at the piece of paper that I was holding, and with the stroke of my pen, I wrote "Jennifer!"

When the ballots were all counted, I found out the news. About 99 percent of the people in the room voted for the same person that they wanted to see on stage. Yep, you guessed it, it was Jennifer! At least that's what I wished the results were at the time. When Greg Knight turned to congratulate me on being chosen, I was furious.

"I am NOT going on stage tomorrow. I am not speaking in front of all those people."

"Why not?" He asked.

"Because!"

"Because why?" He said.

"Because... Because!" I answered.

I couldn't tell him the real reason why I didn't want to do it. The truth was I was scared out of my mind. With everyone in the group now staring at me after voting for me, Greg said, "Like it or not, you are going on stage. You can't let all of these people down. They all voted for you, they believe in you. As a matter of fact, the only person in this room that doesn't believe in you is you, Morris." With everyone staring at me, I didn't want to look like a coward.

Caving in to their peer pressure, I softly said under my breath, "Okay, I'll do it."

The truth was, there was a girl in the room that I had a crush on. Her name was Trina. I didn't want to ruin any chances of impressing her. That was the real reason why I said yes (once again, there's always a girl... there's always a girl)!

I stepped onto stage on the first day and I thought that I was going to faint. It took every ounce of strength that I had to stay up on my feet.

By the end of the first day, let's just say I was glad it was over. One day down, two more to go. By the second day, the anticipation was even worse and I barely got any sleep the night before because I was so nervous.

Once I got on stage during the second day, I felt a little better - at least by then I knew what to expect. By the end of the second day, I am not sure what happened. But all of a sudden, things started to click. Everything started to feel natural to me.

Speaking in front of all those people felt so good, and I went to sleep that night excited about the next morning. On my third and final morning on stage, I felt amazing. All of the nervousness had gone away. The nervousness was replaced by excitement, and all of a sudden, I didn't want to leave. I didn't want the day to end. I didn't even want to hand over the microphone when it was time to step off stage. I felt great, and the best part about all of it was the enthusiasm that I generated from my peers.

After three days of being there, I connected with many people. When you are at a conference like that, people are quick to share their story as well as their dreams, because everyone is so pumped up and energized. Many of the students at the conference knew my story as well. I guess that's what made the comments even more fulfilling.

"Dude, you killed it. You were great up there!" said some.

"Man, you have so much energy. You really know how to get people motivated." said others.

But the majority of comments sounded like this: *"This would be a perfect job for you! You are so good at being on stage, you should be an entertainer, or a speaker or something!"*

And that was it. That's how it happened. That's how my dream to be a speaker was born.

I learned a very valuable lesson in life when I decided to say yes to attending that conference. I learned that amazing things *CAN* happen *when you just show up.* But I learned an even more important lesson by agreeing to speak on stage. I learned that amazing things *WILL* happen when you *show up and participate.* I showed up at that conference during a time in my life when I was lost.

By the time I left the conference, I discovered something else inside of me – my gift. And none of it would have ever happened without my Driver's Ed teacher, Mr. Joe Cavalier.

SO I DECIDED NOT TO GIVE UP

After experiencing the adversity that I faced as a teenager, I realized two things. The first was *it's amazing what a person can do when they have to.* Adversity can reveal things about a person's character that nothing else can. If given the option, I would never have chosen to lose both of my parents in New York City when I was a child. And I certainly would not have chosen for my only remaining father figure, Chuck, to be sentenced to nearly 100 years in prison and taken out of my life.

I definitely would not have willingly chosen to stand in the middle of that parking lot at Ruby Memorial Hospital and whisper goodbye to my Angel, Gwendolyn Sanders.

I would never have willingly participated in any of those moments if given a choice. But I didn't have a choice, and as a result, those moments produced an emotional response in me that gave me focus and a purpose. That's why I truly believe that one of the greatest motivational principles of life is *it's amazing what a person can do when they have to.*

The second lesson that I learned was *the impact that relationships can have in our lives* . Rather than dealing with the pain in my life, I wanted to hurt myself very badly. But I had people like Eddie White, Big Jay, the Chocolate Johnson family, the Vanilla Johnson family, Coach Gerarde, Linda Morgan, and even the most unlikely of characters – my driver's ed teacher Mr. Joe Cavalier – there to cheer me on. I call them my Board of Directors. Each one of them, in their own way, instilled something in my heart that made me want to live during a time in my life when I wanted to end it all. They taught me the importance of having the right people in your corner.

I slowly began to see myself the way my Board of Directors saw me. Once I did that, it was on.

There is only one real form of *Overnight Success* – it's the success that you feel in your heart when you finally start to see yourself differently. So the question is, "What happens when you make a decision to finally live your life? What happens when you decide to live knowing that your future could not possibly be as painful as your past?" That's when your life changes. That's the exact moment in a Hollywood movie when the main character finally decides to step up and fight off his biggest challenges. You know, the moment when the Rocky theme music starts playing in the background. Well go ahead, get the music ready, because here comes the good stuff. ...

Chapter

5

Pretending

If there's one thing that bothers me more than anything in life, it's pretending. Now don't get me wrong, I don't mind pretending when I'm playing out a character or playing a game or having fun. But that's not what I'm talking about. I'll give you an example. I absolutely *cannot* stand it when I'm forced to engage a person with bad breath in close proximity - especially when I don't have a choice and I can't leave.

My boy Germaine used to tease me all of the time. He knew how sensitive my nose was to bad breath. When we were in college, he would notice from a distance whenever I was talking to someone who had bad breath. He would call the rest of our friends over, and he would just point towards me and say, "Look at Morris, look at him over there. He's trapped in a conversation. I can tell he doesn't like that person's breath. Let's see how he handles this."

After the interaction, I would walk back over to him, and he would laugh and say, "So, on a level of one to ten, how bad was it this time?" If a person's bad breath was minor, I would say, "Man, their breath was humming." But if their breath was firing in the medium range, I would look at him and say, "Man, it was on the double," meaning it was twice as bad as regular bad breath. And then there's the granddaddy of them all. If I ever looked at them and said, "Man, his breath was on the triple," then that was the ultimate. It didn't get any worse than that. As a matter of fact, if I designated you as the person who was *on the triple*, we looked at you differently.

Why am I talking about bad breath? Because we all have our thing. We all have things that get up under our skin and ultimately, these idiosyncrasies make us who we are. Bad breath, well, that's just something that I've never been able to deal with much. It's not really the smell that I can't deal with. I just don't like pretending. It's the fact that I have to stand there and *pretend* that I don't really smell it. It's the fact that most likely, I really need something from you at that moment and I do not have the liberty to just walk away. I hate it! Do you know how tough that is? I think that's why I have been able to grow my delivery skills on stage as an entertainer and a speaker, because some of the best Oscar-worthy roles I've played in my life, were when I was trapped in a conversation with a person who was "firing and humming on the triple" and I couldn't escape.

YOU NEVER SAW THIS ONE COMING

I'll give you another example of how tough it's been for me to pretend. I gotta tell you about my Aunt Sasha. My Aunt Sasha was probably one of the brightest people that have ever been in my family. Her IQ is on a whole other level.

When I was a kid, I remember watching her graduate from high school and become the first person in our family to go to college. I also remember when she became pregnant and had to drop out of college to start working and taking care of her daughter. Once my Aunt Sasha got into her mid-20s, something interesting started to happen to her physical appearance. My Aunt Sasha started to grow…a mustache. That's right, you heard me. My Aunt Sasha had a mustache. And it wasn't a little mustache either, it was big. I mean don't get me wrong, *it started out as a small concept at first*, but as she got older, it really took on a life of its' own.

Now trust me, there is nothing wrong with a woman having facial hair, especially if that's your thing and you enjoy it. I'm not judging you. But as for me, I've found that there is nothing tougher than dealing with bad breath, or standing in front of someone, anyone – it doesn't matter who it is – who has anything on them that draws attention to them, especially when you have to pretend like you don't see it. It could be food on their face, something on their teeth, maybe an eyelash is falling off and it's a little crooked. It puts you in a predicament because you are forced to ask yourself, "Should I tell them?" Then you have this long internal debate going on about whether or not you should tell them. You may even ask yourself, "If it were me, would I want the other person to tell me?"

Any time I would visit with my Aunt Sasha, I would just stare at her mustache. Since I was younger, I didn't know any better and couldn't exercise the self-control that it took to just "look away." I would just stare at her mustache and would think to myself, "Why? How? When?" I'm sorry, I'm just a naturally curious person, that's just who I am. But I could never really bring myself to say anything to her about it!

To make this situation even worse, my Aunt Sasha decided to take matters into her own hands. She finally made a decision to shave it off. I think we all thought to ourselves, "Oh noooooooo, don't do that!" But she did it anyway and I think you know what happened next after she shaved it. The same thing happened to her mustache that happens to any human being when they shave any hair on their body: it grew back thicker! Finally, I couldn't pretend anymore.

One day, I just said, "Aunt Sasha, where does that come from?" I said it just to mess with her, and throughout my life I continued to bring it up occasionally whenever I saw her. And she would always respond, "Boy, get out of my face! You always trying to be funny. You need to go somewhere with your little big-head-self."

Well, we talk about it today and we laugh about it. I even talk about Aunt Sasha's mustache on stage sometimes. I hated all of the years when her mustache was the big elephant in the room that no one wanted to talk about, as if everyone wasn't thinking the same thing. I mean, "How in the world could everyone possibly ignore the fact the her mustache was thicker than anyone else's in our family - *including her brothers*? I am glad that we can all joke about it now as a family, because like I said, *I can't stand pretending!*

WHEN YOU CAN'T PRETEND ANYMORE

As I prepared to transition out of high school into college, I was focused. I had a clear vision of what I wanted to do with my life. I knew that I wanted to be a speaker and an author and travel the world helping people and companies stay motivated. But I still hated the pretending that I had to do. I pretended like Chuck being in prison didn't hurt me as much as it did.

I pretended like I was strong every time I drove up to that prison and every time I was searched by the guards and put through the metal detectors just to pass clearance. I pretended like I didn't come up with every conceivable plan in my mind to break him out and take him with me so we could ride into the sunset together, happily ever after.

During my junior year in high school, I was a part of the state championship basketball team, and it was one of the best experiences of my life. I loved basketball, and basketball is one of the things that really kept me off the streets, and it kept me from selling drugs and getting into other types of trouble because it occupied my mind and gave me something to focus on.

After beating Beckley Woodrow Wilson in the semifinals, we went on to face Robert C. Byrd in the state championship game. After winning the state championship that year, I never forgot how great it was to see that smile on Coach Babe Stingo's face. And as I looked over at Coach Dave Ricer and Coach Joe Gerarde, I was just happy that we were able to do it for them. But I can't lie. I felt great also. There's nothing better than being a champion and being recognized as being a part of one of the best teams.

As soon as we got home from the state championship that day, I went to visit my Aunt Dot. She was the sister of Gwendolyn, the lady who raised me in West Virginia.

I spent a lot of time visiting Aunt Dot when I was younger. Ultimately, Aunt Dot took me in and allowed me live with her during my last year of high school when I had nowhere else to go. After returning from our victorious trip to states, the glory and the amazing feeling of winning a state championship were overshadowed by what I heard Aunt Dot say when I entered her house that day.

As soon as I walked in, she motioned to me to be quiet because she was on the phone. Aunt Dot was talking to Aunt Katherine. Aunt Katherine was one of the sisters of Gwendolyn and Dot who lived in Harlem. I had always heard about Aunt Katherine, but I had never met her before because she never visited West Virginia. All of the family members used to say things about how crazy she was and how much she despised West Virginia and never wanted to return. I never really knew the lady, I just heard some stories about her. I just thought she was a distant aunt, just a relative. I had no idea who she *really* was.

You can imagine how tough it was for me to pretend that I didn't hear what Aunt Dot said that day. "Hey Katherine," she said on the phone with a smile. "I just gotta tell you, that grandson of yours is doing so well. He takes advanced classes, and he really pushes himself in school, and he is doing so well. He keeps that Bible in his hand, and he's always dribbling that basketball. You never gotta worry about him being out in those streets. I wish you could meet him one day Katherine - you would be so proud of your grandson these days. He's just growing up to be such a fine young man. Yep, Billy's boy is growing up, and Billy's little boy is turning into a young man himself."

I sat in the other room, shocked. I couldn't pretend that I did not hear what Aunt Dot just said. I tried to listen to the rest of her conversation, but I couldn't take it. I packed my things and I left the house. As I walked into the night aimlessly, I could not pretend that I was okay.

"Did she just call me Katherine's grandson?" I asked myself. "What the *heck* is she talking about, and who the *heck* is Billy? My dad is CHUCK, and he is in jail."

I was Furious, so I walked back to Aunt Dot's house. I waited for her to get off the phone.

When she hung up the phone I said, "Aunt Dot, who is Katherine? And why did you call her my grandma? I thought Gwendolyn was my grandmother. And who is Billy? Billy is not my father, Chuck is my dad. Aunt Dot, what is going on?"

There was a long pause from Aunt Dot. As she stood up, she turned towards me and she started to cry. Every time she tried to talk, she couldn't get words out. She just cried. Aunt Dot fell back down onto her bed and she motioned for me to leave the room.

I could tell by her tears that something was up. I went back to the other room, and I cried too. I've never missed my dad Chuck more than I did in that moment. I expected Aunt Dot to enter the room at any moment, but she didn't. She cried off and on for about three days, until finally, she had the strength to talk to me.

"I cannot believe that my sister Gwendolyn died without telling you the truth about who you really are," she said.

Now let me tell you this: any time a person begins a conversation by saying something like that, whatever they say next is something that anybody needs to prepare for. So immediately, I braced myself for what she was about to say.

Aunt Dot looked at me and said, "Morris, Gwendolyn is not your real grandmother, and Chuck is not your real father. Morris, your real father's name was Billy. He's was my nephew in New York City. And his mother Katherine, my sister...she's your biological grandmother."

I just stared at Aunt Dot. You know those moments when someone tells you that a family member just died or something traumatic just happened, or you receive news that you don't want to believe or process? That's how I felt. All of a sudden, my mind went somewhere else, and I saw Aunt Dot speaking, but all I saw was her lips moving.

As soon as she said those words, a part of me died. The first thing that I thought about was my dad – not my biological dad that I just learned about, Billy, but the only real dad that I've ever had in my life, Chuck. I thought to myself, "How could he not be my real dad? He has to be my real dad. I mean, just look at him, and look at me. What does she mean he's not my real dad?" I thought to myself.

None of it made sense because, for the life of me, I could not understand why any man like Chuck would choose to open up his heart and share his time, money and resources with a kid that wasn't his. Heck, in the hood where I'm from, I've seen plenty of black men run out and escape their responsibility of being a father. And this man did the opposite? This man, Chuck, actually *stepped in*…to be a *father* to someone who wasn't even his? What the heck are you talking about, Aunt Dot? Get out of here, you must be crazy.

When I finally snapped out of it, Aunt Dot could tell by the look on my face that I was heartbroken. And the truth is, I had a mix of emotions. I was angry at Gwendolyn for lying to me, but at the same time I was thankful that she loved me and gave me the life she did. I was angry at my dad Chuck for lying to me. As a matter of fact, I was angry at everyone. I thought to myself, "How could everyone live this lie and let me go through my whole life not knowing who I really am? What kind of monsters do I live with? What kind of people are around me?"

Aunt Dot knew that I needed some time to process what she had just shared with me. So she stopped talking and she let me go.

A few days later, Aunt Dot said, "Morris, there's only one person who can really explain this to you accurately. There is only one person who can tell you the truth about who your parents *really* were and how they really met in New York City, because there was only one person who was there with them during that time. Morris, do you think you would like to talk to your real grandmother, Katherine?"

Huh? I stared at her with a confused look on my face.

Finally I said, "Talk to who? Talk to Katherine? Talk to my grandmother?

She said, "Yes Morris. I think it's a good idea. You should talk to Katherine.

I didn't know what to do. I had a big decision to make.

It's the same decision that every foster child goes through at some point in life, if they're lucky. I had to chose rather or not I wanted to find out the true identity of who I really was.

After walking around angry for a few days, I finally decided to take the step, I decided to have a phone conversation with my grandmother Katherine.

"Okay, Aunt Dot. I'll talk to this lady. I think it's time." Aunt Dot connected me on the phone with her sister, my grandmother, Katherine.

AN UNEXPECTED PHONE CALL

Within the first few minutes of talking to my grandmother Katherine on the phone, I realized I had never heard a woman curse so much in my entire life. This lady was brass, she was direct, and she lacked manners. But what she lacked in politeness, she more than made up for with honesty.

"Boy, I'm not gonna sugarcoat it," she said. "I'm not gonna tell you some story about who your parents were just to make you feel good. So I'm just gonna tell you straight like it is. Your father was a no-good pimp and a hustler, and your mother was nothin' but a hooker. Your mother was a junkie, and your father ended up puttin' her on the streets to work for him. Somewhere in the midst of all of that, you came along."

I stood there on the phone frozen. I was paralyzed. I could not move. Everything around me turned blurry. And as soon as she said that, my mind went to a dark place. I heard her voice speaking to me on the other end of the telephone, but – just like when Aunt Dot first broke the news to me – I could barely hear what she was saying. I couldn't help but picture my drug-dealing father in Harlem and my mother, a junkie prostitute.

When I began to focus back on what Grandma Katherine was saying to me, she said, "I don't know what those people done told you about yourself, and I don't know what those people done told you about where you come from, but that's it. That's the truth. Ain't nothing else to it. Your mother died in those streets and your father did too. I know you and I ain't never really talked much, but I'm just gon' tell you straight up that I don't much like kids. I never have."

And you know what? My grandmother Katherine wasn't lying to me either. Nevertheless, she still had two kids of her own: Billy and my aunt Tess.

My Aunt Tess lived a crazy life in the streets also. I remember hearing the stories that Grandma Gwendolyn and all my family members would tell when they talked about how crazy their sister Katherine was and how her kids, Tess and Billy, were the same way. And when my grandmother Katherine said, "I don't much like kids. I never have," it all clicked and it began to make sense.

My Aunt Tess had at least five kids: Thomas Michael, Little Tess, Joseph, Tiffany, and Romanita. She probably had more children, but those were the five that I knew of. I always wondered why all of my Aunt Tess's kids were either adopted, put into foster care, or raised by other families. I used to wonder why somebody in New York City didn't take those kids. But now the story was coming full circle.

It's because those kids, the children of my Aunt Tess, were just like me. As a matter of fact, my grandmother Gwendolyn also raised one of Tess's oldest kids - we called him Thomas Michael. Gwendolyn raised him in West Virginia before she raised me. I always thought Thomas Michael was her son, but I never really knew the truth. I also wondered why they called him by his first AND his middle name. It was because Gwendolyn already had a biological son named Thomas. His name was Thomas Allen Sanders. And when Gwendolyn took in Thomas Michael Gilbert, her great-nephew from New York City, they had to find a way to distinguish between the two 'Thomases'. So, they started calling them Thomas Michael and Thomas Allen. But many of Tess's other kids in NYC were raised in foster care. They were raised in the same foster care/orphanage type of system in New York City that I would have been raised in if Gwendolyn, my Angel, would not have adopted me, taken me in, and raised me in Fairmont, West Virginia.

AN UNEXPECTED RELATIONSHIP

Over time, I formed an odd relationship with my new grandmother, Katherine. She was not the easiest person to talk to, but I'm glad we got to know each other, and I'm glad I had a chance to talk to her before she died.

God's blessings in life often transcend any medical predictions because the funny thing is, about a year before I first talked to her over the telephone, my grandmother Katherine was only given approximately six months to live. Although we never got a chance to meet face-to-face, I was able to interact with my grandmother over the telephone for a period of almost a year and a half before she died in New York City.

If I would not have had a chance to talk to my real grandmother, I would have never known the truth about my life – the truth that many people chose to spare me from ever knowing. No one else had the courage to tell me who my mother really was, and no one else had the courage to really talk to me about my father. And all attempts to do so were cut off by my grandmother Gwendolyn.

After my grandmother Katherine exposed the truth about my parents to me, I had some really good conversations with my her during that year and a half that we communicated to each other. I learned a lot about who she was as a woman. I learned about the vision that she had when she went to New York City after leaving West Virginia.

She said, "I'm just gon' tell you straight. Those Negroes down there in West Virginia ain't never been nothin' and they ain't never gon' be nothin' and I knew that at age 18. That's why I got outta there. West Virginia's a place for white folks and it ain't no place for a black woman that wants to do something with her life. I had a plan for my life, and I had to go someplace where I could make things happen for me,"

My grandmother Katherine felt like Harlem was the place that any black person could go to pursue their dreams - so that's where she went. And she found much success once she moved to Harlem - she ended up owning and operating several nightclubs and restaurants in the Harlem, and she made a lot of money.

I asked my grandmother Katherine why she was so interested in owning her own businesses, and she said, "Boy, I don't know. It's been in my blood."

"Been in your blood? What do you mean by that?"

She said, "It goes back to that good old Bessemer, Alabama barbecue. It's been in our family since day one. Our family has always known how to make money. Mama Hattie always said that all you gotta do is find something that people want and something that people need, and put it right in front of them and they'll buy it. And don't stop until you get what you want, cause it ain't gon' be easy, but it's not supposed to be. If you can make it through the hard parts and get to the other side, anyone can run a successful business if they want to."

I gotta tell you, as tough as it was to hear about the truth of who my parents really were, it was also inspired to find out the truth about the many generations of black slaves in the South who, after they were freed, all pursued a greater life. They were the generations that Mama Hattie came from in Bessemer, Alabama, after she shot her husband, she came to Fairmont WV to create a new life and to start her own businesses. While they weren't exactly legal, they were still her's, and she still used her business instincts to grow them. And thankfully, I was able to hear directly from her daughter, my grandmother Katherine, about where I came from. And *that...* inspired me.

SOMETIMES YOU HAVE TO PRETEND

As I said at the beginning of this chapter, I never really have been a big fan of pretending. I never liked pretending like bad breath isn't *that bad*, and it was always tough for me to pretend like Aunt Sasha's mustache wasn't *that thick*. Once I found out the truth about who my parents really were, it was tough for me to walk around Fairmont, WV, pretending like I didn't know where I really came from. As you can imagine, the hardest part of it all was the frequent visits that I made to Mount Olive, West Virginia, every time I arrived at the Mount Olive Correctional Center to visit my dad Chuck in prison.

Within days of hearing the news that Grandma Katherine shared with me, I sat in the visitation room across from my dad. The entire time, I contemplated whether or not I would ever tell him that I knew that he was not my real father.

Every time I made the drive down to the prison, I would ask myself, *"Is today going to be the day, is this going to be the day that I tell him that I know that truth?"*

I knew that no matter when I told him that I knew the truth, it wasn't going to change how I felt about him. Yet, on every visit, I couldn't bring myself to tell him that I knew the truth.

Shortly after I found out that Chuck was not my real father, I ran into a guy that was once locked up with my dad in jail. He said to me, "Boy, you have no idea. You are the apple of your father's eye. You are all that he talks about. You should see his prison cell. He's got pictures and articles of you everywhere, all over his cell. You are all that he talks about. I've never seen a man do a life sentence in prison and be so positive like your dad - and *you're the reason why he's always so positive* - he loves you so much."

Deep down inside, I knew that Chuck really did love me. And I did not have to pretend anymore. He may not have been my biological father, but he was my dad.

I made up my mind that day that I would never tell him that I knew he was not my real father. If being connected to me and being my dad was enough to help him make it through his days in prison, then that was the least I could do to repay him for taking care of me when I was a kid – when he stepped up to be a father to me even though he didn't have to. I knew in my heart on that day that I would never make mention of it again, and I would never have to *pretend* again.

OVERNIGHT SUCCESS》》

Chapter

6

The 1 Thing That Everybody Wants

I once heard a story about a lady named Mary who found out that she had cancer. After receiving a fatal cancer diagnosis, her doctor informed her that she only had a few months to live. Instead of being heartbroken, Mary made a decision to do two things. First, she tapped into her faith by reading her favorite Bible verses. She wanted to remind herself of everything that God had promised her. And second, when she wasn't reading her bible, she spent a lot of time watching funny movies and funny TV shows.

And that's all she did - she prayed a lot and she laughed a lot. After a few weeks, she noticed that her health was not getting *worse* as the doctors had anticipated. Instead, she started to feel *better*. When she finally went back in to see her doctor, he said to her, "Mrs. Mary Beth I have to be honest with you. We didn't expect you to make it this long."

"I know you didn't expect me to," she said with a smile. Eventually, Mary lost all symptoms of the disease that tried to take her life, and the doctors could not find any trace of cancer in her body because she beat the disease. She won... Mary beat cancer.

Mary's story taught me something. It taught me that a diagnosis is never a destination, unless you choose it to be.

Let me repeat that again... *a diagnosis is never a destination, unless you choose it to be.*

A diagnosis is just an opportunity to *dance to music* that no one else hears but you. Sometimes you have to find a way to dance, even when no one else hears the music. The moment you let a diagnosis change the way you live your life, you're done. The moment you stop choosing to dance, you're finished.

TAKING MY OWN ADVICE

I won't lie to you, my grandmother Katherine told me some things about my parents that weren't easy for me to take, and it felt like I got hit with a hammer. I felt the pressure and the weight of many years of generational cycles and bad choices coming down on me.

At first, I felt like I received a diagnosis that pretty much guaranteed that I would have the same thoughts and behaviors that my parents did. But I learned something from Mary when she beat cancer. I learned that I could choose how I wanted to respond to any news that I received - that part was up to me.

My grandmother Katherine's sister, my Aunt Dot, eventually came to my rescue.

She said, "Baby, I know all of this ain't easy to process. But it's time for you to make a choice. Your parents did what they wanted to do with their life. Now it's time for you to choose what you want to do with yours."

Aunt Dot could tell that I was still discouraged.

She said, "Okay, you can look at things however you want to. But all I'm going to say to you is this... God knew you before you were born and he put you in your mother's belly. He gave you everything that you needed to be the person you were created to be. We can't choose who our parents are, and we don't always get to choose everything that happens to us. But you can choose how you respond – that part is up to you."

Aunt Dot said her peace, then she walked away. Let me help you to connect it all. Make sure that you pay close attention to this next part...

EVERYONE WANTS SOMETHING

Everyone wants something. Even people who don't know exactly what they want still want *something*. And everyone usually wants the same thing – some type of results. We all want to see results in whatever it is we're doing. We want good results from the work we do in the classroom, in the workplace, in our relationships, and for many athletes, on the field. Even though we don't necessarily like it when we don't get the results that we want, the thing that keeps us coming back and the keeps us focused is progress.

There is nothing wrong with not seeing immediate results. The most important thing is HOW we make progress. Many of us are so distracted by our phones and devices all of the time that we leave very little time to be unconnected. That's one of the major reasons why we are attracted to the idea of instant gratification and *Overnight Success* - because want to experience progress, but we don't have a lot of time to do it. That's why many people (including me at times) want to skip as many steps as we can, just to get results.

The culture that surrounded me all of my life has granted me access to many different types of people. I have known drug dealers, pastors, CEOs, stay-at-home moms, and every type of person in between. Today, I speak to many different types of audiences – everyone from teenagers to Fortune 500 companies. I stand at the intersection between multiple generations of people all coming together, and I notice things. The biggest thing that I noticed is that it doesn't matter who you are, how old you are, or where you're from – many people can relate to Clyde Randall, the guy that you first met in the introduction of this book. Many people feel just like him – *they just want more out of life.* They want better results and they want to see some sort of progress in what they're doing because *progress inspires hope and commitment.*

People always ask me if there was a specific system that I used or some type of process that I had in place to help me progress and get to where I am today. The truth is, I had no recipe or framework to follow when I was young. All I had was *my faith, my instincts and the work ethic of a West Virginia coal miner in my heart* – that was it.

Today, after making the transition from where I was many years ago, I get to work with some of the brightest minds in the world. Because of that, my perspective is very different. Why? Because every time you learn something from someone, you equip yourself with new plays to run.

As I surround myself with great husbands, fathers, business leaders, church leaders, and neighbors, I keep learning. That's what life is all about – living, learning, and growing.

I know that my experiences and my perspective have been shaped by some amazing people. I cannot take credit for my life - *I give credit for my life*. I give credit to the people that God has blessed me with. As I take the time to step back and connect the dots to see where I really came from and how I really got here, I am humbled and thankful. Every time I reached critical moments in my life where I was just about to mess things up, I was blessed with someone who stepped in to help me.

And that's what the rest of this book is about. After connecting those dots, something really big stood out to me – *something simple that had been there all along*. I realized that the only thing that helped me survive when I was younger, the main thing that others taught me is the importance of *being intentional* about everything that you do if you want to get better results in your life.

Once you become intentional about your life, everything changes. When you live intentionally, you make every choice and decision in your life based on the results that you want to have in the future. Being intentional begins with being focused and clear about what you want. Being clear about what you want and where you are going gives you an advantage over the powerful effects that culture can have in our lives.

Culture is powerful and it can strip you of your voice if you let it, so you must be able to *see your way through it*. You must be able to see your way through all of the cultural stuff that causes us to think and act the way that we do. Most importantly, you must have something to help you achieve the life that you desire to have - *not the life that others expect you to have*. Because my Aunt Dot was right, *my diagnosis wasn't a destination,* and neither is yours.

You can choose whatever type of life you want to live moving forward. And that's what this book was written to help you do.

The 7 Steps to "C" Your Way Through is a framework that any individual, organization, or team can use to intentionally pursue the results they want. The rest of this book will break down each one of the seven steps for you.

The seven steps will help you to escape the negative pull of that culture can potentially have on your life. *The 7 Steps to "C" Your Way Through* **will help you see through distractions** to stay focused and they will also help you to defeat the attraction of instant gratification and *Overnight Success*.

SOMETHING EVERYONE CAN RELATE TO

In chapter 3, the night that I stood in the parking lot of my grandmother's hospital was one of the toughest nights of my life. When I looked up and I saw them cut the light out in her hospital room, a flip was switched inside of me. I stood there in that hospital parking lot thinking to myself, *"What do I have to do to fulfill all of the promises that I just made her in the hospital room?"* The *emotional capital* (motivation) that came in that moment was enough to light a fire under me, forever.

I do not expect you to be able to relate to *my story.* You have your own story. You probably can't relate to what it must have been like losing two sets of parents. But you can relate to the question that I asked myself as I stood in that hospital parking lot – **"Why is it that some people are successful and others aren't?"**

I asked myself that question over and over again, because I didn't want to fail.

From that moment on, I became obsessed with finding any advantage that could help me to successfully transition from where I was, to where I really wanted to be.

The irony is, after finishing my bachelor's and master's degrees, then after working in *corporate America*, and after launching my own company, I realized something: **our clients that we work with are worried about the same thing** that I was worried about when I stood in that hospital parking lot that night. They're worried about finding ways to continuously change, grow, and transition their culture to the next level and produce better results.

After working in the youth, college, and corporate markets, I realized something else: **today's youth** are also focused on the same thing – *transition*. Progressing from one grade to the next and continuing to grow and achieve each year are important steps for all children. As adults, it's easy to forget how tough it really was for us when we went through those same transitions.

Then I realized something else. I realized that *college students* have the same topic - *transition* - on their minds. Their transitions may be a bit more complex as they manage the idea of new careers, relocating to new areas, dating relationships, and officially being off of mom and dad's payroll for the first time in their lives, but it's all connected back to the same thing – *transition*.

Transitions are critical time periods for everyone, no matter who you are. The people and organizations that experience the most progress, growth, and results are the ones that are *intentional about every step in the process*.

When I started sharing my message as a professional speaker, I studied hard to learn specific speaking skills that would allow me to connect with audiences. Eventually, my ability to connect with audiences became intuitive once I realized that although every person will not be able to relate to my story, *every person can relate to one thing* - the desire to change, grow, and transition to the next level, *because that's the 1 thing that everybody wants - everybody wants to get to the next level in what they are doing*.

Everyone can relate to wanting better results in their life, and everyone can relate to what it's like being in transition – everyone including kids, college students, corporations, churches, and even sports teams.

Everyone wants to transition from where they are to where they really want to be. Transitioning takes focus and it takes commitment. And you must have a structured plan that will get you to the next level and keep you focused during the process.

That is what the *7 Steps to "C" Your Way Through* is all about.

Get ready to see what the seven steps are all about.

Chapter

7

CULTURE
CULTURE
CULTURE

The Influence of Culture

I love cars. I always have, ever since I was a little kid. My family never consistently owned a car when I was growing up. I made a promise to myself that I would always work hard and have a great career so that one day, maybe one day, I could buy the car of my dreams. I didn't like cars simply because our family did not have one, I was just really into cars. Ever since I was little, I have been able to name the make and model of the majority of cars just by looking at the way the lights were shaped, even in the dark.

After I finished graduate school and started my corporate career, I could not wait to buy my first real car. Several cars later, one of the biggest experiences of my life happened after a recent car purchase. When I left the dealership, I had a long, four hour trip to make home. During my trip, the weather changed instantly - turning a beautiful trip full of amazing sunlight into a dark, cloudy day.

I hate driving on muggy days, and I wanted to lift the energy and the mood inside of the car so I did what I normally would do... I reached for my CDs. I wanted to play some of *my music.* And when I say *my music,* I'm talking about classic music. Nothing but the best. I wanted to listen to some Jay-Z or Biggy (The Notorious B.I.G for those of you who do not know). As I searched for my CDs, I realized that I had a problem - there were no CDs in the car because I just purchased the vehicle, and I also didn't have my iPod with me.

My first instinct was to check the glove box or inside the door to see if I left any CDs in the car somewhere. There was nothing. I thought to myself, *"Man, this car is too new - I just drove it off of the lot and I haven't had it long enough to junk it up and stash CDs everywhere yet!"* And you know exactly what I am talking about too - every person keeps a few CD's crammed in between their seats or down inside of the door. But on that day, I had nothing.

I was frustrated, so I began to search through the radio to see if any station would come in. I was driving through the mountains and signals were pretty bad there. I kept searching for stations, but there was nothing. First, I had no CD's to listen to, now, I couldn't even get radio station to come in! After I drove in silence for a while, I couldn't take it anymore. The only thing I could think of doing was the same thing that many of us do when we selfishly want something. I looked up and I said, *"God, please, come on, help a brotha out. Please at least give me a radio station to listen to. I don't care what it is, just give me something to listen to, anything. I'll listen to it, I promise – I don't care what it is!"*

Today, as I look back at that moment in the car, I have no idea what led me to do that. Have you ever heard the saying "watch what you ask for?" Well, all of a sudden, in the middle of nowhere a radio station finally came in, but it was not *my music* that I was used to listening to. As soon as I recognized the twang from the guitars and the banjos, my first instinct was to reach up as fast as I could to hit the power button and turn it off. I remember thinking to myself, *"Nope, this ain't happening... I am NOT listening to country music. I'm black, and we don't do that!"*

You may be reading this right now and thinking to yourself, *"What are you talking about Morris? I like country music. Nothing is wrong with country music!"* I am not saying that there is anything wrong with listening to country music. To each his own! It just wasn't *my music.* As I drove my car further down the road, a small part of me thought about turning it back on. But I said to myself, *"There is no way that I am going to listen to some stupid country music."* I was just not used to listening to anything like it. I was raised listening to all R&B and rap music. And that's what I loved! All of a sudden I heard a little voice inside of me trying to get my attention.

"Psssssssst. Pssssssssstttt!"

At first I ignored it. But it kept trying to get my attention.

"Pssssssst. Pssssssssssttttt!"

And you know what voice I'm talking about too. That little voice inside of you that sometimes causes you to follow your gut and your instincts. All of a sudden I remember telling that little voice inside of me, *"Shut up! Shut up Craig. Leave me alone!"*

I know what you're thinking. You're thinking to yourself, "Did he just call the voice inside of him Craig?" And to answer your question, yes. Yes I did! Ever since I was young I've learned to follow my gut. I didn't always have parents or adults to tell me what to do, and I had to make a lot of decisions on my own. My survival instincts began to kick in at an early age, and I got so used to following the voice in my head that eventually, I just gave him a name: Craig!

While I was driving down the road, as soon as I cut off the country music, all of a sudden Craig said, "Hey... hey... why did you turn the country music off?"

"Shut up Craig, we are not listening to country music."

"Why not? What is the worst that can happen? Why don't you want to listen to it?" asked Craig.

I remember thinking to myself, *"Why am I listening to this fool?"*

But Craig was right. Why didn't I want to listen to country music? Why was I never willing to try it before?

I didn't have to wonder very long. It doesn't take a genius to figure out that when you are black and you are raised in an all-black culture, nobody around you really listens to country music. I'm not saying that black people don't listen to country music. What I am saying is that my family, friends, and the entire black culture that I interacted with did not listen to country music – including me!

Eventually, I got so tired of driving on that dark, cloudy day that I needed something just to lift the mood a little bit in the car and I was desperate - so I turned the stupid country music station on.

The song that came on the radio that day was a popular song by Billy Currington called "Good Directions." In the song, he was talking about turnip greens, pork rinds, rednecks, and sweet tea. I was thinking to myself *"What the heck is this guy talking about... what am I listening to?"* Then he started talking about a girl who was lost, and all of a sudden I started to wonder why he was talking about this girl who needed directions.

Before you know it, I got caught up in the song. I mean, it's not like I started to like the song or anything like that. I just got caught up in the words and what he was saying because I wanted to know what was going to happen next.

It's not really my fault, it's my wife Lisa's fault. She has a theory about all great movies and songs. She says, *"Every great song and every great movie is always about a girl. Even if a guy is the hero, he would never be motivated without a girl to save because there's always a girl!"*

As I got caught up in the song, I had no idea what was happening. All of a sudden, halfway through the song I looked down and my left shoulder was moving up and down and my body was swaying from side to side in my seat. To make things worse, I glanced in the mirror and I noticed that I had the stupidest smile on my face.

By the time I realized it, it was too late. I began singing along with the song, and of course I didn't know any of the words because I had just heard the stupid song for the first time. It still didn't matter though, because at that point I was already too far gone.

It was so sad.

Yep, the country music angels that sit up in heaven must have really been smiling down at me that day. I can just picture one of the country music angels saying to one of his friends, "Hey Bubba Ray, lookeeey here, we got ourselves another brotha! Yeeeeehaaaaaw!"

And boy oh boy did they have me – I was done. If I wasn't addicted to country music yet after listening to "Good Directions," Bubba Ray and his angel friends made sure they gave me a double dose. After "Good Directions" went off, the very next song that came on the radio was Tim McGraw's "Don't Take the Girl!"

For those of you who don't know, "Don't Take the Girl" is one of the most emotional songs ever written. I can't even explain it to you without tearing up.

Just a few minutes before this whole episode went down, I was just driving in my car, minding my own business. I had no idea that my life was changing right before my eyes. I fell in love with country music that day. I listened to that country music station for the rest of my four-hour trip, and I turned the station back on again on the way home. I could not get enough country music. And then I started to listen to Brad Paisley, another country music artist, and I found out that he was originally from West Virginia. I thought to myself, *"I have to support this dude, he's a West Virginia man - I have to support my fellow mountaineer!"*

And guess what. My rap and R&B music had to move over and make room for some country. But the main problem with switching to such a different genre of music wasn't the fact that I had to purchase all new music. The biggest problem with falling in love with country music was that I had to hide it from my friends and family for so long.

I guess looking back at it I didn't really have to hide anything. But *I felt like I did,* because where I was from, black people didn't listen to country music.

I believe that *the quality of questions that we ask ourselves determines the quality of decisions we make in life.* Sometimes you have to ask yourself some tough questions if you really grow. After my country music experience, I asked myself, *"Why did it take me so long to be willing to just TRY listening to new music?"* The truth is, I already knew the answer. I wasn't willing to try listening to new music for the same reason that most people aren't interested in trying anything new… I was closed-minded.

Listening to country music completely changed my perspective and my approach to everything that I do, because country music taught me the power of being open to trying new things.

Ever since that day, I have applied the concept of "being open" to just about everything that I do. As a matter of fact, after I started listening to country music, I began to ask myself if there were any other types of music out there that I might be interested in. I did not want to take any chances of missing out on something big, so I began to listen to every single type of music I could get my hands on. I started to listen to older music from groups like The Platters, Sam Cooke, Frankie Valli & The Four Seasons - and my favorite music discovery of all-time was Creedence Clearwater Revival's greatest hits… man, I love that CD!

Could you imagine going through life without having the chance to listen to music from artists like The Temptations, Earth, Wind & Fire, The Eagles, Journey and the sweet, precious sound of Nina Simone? Of course not. And that's exactly what almost happened to me. I would have never experienced the amazing talent of those artists because I was so closed-minded before I started listening to country music.

Music is universal - everyone likes *some type* of music. I couldn't have used a better example to share at the beginning of the 7 Steps to "C" Your Way Through.

Music is a powerful example of culture. There are plenty more examples that show how powerful culture can be in our lives, because culture is all around us – it's in the things we hear, the things we see, the places we go, the things we do, and the people we do them with.

We experience culture through our friends, our families, our workplace, at school, and where we hang out. And every place has its own culture – even a grocery store. Hospitals also have their own culture, prisons have their own culture, and the neighborhood you were raised in definitely has (or had)… *its own culture.*

I realized right away that the experiences that shape our lives will always have some type of effect on us. Unfortunately, the culture around us can absolutely dominate and control our lives if we let it. On the other hand, culture can shape our lives and give us a platform to stand on if we utilize it the right way…

WHEN CULTURE TAKES YOU TO THE NEXT LEVEL

When I was a kid I dreamed of playing basketball one day. I ran hard, I played hard, and I practiced every moment that I could when I was young. I even had the opportunity to play in high school with one of the most talented teams that ever played at my school.

We won a state championship because we had guys on our team like Bryan Garcia, Cory Bridges, Rashod Kent, David Miles, Jonathan Reid, Ryan Rowland, Eric Wilson, Josh Keener, and Andy Johnson, just to name a few. We had a great team and we had a great time pursuing our championship. We had great talent, but most importantly, we had a culture that enhanced *HOW* we played.

Even though I had the pleasure and the opportunity of walking on and playing basketball at Fairmont State University, I still had a tough reality to face in terms of my NBA dreams. The fact was... I was not good enough. *I wasn't even close.*

The NBA had a specific culture surrounding the league and its' players. If you had the talent to make it to the league, the NBA could use your talent to take your game to the next level. I was barely good enough to play in college, and I definitely had to squash my dreams of ever playing professional basketball.

I had another dream too though – a dream that no one else could take away from me no matter what - I wanted to be a *professional speaker.*

The interesting thing about professional basketball players is that they play in a league called the *National Basketball Association.* The irony is that today, as a professional speaker I play in a league called the *National Speakers Association.*

So I did go *PRO*... in something else.

One day, both of my dreams collided when I got a call from the National Basketball Association. They were finally ready to see what I could do. They were finally ready to make me a first round draft pick. Well, kind of. They hired me to be their speaker for the Rookie Transition Program, the NBA's highly respected program which helps their first and second round draft picks transition successfully to the NBA. I had the distinct opportunity to utilize my message about being intentional about developing great habits and behaviors to *transition* their leadership skills to the next level in the NBA. These guys were in the middle of living a true super-hero type of American Dream, and I was there to participate in their process - wow, what a blessing!

When the NBA paid me, as I looked at the check that they sent me, the first thing that I thought to myself was *"Look, I achieved one of my other dreams too! I still got a check from the NBA and I did not have to dribble a basketball to do it."*

It was a bittersweet victory that I was certainly thankful for.

ONE OPPORTUNITY LEADS TO ANOTHER

When the University of Notre Dame was looking for a speaker to engage their student athletes, a representative from their athletic department spoke with one of my clients at the National Basketball Association to get input on which speaker they should choose. They just happened to recommend me as a potential speaker. Before you know it, the contract was signed and I was headed to Notre Dame.

I have to tell you the truth about Notre Dame. I absolutely hated the University of Notre Dame before they first hired me to work with them, and my reasons were fully justified. I am a West Virginia University fan for life and when I was a child, the University of Notre Dame played against West Virginia University in the national championship game, and they crushed my hopes of celebrating a national championship with my WVU Mountaineers. The only thing I remembered people saying throughout the years was, *"The luck of the Irish, the luck of the Irish, the luck of the Irish"* ... and I hated Notre Dame.

It's funny how money changes things though - it always does. Once the University of Notre Dame started paying me and sending me those checks, I started to like them *much better.*

Notre Dame hired me to speak to every single one of their student athletes. As soon I arrived on campus, it was easy to see why people talked about how special the school in South Bend, Indiana was.

There was something different about Notre Dame. There was a different spirit in the air. As I continued to develop my relationship with Notre Dame I couldn't help it - I became an instant fan. Now usually, *Overnight Success* and instant results can be a dangerous thing, but I could not help it. I felt the emotional connection that everyone talked about when they described the Notre Dame tradition. It was a special place. It wasn't something that was all hyped up.

It was real.

People really did buy in to the culture at Notre Dame.

I began to understand that Notre Dame was special because of the culture that it developed over the years. It didn't matter who you were - it didn't matter if you were a medical student or football player - every single student at the University of Notre Dame had huge expectations regarding their conduct, their character, and their work ethic.

Students at Notre Dame are expected to achieve astounding results when they walk onto that campus. As a matter fact, the expectation for excellent performance extended *beyond* campus. Notre Dame graduates are expected to go out and make an immediate impact in the world that they live, work and serve in. Do you want to know WHY everyone buys into Notre Dames culture right away? Because they don't have any other choice. Notre Dame's culture has standards that are expected to be followed by everyone. If people don't buy in to the culture at Notre Dame, they are kindly asked to leave.

I have worked with many student athletes throughout the country. I have never met a more focused and engaged group of students and student athletes in my life. I have also never participated in any culture, anywhere, with any organization, that is better at driving a commitment to excellent results like the University of Notre Dame. Working with Notre Dame as a client completely changed the opinion that I once had of them as a child after they defeated my WVU Mountaineers in the national championship game. And it completely changed my approach and my beliefs about the power of culture and the ability for culture to take a person's game to another level.

When I spoke to the football team at Notre Dame, I had a great time getting them all fired up. I delivered a message to them about ways that great teams can *Position Themselves for Success.* I spoke to them just days before they kicked off their season.

After they won their first three games in a row, people said to me, "Wow, you must have really got them motivated and ready to play!"

I said, "No, it wasn't me – I am NOT the reason why they are winning - they are."

Eventually, they kept winning more games.

In the middle of the season they found themselves still undefeated. After they won their first 7 games, people still kept calling me.

"Hey Morris, you must have REALLY got them motivated to play, they still have not lost a game!"

I said, "No, I am NOT the reason – those boys go out there and fight hard every week - they are earning everything they get on their own!"

Eventually, Notre Dame found themselves undefeated at the end of the regular season and my phone was ringing off of the hook!

People said, "Wow, congratulations! It must feel really good Morris - you really inspired them to play their butts off this season, you really motivated them!"

And of course, you know what my response was.

"Yep, it was me – I'm the reason!"

I had a great time telling that joke and it always brought a smile to my face. Even though I knew that I was NOT the reason. I was thankful for the opportunity to partner with Notre Dame and the opportunity to work closely with one of the best organizational cultures in the world. It was an amazing experience.

USING CULTURE TO ACCELERATE YOUR RESULTS

There is no such thing as *Overnight Success*. The University of Notre Dame did not develop their culture of success overnight, and you won't either. *The 7 Steps to "C" Your Way Through* will help you change your results by helping you to become more focused and intentional about everything that you do. Your focus begins and ends with culture.

The culture that you live, work, and play in will have a major influence on the results that you achieve, because culture influences how you pursue everything.

Let me ask you a question…

Do people around you take shortcuts to get what they want?

Do people around you act entitled (do they expect to get everything they want – always?)

Do people around you complain at the first sign of adversity?

If people around you have of the habits and behaviors that I just mentioned, over time you will too, and you will destroy your ability to be great. If you are not intentional about the culture you surround yourself with, culture will eventually strip away *the best part of you*

You must have the courage to stand up and reject the things you don't like about the culture around you. Remember, if you don't like something, your instincts are making you feel that way for a reason. That is why I listen to my "Craig" whenever my instincts tell me something.

Once you develop the habit of *following your instincts*, you have to have the courage to get rid of the things or people around you that are killing your ability to be your best.

Your ultimate goal should be to live, work, and play in a culture that helps you thrive. But first, you have to surround yourself with a culture that helps you to experience small amounts of growth and progress. If you keep making progress in a certain culture or situation, stay there because that culture will help you to *ACCELERATE your results faster* than you would somewhere else. So the question is simple: is your current environment making you better... or worse?

~ ~ ~ ~ ~ ~ ~ ~ ~ ~

I was recently in Gainesville, Florida for a speaking tour at the University of Florida. I decided to join Keith Carodine, Senior Associate Athletic Director at UF, for a quick workout in the Heavener Football Complex. The facility was absolutely amazing! As Keith and I began our workout, he looked at me and he said, "Hold on, I'll be right back." When he returned, he had two Nike dry-fit workout shirts with the official Nike and Florida Gator emblem on it. He threw them both over to me and he said, "I wasn't sure which size you wore so I got you two shirts. Go ahead and try them on to see which one you want."

I said, "Thanks Keith, I love these official UF Nike shirts - this will be great to wear when I travel!"

As he looked down at the *West Virginia University* workout gear that I was wearing, he looked back up and at me and he said, "That's fine Morris, you can wear it when you travel, but first I need you to put that shirt on now if you want to work out in this facility. I should have given that shirt to you when we first walked in, but I forgot.

I said, "Huh?"

Keith said, "You absolutely cannot exercise in this workout room without wearing some type of official Florida Gator apparel."

At first, I thought he was joking with me. But as I looked up at everyone in the fitness room, I realized that I was the only person that was NOT wearing official Florida Gator gear.

As I looked back at Keith, he looked at me with a slight smile and he said, "See I told you, we don't play around here!"

~ ~ ~ ~ ~ ~ ~ ~ ~ ~

Sometimes you don't have a choice about the culture you're in. You might be reading this book right now while you are stuck in a relationship, a job, a neighborhood, or a situation that you just can't *get up and walk away* from.

You also might not have any authority whatsoever to do anything about your situation, or make any changes to your environment.

I realize that everyone's situation is different.

You might be locked up in jail or in prison as you read this book right now.

Regardless of who you are or where you are, even though *you might not have the ability to change the culture AROUND you, you always have the ability to change the culture INSIDE of you.* You just have to want it bad enough, and you must be intentional and focused about everything that you do.

Never forget how unique you are – *there is no one else like you.* No other person in this world has your ability. But it doesn't matter what abilities you have or how good you are if your talents aren't being utilized. When you participate in a culture that's right for you, you will be able to use your abilities to make the culture and everyone else around you... *better* - *w*ithout losing the best part about who you really are.

I surround myself with great husbands, fathers, business leaders, church leaders, and neighbors – and you know what happens? I keep learning.

As an athlete, used to love learning new plays that would help me score points. And today, I love learning new plays that will help me make better choices and decisions when life throws challenges my way. But the credit goes to the other people that I surround myself with.

I surround myself with people that I call *CULTURE CRASHERS.* Culture Crashers are **people who crash cultural expectations** by not buying in to the same negative thoughts, habits, and behaviors as everyone else around them. They take all of it and they crash it, especially if it's something that isn't good for them or if it's something that gets in the way of their growth and progress.

I do not surround myself with *CULTURE CARRIERS.* Culture Carriers aren't tough enough and their level of resiliency is weak. Culture Carriers just **carry the same thoughts, habits, ideas, and behaviors as everyone else**. They are also the same people that die with the best of them either still inside of them, or they die knowing that the best of them has already been wiped away and diminished by the crowd and culture they surrounded themselves with their whole lives. Either way, it's a shame.

I know that I will never be perfect, but I still want to make progress and feel like I am fighting for something - and surrounding myself with *CULTURE CRASHERS* helps to keep me focused and it helps me experience the feeling of progress in my life.

If you would have looked at my life at the very beginning, I had a much higher likelihood of going to jail or dying at an early age, than having plans one day to have dinner with the President of the United States at the White House.

I'm just acknowledging that the biggest transformation in my life happened after I realized the importance of being intentional about who I surround myself with.

I cannot take credit for my life, I *give credit for my life* – to some of the dopest, most amazing, *CULTURE CRASHERS* that I have ever met. Don't surround yourself with *culture carriers,* because you will be one click away from being average.

Also, there is something else that I want to remind you NOT to do...

Don't take these words for granted.

I wish I had this type of playbook to follow when I was really going through some of my toughest transitions in life.

This framework and the *7 Steps to "C" Your Way Through* are a recipe that you can follow. Even though I have these steps to share with you now, I didn't have them back when I needed them the most. All I had at the time was *my faith, my instincts and the work ethic of a West Virginia coal miner in my heart* – that was it.

And now, I am giving you the plays to run. So run 'em.

~ ~ ~ ~ ~

I am about to connect the next dot for you. Get ready to experience the connection between *CULTURE* and *CLARITY*. Clarity is the second step in the process to help you to *"C" Your Way Through.* But before I do, don't forget to use the culture checklist to keep yourself or your team focused on where you're going.

CULTURE CHECKLIST

- What type of culture do you live, work, learn and play in?
- What inspiring about the culture around you?
- What do you need to have the courage to change, challenge or reject in the culture that surrounds you?
- Are you surrounded by Culture *CRASHERS* or *CARRIERS*?
- Are *Culture Crashers* celebrated or rejected in your culture?
- Do you consistently follow your instincts (*"Craig,"*)?
- What areas of your life do you need to be more open-minded about to enhance your perspective?

Chapter

8

CLARITY

CULTURE

Clarity and Vision

"There will always be a special seat reserved for those who have a clear vision and the courage to follow it. The world has no choice but to make room for you." - Craig

~ ~ ~ ~ ~

On a recent trip to Pittsburgh, Pennsylvania, I met a limo driver who changed the way I saw the power of vision and clarity. I flew into Pittsburgh and hired a driver to pick me up at the airport. As the driver transported me to speak at an engagement, I sat in the backseat going over my notes from a speech, and I had my headphones in my ears as I listened to some of my music. Unfortunately, I did not get a chance to speak to the driver during my trip to the engagement, because I was in the backseat preparing for my speech. Typically I love to engage whoever I am in a physical space with. So when we got to the facility where I was speaking, I got out of the car, turned to the driver, and asked him a question. "Hey, are you going to stay here while I deliver the speech, or are you going to leave and then come back and pick me up later to take me to the airport?"

He looked at me and he said, "Actually I was just going to sit right here in the car and relax a little bit, if that sounds okay with you!"

I said, "Can you do me a favor?"

He responded, "Sure, anything. What can I do to help?"

"Would it be okay with you if you came in to listen to my speech? I would love it if you could take a couple of notes and write down some of your thoughts. Maybe on the way back to the airport you could tell me what you think. I always like to get direct feedback immediately after a speech."

He looked at me and he said, "Are you sure? You want me to write down anything and tell you what I think, even if it's good or bad?"

I said, "Yes, I don't care if it's good or bad. I just want to know what you think about the speech".

He replied, "Sure, of course. I think I can do that!"

At the end of my 60 minute keynote speech, and once I had finished meeting all of the people from the conference I spoke at, I looked up and the limo driver was waiting for me to finish up. As we made our way to the car, he took my bags and opened the door for me. Within minutes of driving down the road I tapped on the back of the driver's seat and asked him to pull over for a minute.

"Sure, is everything okay?" he asked.

"Yes, everything is okay. I just need to get out for a moment."

After I got out of the backseat of the car, I walked up to the front passenger seat. I tried to open the door to sit beside the driver, but he locked it so I could not get in. He rolled the window down and said, "What are you doing? You can't sit up front."

I asked, "Why not?"

He replied, "No one ever sits up front."

"Is there a policy against passengers sitting up front?" I asked.

He said, "I don't think there is. I'm not sure actually. Why do you want to sit up front anyway? My job is to take you to the airport. You do not have to sit up front with me."

I said, "I know that. I know that I don't have to sit up front. I want to sit up front so that we can talk and connect on the way back to the airport."

Surprised, he said, "You do?"

After he opened the door, I began to transition into the front seat. I pulled out my notepad along with my pen and I prepared myself to take notes. I looked at him and I said, "Okay, let me have it Mr. Tom. I am ready to hear your feedback about my speech today. What are your thoughts? What did you like? What can I do to improve for next time?"

Tom the limo driver began to give me some great feedback about my speech. I took some really good notes that day. After we talked about my speech, eventually we started to ask each other questions about our lives. We had an awesome conversation that day. As we got about halfway into our drive, I started looking at my watch because I was a little bit concerned that we would not make it to the airport in time for me to catch my flight. Then I noticed something that made me even more worried. The resort that I had spoken at was located far out in the middle of nowhere, and I began to think that my driver Tom might be lost. "Tom, are you sure you know where we're going?"

He said, "Of course I know where we're going. What would make you ask me a question like that?"

"I apologize, Mr. Tom. I don't mean to question your directions, it's just that I noticed we have passed that sign back there twice already. Are you sure you know where we're going?"

"Do I know where we're going? Do I know where we're going?! Of course I know! We're going to Pittsburgh. I can't believe you would ask me something like that," he said.

Mr. Tom was about 70 years old, and I learned that day that he was a veteran who had served our country. I also learned that he was a proud husband, father, and grandfather. Tom was a real patriot, and he loved the United States of America. I mean this guy really loved our country! On our drive he continued to talk about how "Kids these days just don't have any patience anymore!" I didn't want him to think that I was one of those kids that he referred to, so I sat back and relaxed for another 10 minutes or so. As I looked at my watch, I became more and more concerned that I would miss my flight that day. As my concern grew, I looked up and what did I see? You guessed it, we passed the same sign for the third time.

"Mr. Tom, I apologize for bothering you, but I know for a fact that we have passed that sign back there three times already! And I think you've noticed it also. You keep making the same turn right up here. Mr. Tom, are you sure you know where we are going?"

"Son, relax. Did I tell you that we're going to Pittsburgh? Son, we are going to Pittsburgh! That is all you need to know."

I said, "Yes, that's what you keep saying. You keep telling me that we're headed to Pittsburgh, but I think we are lost."

That's when Mr. Tom turned and looked at me as he was driving. He shared a few words with me that day that I haven't forgotten since. He started the conversation with, "Son, listen to what I'm about to say and listen to me good. Are you listening?"

"Yes sir, I am listening. I hear you loud and clear."

"Son, as long as you know where you're going, you are never lost. Do you understand that? Listen to me son. As long as you know where you're going, you could never be lost. I may have taken a wrong turn or two, I may have even taken a few wrong turns. But you can never be lost as long as you know where you're going."

As much as Mr. Tom attempted to reassure me, I was still worried that I would miss my flight. Guess what, I was wrong. Mr. Tom got me to the airport just in time for my flight and everything was okay. He got my bags out of the car and then he pointed at my notepad, towards the notes that I had written while I was in the car with him. "Did you write that down son? Did you write down what I told you? Mr. Motivational Speaker, you get to share whatever you want with people on the stage, so make sure you tell people what I told you today. You can never be lost as long as you know where you're going."

THE WISDOM OF AN OLD VETERAN

Tom the limo driver was right. As long as you know where you're going, nothing else matters. If there is one thing that I know about great people and successful teams, it's that they're focused and they know exactly what they want. I am convinced that the main reason why people succeed in getting the results that they want when they are focused is because, no matter what happens, they never feel lost and they never get distracted. The only reason why I was able to transition successfully from where I was when I stood in that hospital parking lot after losing my grandmother Gwendolyn to where I am today, is because I have been focused the whole entire time.

In the first step of the *7 Ways to "C" Your Way Through* , we talked about the power that culture has in shaping our perspective. In the second step of the 7 C's, the words of the doctor at the hospital come back to mind. The doctor reminded me that everyone has equal access to their own version of the American Dream. He also said that one of the critical steps in making progress towards your goal is to take personal responsibility for your life and your actions. Culture does have a powerful impact on who we are, but everyone is fully responsible for figuring out what they want out of life and for establishing CLARITY in their vision.

WHAT DOES CLARITY LOOK LIKE?

How can you achieve something if you aren't clear about what you're after? You can't. When we do see someone that is clear about what they want, we recognize those types of people immediately. You know what it looks like when a person has clarity. They know what they want, they know where they're going, and nothing – no matter what – will change their vision.

Great teams and successful people usually do three things well. First, they decide what they want and they go after it. Second, they take responsibility for being intentional enough to pursue it. Third, they resist the urge to take shortcuts.

I will give you two perfect examples.

One of the clients that we work with, Electrolux Corporation, has recently undergone many changes in its business model over the past few years. The Electrolux Field Operations Team is responsible for the in-store relationships with many big box retailers and small mom and pop appliance stores. Their roles are critical in the training of employees as well as the floor placement and sales of Electrolux appliances. Every store that you walk into when looking to purchase an appliance has been managed and serviced by a specific Electrolux employee. The Field Operations Team directly influences the sales and bottom line of Electrolux in a strong way.

While working with the Field Operations Department, we gathered all of their teams from four different locations across the country. First, we met with their leadership team in Georgia to cultivate vision and direction for the entire team. Next, we met with their Field Operations Training Managers who were directly responsible for taking the vision of the team to the next level by equipping every member throughout the country with the skills they needed to execute. The final two meetings included an east coast meeting in Washington, D.C. and a west coast meeting in San Diego where every member of the field team was present. We started with the leadership team and worked all the way down to the street team level with one goal: to inform, inspire, and equip everyone in the organization with one very specific vision for moving forward. They were extremely clear about what their organizational goal was: to become the BEST FIELD TEAM EVER.

The second example that I would like to share with you is a story about a little boy with a BIG vision.

Many years ago, a young man named Joseph dreamed of being a leader and king of an entire country. When you hear the words *dream big*, this is a perfect example of it.

This kid had BIG dreams.

Unfortunately, the culture that Joseph lived in did not celebrate the clarity and vision that he had - as a matter of fact, his own family members hated him for it.

As their hate and disgust for him grew larger, his own brothers decided to kill him. But before they did, a last minute decision was made to sell him into slavery instead. Once he left his family, the brothers lied to their father and told him that Joseph had been killed by wild animals.

Even though Joseph was a slave, he never lost sight of his vision. But he continued to encounter challenges. As a slave, he was falsely accused of a crime that he did not commit and he was thrown into prison.

While in prison, he still kept his vision clear and close to his heart.

Eventually, his positive attitude and his abilities were noticed by others. The king of the land where he was imprisoned was so impressed by him that he freed Joseph and put him in charge as ruler of his own land.

When Joseph's older brothers and the rest of his family were forced to move to the land where Joseph was now king, they were shocked and surprised when they learned who their new leader was.

They thought that their brother would kill them for what they had done to him, but instead, he thanked them by saying, "If you would not have sold me as a slave, I would not have been recognized, rewarded, and positioned where I am today." Wow!

The examples above of Electrolux and Joseph both have the same things in common – vision and clarity. Organizations thrive when everyone is committed to the same vision. That's why Electrolux placed such importance on getting all of it's employees together at those meetings. They wanted to have everyone on the same page.

Great teams, families, and companies become great because they are clear about what they are pursuing. Vision and clarity in any team, family, or organization must come from leaders. When it comes to individuals like Joseph though, there is only one leader – you. You must create your own vision and purpose for your life. That can't come from anyone else.

CLARITY CAN ALSO BE A VERY DANGEROUS THING

When I was young I had a crazy life full of challenging experiences. But I had many teachers, coaches, and leaders who created an expectation for me to actually do something with my life, and their encouragement made me feel like I could actually be successful.

As time went by, I began to use their encouragement as motivation. When I began to dream really big, I was given some great advice from my dad, Chuck.

One day, while I was visiting him in prison, and we were discussing my dreams and my future, he said, "There are a lot of wounded people out there and sometimes you don't know who they are. Wounded people are dangerous because if they are in pain or unhappy with their lives, they may respond differently when they meet someone like you, because you are always so positive and full of energy. Never forget that Morris."

I followed my dad's advice very carefully, and here's why – aimless people are disdainful people. People without a focus in life are dangerous because they are misguided; they have no direction, and they don't even realize it. It is extremely difficult being around people with no goals or aspirations. There is a great chance that they will not respond positively to you if you are focused. Actually, there is a better chance that they will respond to you the same way that Joseph's brothers responded to him when he shared his BIG DREAMS with them. They most likely won't kill you, but deep inside they might want to kill your spirit.

Be very careful who you share your dreams, goals, and ideas with. If you share them with the wrong people, they will just discourage you. If you share them with the right people, they'll encourage you to fly. This includes friends, family, and people that you THINK care about you. Make sure you know who you can trust enough to share your dreams with. I have one rule when it comes to my dreams, vision, and ideas: I only share them with people who can breathe life into them.

I learned this skill very early in life, and it's never too late for you to reevaluate your path in life and use this technique.

THE BIGGEST KILLER OF YOUR CLARITY

You can't follow your dreams if you don't know what they are. I know that it sounds simple, but it's not. Most people forget their dreams as soon as they wake up – they get dressed, leave their house, and start their day without giving them a second thought. When they return home at the end of the day, they unwind, relax, and go to sleep. Then they wake up the next day and start the whole process all over again.

If you don't take the time to figure out where you want to go, you will end up wherever life takes you. But that is not the intentional model of achieving results that leads to living a life of purpose.

People are so connected to phones, devices, and computers today that no one really takes the time to decide what they really want out of life. One of the first steps to being clear about the results that you want is to put your cell phones down long enough to relax and "think" for a while. Put your phone on airplane mode if you have to. Or maybe just turn your ringer off for a while. There is no law that says that you have to answer every text message or phone call. If you do, you will always be connected. If you are always connected, you will never be present in a moment long enough to capture it.

Most recent studies in the news point to one fact: if you are multitasking, you are not focused. It's just that simple. You must make time every day to quiet your mind and just think. Some people call this meditating, some call it brainstorming, others just call it quiet time. You should aim to do this for at least 20 minutes a day. If you don't have 20 minutes a day to do this, then you are worse off than you think, and you actually should try for 40 minutes!

In the beginning of this chapter I told you a story about Tom the limo driver. When I was riding in his car, my focus was all over the place. I was focused on the road, I was focused on my phone, I was focused on the notes that I was taking as I sat in the front seat – my focus was everywhere. Conversely, Tom only worried about one thing: Pittsburgh – he was focused. Even when we got off course, he never worried. He didn't worry because his mind was focused on one thing: getting to Pittsburgh.

I guess Tom had a different perspective than I did. After all, he was a veteran of the U.S. Armed Forces. How much clarity do you think guys like that had to have? Think about it, when soldiers are in the middle of a battle they're only focused on one thing – fighting. And you better believe that in that exact moment while they're fighting, they know exactly what they're fighting for.

Tom the limo driver said, "Sometimes I wonder if people out there even know what they're fighting for anymore."

~ ~ ~ ~ ~

Current research is alarming. Studies are beginning to show that today's kids (you know, the future of our country) are more distracted than ever because of the constant mental stimulation they have. Constant mental stimulation is one reason why attention-deficit disorder rates today are climbing more than ever. As a result, critical thinking skills are falling.

The craziest thing is that all kids are born with the potential to be geniuses. Over time, life, culture and environment strip their possible genius away. Kids today can't even focus long enough to pay attention in class.

Kids aren't the only ones suffering. Human resource professionals are facing a talent development nightmare. Talent development professionals can't hire new employees fast enough to replace the Baby Boomers who are retiring. But it's not the talent war that has companies concerned. Their main worry is that the new employees they hire are entering today's workforce with a shortage of critical thinking and soft skills.

Remember Clyde Randall, the guy that I met in LaGuardia Airport in New York City? *He was a guy that had it all.* He had wealth, status, success, and the girl of his dreams, but he still felt empty because all of his triumphs came easily to him. He never made a decision to be intentional about pursuing anything in life because everything was just handed to him.

As a result, what he wanted more than anything else was a purpose. He wanted something to set his sights on, something to fight for. Clyde was empty inside because no matter what, you can't fool yourself. *You can never fool yourself.* If you achieve something easily, without intention, it's almost impossible to recreate that success again. Why? Because you don't know how to – you won't know how you got it in the first place.

People who have things given to them or people who just get lucky… deep down inside they know the truth. And they can't fool themselves. They never can.

BENEFITS TO HAVING CLARITY

Have you ever heard the saying, *"People who know what they want usually get what they want?"* People always ask me why that happens. Here is why: there is nothing more exciting than the feeling you get when you talk to a person who is passionate about something. Steve Jobs made Apple a household name because there was nobody more excited about the products that Apple created than he was. But you don't have to be a millionaire to do this. Have you ever seen a young child talk about a picture or piece of art they created? Yeah, that's the good stuff. You can't help but love it. The reason why *people who know what they want usually get what they want* is because they have focus.

The most inspiring conversations that you will ever have are with people that are clear about who they are and what they want. Some people call it passion, but I call it clarity. When people are clear about what they want, they describe it to you in COLOR, not black and white. They describe what they want or where they're going in such vivid detail that you can see it too, right there in front of you. That's why we are so *ATTRACTED* to people who are focused and going somewhere.

Attraction is an interesting thing because having clarity can even help people in their dating lives. Single people are attracted to other people who are clear about what they want in life. If you both happen to want the same things in life, then POW! That's when the magic happens. People are attracted to others who want the same things that they want. It really is that simple. People fall in love with other people based on the vibes that they give off. So if you're single and ready to mingle, make sure you get your game ready by thinking about what you want out of life. Trust me, he or she will ask you about it on your first date!

CLARITY LEADS TO COMMITMENT

Remember the spoiled soccer kids that I talked about at the beginning of this book? Those soccer kids may have developed the bad habit of quitting when they didn't get what they wanted, but at least they KNEW what they wanted. That's what clarity is – knowing what you want. Having clarity won't give you instant success, but it will give you a chance to experience the thing that everyone wants – progress.

Remember Robert and Kim Bryan, the family from chapter 1? Clarity is the reason why Robert and Kim Bryan have produced four high-functioning, well-adjusted adults. Robert and Kim were extremely clear about what they wanted their family to represent: God first, followed by a strong, American work ethic.

I may not have been raised in a home like the Bryan family, but I did have my own clarity – the clarity that I received when I stood in the parking lot of that hospital on a cold, January night.

My mother had clarity too. She knew she needed to be in New York City, and she had to leave Tennessee to get there. My great-grandmother Mama Hattie had *extreme clarity* – she knew that she had to get the heck out of Bessemer, Alabama, before she was arrested.

Eddie White was the first "Real Hero" that I introduced you to in chapter 4. The biggest thing that he taught me and every other kid that he tried to help was to have the "Eye of the Tiger." He said, *"When you have the 'Eye of the Tiger,' you will be so focused that nothing will stand in your way."*

Please try your best to understand this clearly: **You must become clear about what you want.** If you don't, the culture around you will destroy the best ideas inside of you. Many people, organizations, and teams could experience dramatically better results if they just stopped to think about *WHAT* they're really fighting for and *WHY* they're fighting for it.

As a former orphan, previous welfare recipient, and person who formerly struggled to find my place in the world, I wish I could explain to you just how energizing it feels when you finally get a vision for what you want. The feeling of having a laser-like focus, a purpose, and something to fight for is the best feeling in the world. I dreamed one day of falling in love, being a father, and using my God-given talent and ability to inspire and equip others to live their lives.

After achieving many of those dreams, I realized something: *there is nothing more powerful than dreaming about something and holding onto that dream long enough to see it grow right in front of you – nothing.*

CLARITY

CULTURE

CLARITY CHECKLIST ≫≫

- Do you have clarity for the vision that you would like to achieve?
- How do you find your way back to your vision whenever you get off of your path or lose focus?
- Who do you share your ideas with most frequently?
- Name (3) people that you get energized from when you talk to them. How often do you speak with them?
- Do you have 20 minutes each day to think, relax and envision what you want… or do you need 40 minutes?
- Which people, places or situations inspire your *"Eye Of The Tiger"* focus to make you dream bigger?
- Do you share your future dreams and big ideas with others or do you usually talk about everyday things?

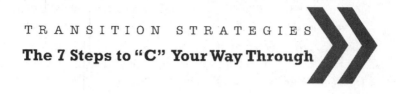
Chapter

9

CLARITY

COMMITMENT

CULTURE

Your Commitment To Dig

My grandmother Gwendolyn was married to Mr. Oscar Sanders. We called him "OT." When I first came to West Virginia as a baby, my grandfather OT took me everywhere with him.

People rarely wore seat belts back then, and OT used to let me sit on his lap when we rode around in his old pickup truck. No matter how many stops we made, we always made a special stop to see OT's older sister, Aunt Bea.

Aunt Bea's house was always a special destination in my mind because she was a really good baker and I loved her food. When I was a little kid, I would do anything to get my hands on some of Aunt Bea's cookies.

Aunt Bea was the type of aunt that every kid loved to have. She would pinch my cheeks every time I walked through her front door. When I became a young man, she still pinched my cheeks every time she saw me! My last visit to Aunt Bea's house was special. As we sat in her living room, she looked up at me and said, "I need to show you something," as she slowly got up from her chair.

She got up, grabbed my hand, and proceeded to walk to the front door of her house. We went out to the front porch, and then she turned to look at me and said, "Did I ever tell you about the time I built this house with my own bare hands?"

"Yes Aunt Bea, you have told me the story about a million times." Aunt Bea wasn't just telling a story either. She really did build her own home with her bare hands. Many years ago when she first dreamed up the vision for the beautiful two-story brick house, she did not have the resources to build a house all at once. She also didn't have enough money to pay anyone else to build it for her. So what did she do? Aunt Bea built that entire house on her own, brick by brick. At times, she would hire certain contractors to help her with areas that she wasn't licensed to do on her own, such as electrical work. Other than that, she did it all by herself.

As we stood out on her porch, Aunt Bea pointed out to her mailbox by the street. Then she turned to me and said, "Did I ever tell you about the time I had to install my own gas line after I built this house?"

"Aunt Bea stop it... you did not install a *gas line*!"

She said, "You are absolutely right, I didn't have to, and that's exactly why I want you to listen really close to what I am about to tell you." Aunt Bea proceeded to tell me the story of exactly what happened...

After she completed the first level of her house, the structure was safe enough for her to move into. Her plan was to live in the bottom part of the house while she continued building the top level. Aunt Bea needed to dig a gas line out to the street before the gas company would supply gas to her home. She had very little extra money, and she could not afford to hire someone to dig the gas line for her.

It was the middle of August and temperatures were in the high 90s *plus humidity*. Nevertheless, she didn't have a choice. She needed a gas line dug from her home all the way out to the street. The gas line had to be 30 feet long by 3 feet wide and approximately 3 feet deep.

If you've ever dug a hole in the ground before, then you know just how big the job was. It was a lot of work for any person to do, and the summer conditions made it even rougher. So what did she do? She grabbed her shovel and she started digging.

After Aunt Bea worked for about two hours digging that gas line, she looked up and she noticed an old man named Mr. Jones walking in her direction.

"Miss Bea, what you doing down there in that hole...digging that dirt in this hot sun? Don't you know how hot it is out here? You gon' hurt yourself," Mr. Jones said.

"Mr. Jones, I don't have a choice. I gotta do what I gotta do. I need to dig my gas line now before the fall weather comes. I know it's going to take me a while so I decided to get a head start. Plus, I ain't got nobody to do it for me, so I gotta do it for myself."

Mr. Jones said, "You get up out of that hole, Miss Bea. Give me that shovel."

As Aunt Bea sat there on the porch telling me this story, she looked at me and said, "Morris, when Mr. Jones reached for my shovel and told me to get up out of that hole, I never moved so fast in my entire life."

Mr. Jones started digging that gas line for Aunt Bea. She was glad that he was willing to give her a break. After she cooled off for a few moments, she reached to grab the shovel back from Mr. Jones and he said, "That's all right Miss Bea, you get in that house and take a load off. I'll take it from here."

Shocked at what he said, Aunt Bea looked at Mr. Jones and said, "Mr. Jones, I hope you don't think I have money to pay you. I can't pay you to do this. I need to do this myself."

The truth was, Aunt Bea had more than enough money. She was just a very frugal person and she didn't believe in paying someone to do something that she could do for herself. But after dealing with that brutal heat on that hot August day, she couldn't help it – she needed a break.

Mr. Jones dug that entire gas line for Aunt Bea. It took him almost 2 days, but he got it done. Once the gas company came to the house and finished laying her gas line, Mr. Jones came back to Aunt Bea's house to put the dirt back into the hole for her. And that was it. The job that would have taken Aunt Bea weeks to finish on her own was finished within a matter of days.

When Mr. Jones was finished, Aunt Bea was so impressed with his work ethic and dedication that she wanted to find a way to express her gratitude. So she was willing to go back on her original decision NOT to pay him.

Aunt Bea tried to pay Mr. Jones but he refused to take her money. Each day, Aunt Bea would sneak up to his house and put a check in the mailbox. No matter what, Mr. Jones would not cash the checks. Eventually she tried to give him cash instead of a check, but the money always seemed to find its way back to Aunt Bea's mailbox. "I helped you because that's what neighbors are supposed to do," said Mr. Jones. "I did not help you because I wanted your money. You take that money and you give it to someone who needs it, Miss Bea."

As we stood on the porch, in the middle of telling me this story, Aunt Bea turned towards me, then she paused as she stared directly at me in complete silence, looking right into my eyes. She gave me a chance to take in what she had just shared with me.

I was already familiar with the story of how Aunt Bea built her house, but I had not heard the story of how her gas line was installed.

As we stood on her porch looking out at the area where her gas line was dug many, many years ago, Aunt Bea pointed at the gas line, then turned and looked back at me.

"If I would never have been out there in that hot, August heat doing something for myself and digging that gas line, Mr. Jones would never have seen me that day. And if he didn't see me out there, he would not have had any idea that I needed help."

She just stared at me.

Finally I said, "You are exactly right Aunt Bea, there is no way he would have helped you."

"I know I'm right, why you think I'm telling you this story?"

After a brief pause, she put her hands on my shoulders and said, "Aunt Bea ain't gonna live forever you know."

I said, "Don't say that Aunt Bea, why are you talking like that? I'm trying to enjoy that great story you just told me, and then you go and say something like that! Stop talking like that Aunt Bea!"

She said, "Well it's true. I'm an old lady, and sooner or later you're gonna have to get your cookies from somewhere else. But you just remember what I told you. As long as you are willing to do something for yourself, there will always be plenty of people there to help you dig your ditches and help you get everything that you need."

You know what? Aunt Bea was exactly right.

DIGGING YOUR OWN DITCHES

Aunt Bea could not have introduced the next part of the *7 Steps to "C" Your Way Through* any better – it all comes down to commitment and taking action. We can't blame everything on culture or our surroundings. And even though it's good to be clear and know what you want out of life, at some point you have to be willing to get up and dig your own ditches. That starts with Commitment.

Aunt Bea was clear about what she wanted because she *needed* a gas line and she didn't have a choice. She *had to* do it on her own – so she did. That's just who she was, she was just built that way - just like many other people from her generation. You won't find many people from older generations who are afraid of hard work. That's one of the reasons why many older people in America today are worried about the future of our country. Most of them seem to think that younger age groups are spoiled and act entitled because they have it *too good* and they don't have to work as hard. And I think they're right sometimes. I even feel the same way about myself at times. Sometimes I even wonder how much better I could perform or how much better my results would be if I were willing to work *harder*, just like Aunt Bea.

I always think to myself, "How can anyone understand what it feels like to want something bad enough, if things around them never get... *bad enough?*" I know that sounds simple, but let me ask you a question. Have you ever tried to pretend to be motivated to want something when you really didn't? If you have, then you already realize that you can't fake being hungry. You either want something bad enough or you don't. And when you want something bad enough, you make it a priority in your life. It's just that simple.

All of us should think about Aunt Bea's words more often. There are plenty of people, teams, and companies that have great talent. But there's a reason why the most talented teams don't always win. Sometimes they just have it *too good* and they lose their focus, especially once they start to get the results they want. Sometimes they just aren't *hungry enough* anymore. I mean, they're hungry *sometimes,* but the real question is...can they stay focused and hungry enough until their Mr. Jones shows up?

I had a really big challenge once that tested how hungry I was. My life has always been filled with many friends, family, and community members who had my back no matter what. Trust me, I love having people in my corner supporting me, but holidays were always tough. I knew a lot of people, and I had open invitations to eat holiday dinners at many houses! Hey, don't get me wrong, I was definitely thankful. But once I became a young adult, the question they always had was, *"Where are going to Thanksgiving dinner at this year?"*

I loved the invitations, but it was always hard choosing where to eat. I didn't have the heart to tell any of them NO, so most of the time it was just easier to tell everyone YES.

Do you have any idea how difficult it was eating multiple dinners, on *Thanksgiving* of all days? And I never wanted to disappoint the hosts by not eating their food, because that would just be rude!   So I ate a plate of food *each time,* at each house.

Of course I was already stuffed full after leaving the first house! I tried to come up with all kinds of methods to keep eating all day long.

I even tried to pace myself and take it slow, but nothing worked.

The worst part was that *I really, really, love food*, so I couldn't control myself.

By the end of the day, I got to a point where I just had to come clean with the hosts. *"I'm sorry, I can't eat anymore. I just can't. Maybe I can help you serve the food or clean the dishes afterwards? I will do anything to help, I just can't eat another bite."*

I learned something in the process – ***you can't fake being hungry.*** You either want something or you don't.

WHAT COMMITMENT LEADS TO

The culture around you can destroy your clarity - I see it all of the time. The #1 question that people always ask me is, *"How do I figure out what I really want to do with my life?"*

Trust me I get it. Knowing what you want out of life isn't always very simple. But sometimes it comes down to *wants and needs*.

Aunt Bea *needed* a gas line for her house; she didn't have a choice. In my life, I *needed* to figure out what I *wanted* because I did not have parents to do it for me; I didn't have a choice either.

But what about everyone else in this world?

What about the people that don't necessarily *need* anything?

I work with many winning teams that only *want* one thing – **to keep winning**. I work with many companies that perform very well in their industries and they only want one thing – **continued performance.**

I also see many parents who provide their kids with the best of everything and they just want to get the *best effort* from their kids.

What do they all have in common? In the examples above, each of of them are already *doing well*, but they still want more - and there is nothing wrong with that. But the question is, *"How does a person, team, or company that is already performing well, perform better?"*

The answer comes down to one thing and one thing only – COMMITMENT.

~ ~ ~ ~ ~

It doesn't matter if you *need* something or if you *want* something. The only thing that matters is your ability to take action towards what you want. That is what commitment is all about.

Once you figure out what you want (Step 2: Clarity), or once you even *think* that you know what you want, you have to fight to keep that vision alive in your heart. And what's the main thing that you are fighting to keep alive? It's progress.

When you are making progress towards your goals, it will keep your vision alive in your heart no matter how long it takes you to achieve it.

FIGHTING TO KEEP YOUR VISION ALIVE

Every time you do something, your brain responds. When you take action towards your goals – even if it's a small step – you will keep your vision alive in your heart and mind, literally. We develop *neural pathways, or* patterns, in our brains every time we think about something, every time we say something, and every time we do something. Everything we think, say, and do reinforces neural pathways in our brain. I will give you an example. There's a reason why we don't have to relearn how to ride a bike every time we get on one – it's because our brains access information that we already developed in our neural pathways.

There is a reason why we don't have to learn the meaning of certain words every time we use them in a sentence – our brains do it for us. Once you create a neural pathway in your brain, you go back down the same path each time you use it. That's why it is so important to think positive thoughts and ideas. Every time you think about something, your brain produces chemicals called neurotransmitters that *transmit information* in your brain.

When your brain is activated, it uses glucose and oxygen to send information along neural pathways. This happens every time you think about something. This also happens every time you talk about something and every time you do something. Each time your brain releases neurotransmitters and utilizes oxygen and glucose to make the action happen, you reinforce the same neural pathways.

The same thing that happens when you walk across a grass lawn happens in our brains. The more you walk across a yard along the same trail, the more you will begin to see a path created in the grass. Over time, that same path will eventually destroy the grass and all you will see is dirt. As long as you continue to walk along that same path, grass will never grow again. But if you do want the grass to grow again, you have to stop walking on the same path – you have to give it a chance to grow back again.

As human beings, our brains evolve in the same way. The more you reinforce a neural pathways in your brain by repeating the same thoughts and doing the same things, the more you will continue to develop habits and behaviors based on those thoughts and actions.

REASONS WHY WE LOVE INSTANT GRATIFICATION

Many people today do not give themselves a chance to really fight for what they want most. Why? Because they are too distracted. A large majority of people are constantly producing *disruptive* neurotransmitters in their brains that break their focus and attention. Our connection to phones, computers, and TV screens keeps us distracted during much of the day. As a matter of fact, the only time that most people are not looking at some type of screen or device is when they are asleep.

Studies are beginning to show that the main reason why many people are always connected is because of FOMO. Yep, you heard me...FOMO. FOMO stands for *Fear of Missing Out*.

Researcher Dr. Andrew Przybylski of the University of Essex, recently published a study in the *Journal of Computers in Human Behavior*. His findings made it clear that people who suffer from FOMO have a strong desire to *stay connected* with everything that people around them are doing because *they don't want to miss out* on anything."

At the beginning of this chapter, my aunt Bea clearly illustrated the value of what happens when you are focused. She also showed us what could happen when a person finally decides to take action and commit to something. But if Aunt Bea was focused on what other people were doing, she would've been distracted from her project. She would've never walked outside, grabbed her shovel, and begun to dig her gas line. Her project would never have started, and it definitely never would have been completed.

When I think about what's going on in the world today and how many people are suffering from FOMO, the irony is undeniable. We don't want to miss out on what everyone else is doing, but FOMO is causing us to miss out on what we could be doing in *our own* lives. FOMO isn't the only thing that's keeping people from committing and taking action towards their goals. Here are a few more examples of things that are keeping people distracted today...

- Nearly half of people ages 18-30 check their phones every 10 minutes.
- 8 out of 10 smartphone users use their phones *all the time* while on vacation.
- 3 out of 4 young smartphone users check their phone as soon as they wake up in the morning.
- On average, smartphone users check their Facebook account 14 times per day.
- Half of cellphone owners keep their phone within arm's length at all times.

I have a couple of quick questions for you. What would happen if you focused on what you wanted, *all the time*, even when you were on vacation? What would happen if you created a list of goals every morning as soon as you woke up? What would happen if you analyzed and revisited your goals every 10 minutes?

What would happen if you stopped everything you were doing 14 times per day just to DREAM about what you wanted out of life?

What would happen if you were so clear about your goals that you kept them within arm's reach of you at all times, just like you do your cell phone?

I'll tell you exactly what would happen...

If you focused on growing and becoming a better person just as much as you focus on other peoples' social media timelines, you would automatically begin to grow instantly. Why? Because of those neural pathways in your brain. Every time you focus on something, you reinforce that mindset. And every time you GET what you want, your brain releases a chemical called dopamine. Dopamine is responsible for making you feel good every time you get what you want. Every time you get a "ping" or a message notification on your phone, your brain releases dopamine.

Your brain also releases dopamine when you receive a package or a letter from the mailman at your house. The difference is that you may get a package in the mail every now and then, but you get pings and message notifications on your phone all day long, which means that small amounts of dopamine are constantly being released into our system - continuously.

That constant release of dopamine in our brains is causing new forms of addictions that are distracting people from making progress towards their goals, and if you are distracted from your goals, you will never do what Aunt Bea did –you will never *take action and commit to your goals.*

Electronic Screen Syndrome, or ESS, is what scientists and researchers are using to describe our current addiction to devices. Electronic Screen Syndrome is changing the way our brains function, literally. ESS is also disrupting the way that people think.

We get a hit of dopamine every time we get a new like or comment when we post a photo or status update on social media. When we start to feel low and we need another hit, what do we do? We post something else.

It's such a big deal that a new psychiatric diagnosis called *Disruptive Mood Dysregulation Disorder* has been introduced into the medical community. It's also part of the reason why cases of Attention Deficit Hyperactivity Disorder have increased almost 800% over the past 30 years.

Think about it - a 800% increase in the number of people who are walking around distracted all of the time - if people are so distracted, how can they ever be clear enough to figure out what they want to do with their lives? They can't.

If you can't figure out what you want, you will never get the results you want - it's just that simple. You will never be able to experience what Aunt Bea experienced when she built her own home. Most importantly, if you are too distracted to take the next steps towards your goals, you will never experience the best part about life – the moments where Mr. and Mrs. Jones' will show up to help you build your dream.

I believe that the #1 enemy of greatness in our culture today is distraction. Distraction is killing our country's ability to grow and become great. Distraction is the new Civil War that each of us are facing. The difference is, this war isn't being fought on a battlefield with brothers fighting against each other. The war is being fought in everyone's minds... with each click of our devices.

The *7 Steps to "C" Your Way Through* is a framework that was created to help you become intentional about how to live your life. The end result that I want people to experience is clarity of vision and a high level of commitment that will help them experience progress towards their goals. So it all comes down to progress.

Every time you experience progress, your brain releases a small amount of dopamine that makes you feel good about what you just achieved. But that's the ironic part about the dynamic we are facing – the dopamine that your brain releases into your system when you make progress towards your goals is in competition with the dopamine that your brain is releasing when you are constantly connected to your phone. That means your brain is being overstimulated... all of the time.

And I mean *ALL OF THE TIME*.

I believe that this is the main reason why people are so willing to take shortcuts to achieve their goals. I believe it's the reason why the idea of instant *Overnight Success* is so attractive today.

Not only are people distracted, but their minds are already overstimulated with feel good chemicals like dopamine. People used to only get those types of feelings after they completed a tough job or assignment. Today, that same feeling is being generated all of the time whenever you reach for your cell phone. That's one of the biggest differences between older generations and younger generations throughout the world today. Older generations of people had to work hard for a very long time just to experience similar levels of dopamine highs when they made progress towards their goals. But today, people don't have to do that.

Why would they be willing to make sacrifices for or commit to doing something that would take 100 times longer and 100 times more effort to achieve when they can just log on to their devices and get an instant high every time they get a new like or comment on social media?

Many people today aren't willing to do that work simply because they don't have to. So they don't.

RUN THIS PLAY

I will tell you the #1 play that you need to run if you want to get focused and committed to your vision.

Every day you need to find time for silence and solitude.

When you are intentional about finding solitude everyday (which is basically peace and quiet in your life), you will have time to unplug from the constant connection of life. You should be intentional enough to find at least 20 to 30 minutes per day of uninterrupted time to sit, relax, and just think. If you do this, several things will happen.

First, your brain will release the built-up oxygen and glucose in certain areas of your brain that are constantly connected. When you focus on something, it takes energy, resources, and chemicals in your body to make that happen. The immediate release of those chemicals will help your brain to reset and refocus, because that energy can be used for other essential functions in your brain. Once those chemicals are emptied in those neural pathways, your brain will immediately began to calm down in amazing ways.

Second, by finding time for a few minutes of quietness you will achieve greater clarity of your vision by disconnecting from the culture around you – at least temporarily.

Disconnecting from your surrounding environment will give you a few moments to come up with your own thoughts every day. If you want to live your own life and achieve the *results that YOU want*, you need to be able to think for yourself and generate your own ideas. We are so distracted today that even when we do come up with a good thought or idea, chances are, we didn't really come up with it on our own. We probably got the idea from someone or somewhere else, we just don't realize it. I'm just being real, because it happens to all of us.

It would be sad to go through your entire life and never experience what it's like to use your God-given talents and abilities and really feel like you are living YOUR LIFE. But that is what most people do. If you don't take the time to unplug from everything around you and come up with your own thoughts and ideas, you will end up thinking like everyone else. If you end up thinking like everyone else, your habits and behaviors will be JUST LIKE everyone else's, and so will your results. You were never created to be generic, so don't act that way - you deserve better.

Third, taking the time to unplug and quiet your mind will give you the upper hand. You will develop an advantage by practicing a new success habit called *metacognition*.

*A **metacognitive person** takes time to think about what they think about*. Practicing metacognition is the ultimate form of being intentional. Any time you focus on thinking about what you think about – or evaluate the thoughts in your mind – you give yourself a fighting chance to create newer, healthier neural pathways that will help you reinforce new thoughts and habits. And trust me, you better be ready to fight if you want to defeat the current culture in today's world that's destroying the opportunity for many people to grow and become better.

Think about Aunt Bea again for one moment - she was clear about what she wanted and she did it. What did she do? She started to dig her own gas line. Why? Because she didn't have a choice. She had to dig her gas line, so she wasn't distracted and did not hesitate. But most people today aren't like Aunt Bea. People really only do things for one of two reasons: because they have to, or because they want to. Either way, you owe it to yourself to figure out what you want to do with your life (clarity), and you owe it to your family, your community, your coworkers, and your teammates to commit to taking action in order to become better at what you do.

As I close out this chapter about commitment, I want to share with you one of the craziest things about how challenging it is to stay focused. Recent studies indicate that *75 to 90% of people check their phone constantly throughout the day, **even when it doesn't ring or vibrate**.* Can I tell you why I think that's sad? Because checking your cell phone even when it doesn't ring or vibrate is the same as going outside to check your mailbox ten times a day to see if someone sent you a check in the mail... even though you have no reason to receive a check at all. Who does that?

What if Aunt Bea would have just sat inside of her house all day and looked out the window expecting someone to just show up and help her? Do you think help would have arrived if that's all she did? Nope! Even if Mr. Jones had been walking down the street, he would not have seen Ms. Bea if she wasn't outside working. We won't make much progress on our goals either if we just sit around distracted, playing on our phones all day long. So take a few minutes each day to put your phone down and figure out what you want, then pick up your shovel and start digging.

Don't worry about how to achieve your goals or how to get better results, just get started. Once you commit to taking action, help will always show up along the way - I promise. That's just how it goes.

COMMITMENT CHECKLIST

- Name one thing that you have put off doing that will increase your results once you take action on it?
- Are you hungry & self-motivated or are you motivated by the expectation of others around you?
- What old habits do you need to discontinue?
- What new habits do you need to develop to reinforce new neural pathways in your mind?
- How would you describe your addiction to technology?
- What time during the day is the best time for you to practice the habit of metacognition to focus and clear your mind?

Chapter

10

CLARITY
COMMITMENT
COMPETENCE

CULTURE

Competency and Skills

When I began to transition to young adulthood, I missed my dad a lot. The only time I got to see my dad Chuck was when I made the trip to Mount Olive Correctional Center to visit him.

Prison visits are always interesting.

From the moment you drive through the gates of the prison, you can't help but think to yourself, "People actually live here, like this... wow."

Everything about visiting a prison is unique and unlike anything else you could ever experience.

Prisons smell kind of like hospitals - *only colder*. Everything seems like it's black and white, with very little color and there is no energy... at all.

Even the prison workers seem to have been stripped of their personalities and humanness.

Every time I visited with my dad we always had the same routine. He would ask me questions about my personal life, then school, and last we would talk about my vision. My dad was an amazing father figure. In fact, he was so amazing that he continued to encourage me, and he took on the position as *chief encourager* for all of the other prison inmates that he lived with. Chuck was a real blessing for many inmates in prison, because he kept everyone around him focused on being positive. His motto was, *"In here you have to be positive and do your time – you can't let your time do you."*

My dad taught me that some of the smartest and brightest people in the world were locked up in prison because they chose to use their gifts the wrong way. My dad even had a theory. His theory was that most men were in prison for only two reasons – women or money. He said that most crimes could be traced back to the illegal things that men do to boost their ego and attract women. He also concluded that most crimes were committed because of some illegal scheme that people came up with to make *fast money*. Either way, the message to me was clear: treat women right and resist the urge to get things the fast way. Point taken!

DEVELOPING YOUR MINDSET

I have always been hungry and focused. But remember, I didn't have a choice. I didn't have people to do things for me, so I had to be focused about everything I did if I wanted to stay out of prison myself. In my head, I repeated the same words over and over just to stay focused. *"Faith, family, focus, fight... faith, family, focus, fight... faith, family, focus, fight."*

Faith reminded me that God had my back, no matter what.

Family reminded me to never lose my vision of one day having a beautiful wife to share my life with, a bunch of kids to spoil rotten, and maybe, just maybe, even the chance to help free my dad Chuck from jail.

Focus reminded me to be intentional about everything I did and to not get distracted.

Fight reminded me that it wasn't going to be easy, and that I couldn't give in to anyone else's influences or expectations for my life, especially if I didn't want to continue the same generational cycles in my family. I had to always fight to keep me vision alive no matter what.

"Faith, family, focus, fight... faith, family, focus, fight... faith, family, focus, fight."

The more I repeated this to myself, the more I reinforced this mindset in my brain. My dad was more than okay with what I wanted for my life and he fully supported it. He didn't take offense to the fact that I didn't want to end up where he did. I'm glad because I needed his guidance and continued support to stay focused on my vision.

My dad and I both knew that the only way that I could make progress towards my goals and stay out of prison was by reinforcing the right habits and by equipping myself with skills that would help me advance. That's all we ever talked about during my visits. As a matter of fact, today when I step on stage as a motivational speaker or when I sit down with clients that I work with, I replay many of those conversations that I had during my prison visits with my father.

Imagine if you had monthly visits with a person – any person – where all you did was update them on your progress towards your goals - and imagine if they actually listened to you. Now imagine if you had three to five hours to have that conversation, when the person sitting across from you was not distracted by his cell phone or computer screen. Imagine if that person's main job was just to... *listen to you*. If you did have that, it would be easy to generate the motivation that you need to keep working to achieve your goals, especially if you didn't want to be embarrassed by displaying a lack of progress.

Those prison visits gave me an early advantage in life, and I didn't even realize it at the time. I didn't realize that if my dad would have never gone to prison, we probably would not have had the time to sit and have those conversations. If he were a free man there was no way that either of us would have been able to sit for hours on end, talking and listening to each other. That would have been impossible - because the busyness of life would have gotten in the way.

My dad's prison sentence became a part of who I was, and it affected me in both positive and negative ways. It affected me negatively because I was lonely and I missed him... a lot. But it affected me positively because it helped me to defeat the culture around me – it helped me become crystal clear on what *I wanted to do with my life* and it helped me commit to taking action towards my goals. How could that NOT be a positive thing?

Before I left each prison visit with my dad, he always made sure that I took action on what we talked about when I got home. There were many days in between the visits that I had with him, I had plenty of time to make things happen, and I was always working. Always. When I started cutting hair and doing landscaping work as a kid, I worked every day. As a result, I developed skills that were valuable to people around me. I was actually pretty good at what I did, and it made me feel good about myself. As an athlete I worked hard too. I was a pretty decent competitor and I had a few skills on the basketball court.

Having skills and the ability to do something – anything, it doesn't matter what it is – having at least a small amount of skill or ability makes a big difference in how you see yourself and how you pursue your goals. When I began to establish my plans to take my vision to the next level, I was always confident enough to at least try my best because I was never afraid of doing the work. When you are raised in West Virginia and you witness the work ethic of West Virginia coal miners around you, it's easy to understand what hard work looks like. I was never the smartest person, but I wasn't afraid of working hard and taking initiative, so I didn't dream small at all – I dreamed BIG.

My big vision sounded like this: *go to college, get a job, fall in love, grow my skills, start a business, start a family, and then... change the world.*

You are probably thinking, *"Wow, anything else? Would you like fries with your order?"* At least there was one thing for certain: *I knew exactly what I wanted.*

CHECKING THINGS OFF OF MY LIST

My dream was to go to the University of Southern California in Los Angeles. I wanted to be a Trojan, and I wanted it bad. The only problem was that I couldn't even afford the application fee or come up with the money to make the trip from West Virginia to the west coast. So I had to scratch those plans.

I ended up going to West Virginia Wesleyan College instead. After seeing the nearly $23,000 per year price tag compared to other schools in the state, I decided to transfer after my freshman year to Fairmont State College.

Fairmont State cost me less than $3500 per year to attend, so the choice for me was a no-brainer, especially since I had already made up my mind to go to medical school, law school, or at least get my master's or Ph.D. one day. For that reason, I wanted to spend as little as possible on my undergraduate degree.

No one had ever graduated from college in my family, which is something that absolutely boggles my mind even to this day. This trend really changed my mindset – I had to graduate. But I didn't just want to graduate, I wanted to get the most out of college that I could.

Someone once told me, *"Everyone on a college campus is paid to serve you, everyone. So take advantage of the resources at your disposal because you will never be catered-to or waited on like that again for the rest of your life!"* And trust me, I took advantage of every resource that I could. By the time I graduated from Fairmont State, my experiences on campus dramatically changed the direction of my life.

I was voted Student Body President, Homecoming King, President of Alpha Phi Alpha Fraternity, Incorporated, and I even had a chance to achieve my dream of playing college basketball. By the time I finished my undergraduate degree, my college experiences gave me a better understanding of who I am and I realized that I really could do anything as long as I was willing to stay committed to my vision.

WHEN COMMITMENT LEADS TO COMPETENCY

Life can be really simple if we let it. Especially if we understand life's *Gravity Principles*. I call them gravity principles because gravity is constant – it's permanent and no matter what, there is nothing you can do to change it.

Here's a Gravity Principle: ***when you grow your skills you grow your ability*** because when you get better at one thing, you get better at everything else that you do. That's just how life is. When you are *competent* and you know how to do something, it changes your mindset.

I am glad that I was committed to going to college. The biggest thing that I learned in college actually had nothing to do with what I learned in the classroom – it had more to do with what I learned about what was inside of me. I became more *self-aware*.

When you have to cook your own food, wash and fold your own clothes, make important decisions about classes, decide which activities and organizations to join, manage important deadlines and *find a way to pay for it all,* you learn a lot about yourself. As a result I became extremely emotionally intelligent, which is a fancier way of saying, *"I learned a lot about myself."*

I later learned that emotional intelligence was an attractive skill that many companies look for. Harvard University researchers such as David Goleman, and many Fortune 500 companies began to identify emotional intelligence, or what they call "EQ" as a valuable skill that companies could use to create a competitive advantage. HR Leaders and Talent Development Professionals began to realize that really effective leaders who have the ability to get great results from others, those leaders all have one thing in common: *they all have a high degree of emotional intelligence.* That's why many HR leaders in companies have begun to develop competency models to help them identify, train, and promote the best and brightest stars in their companies – the employees with high EQ.

People always told me that being on my own and learning how to survive at a young age would help me one day, but come on... *even researchers at Harvard thought so?* Their research shows that over the next few decades, EQ will continue to emerge as an even more valuable skill set to have than IQ. Intelligence is still important to have, but emotional intelligence will take you farther in life. And I think I understand why. The more you know about yourself, the more you begin to think differently. When you can think differently, you become a unique individual and an attractive recruiting prospect.

Emotional Intelligence can also help you to develop better critical thinking skills. Critical thinking skills used to be something that you assumed everyone had. Not anymore. People are constantly connected to their devices, and most of the new technology can do everything for you if you want it to. People are being forced to think for themselves less and less today. Thats why many leaders and researchers are worried about today's youth not being able to think for themselves in the future. It's even causing headaches in today's workforce. One of the major concerns among business leaders today is the amount of entry-level professionals entering the workforce with poor critical thinking skills.

So whose fault is it? Actually, it's nobody's fault. However, you are responsible for how you respond to these changes around you. My goal is to help you *"C" Your Way Through* today's culture and stay focused on making progress towards your goals. But you have to remember what the doctor told me on the night that I said goodbye to my grandmother at the hospital – he told me to **take responsibility** for my life if I wanted any chance of achieving my dreams.

You must take personal responsibility for growing your skills. It's your #1 job, and you can't expect anyone else to do it for you.   R e m e m b e r my favorite quote, *"It's amazing what you can do... when you have to?"* Well, how can you really do that if you don't... have to? *You have to stay focused and motivated.*

Many of today's kids do not have to take the same path to get what they want, because previous generations before them had different experiences. People from older generations had to walk to school – they didn't have a choice. Kids today have school buses.

Just 20 years ago, Baby Boomers had to use encyclopedias to research information. Today, everyone uses Google.

Have things changed? Of course they have. But no matter who you are, you still have to choose to be intentional about how you live your life and how you grow your skills.

THE MOST IMPORTANT SKILLS NEEDED TODAY

<u>EMOTIONAL INTELLIGENCE SKILLS</u>

Self-Awareness: The more aware you are about yourself, the more likely you will be to make better choices that will lead to success. You will be able to take better responsibility for your actions by regulating how you make decisions.

- *Tip: Say yes to new challenges. You will develop new neural pathways in your brain, develop new habits, and learn to trust your abilities each time.*
- *Tip: Get real feedback from people who care about you - people who will be honest with you about the areas in life you need grow in the most.*

Motivation: When you are clear about who you are, it's easier to stay focused and energized about where you are going. The more you know about yourself, the more motivated you will be to live *your life.*

- *Tip: Stay focused on where YOU are going and **stop comparing yourself to others**. You will never feel like you are growing if you constantly compare yourself to everyone else around you.*
- *Tip: Eat your dessert first. Sometimes you have to remind yourself that your life belongs to you, and you have the right to do whatever you want to, however you want to. Be yourself.*
- *Tip: Celebrate progress. Take time to really celebrate when you do something well or when you achieve something big. This will keep you focused on doing your best more often. Why? Because you will get a chance to celebrate again if you keep getting results!*

Social Skills: People with high EQ connect well with others. When you are clear about who you are and where you are going, other people will be attracted to your vision – it's sexy. When other people like you, they will want to be around you more. Having high EQ will also help you show more empathy and compassion towards others because you won't be comparing yourself against, or competing with, them.

- *Tip: Put your phone down and turn your shoulders towards someone when you speak to them.*
- *Tip: Stop interrupting people when they talk. Wait until you know they are finished speaking before you start to talk.*
- *Tip: Ask people questions about the stories and comments they share with you. It will help you listen closely, and it will show the other person that you are genuinely interested in what they are saying. Many people just want to be heard and understood. If you practice doing this, it will show others that you have extremely advanced social skills.*
- *Tip: Always smile and make direct eye contact when you speak to others. You will give off positive energy by doing this and make other people feel great about themselves.*

CRITICAL THINKING SKILLS

Interpretation: Can you understand information when someone gives it to you and can you explain it back to them?

- *Tip: Try to understand why information is important. This will help you to remove any opinions or biases you may have about what you are interpreting.*
- *Tip: Every time you hear about something in the news – positive or negative – try to imagine if you were the person that the story was about. It will dramatically change how you interpret what you think you see and hear.*

Analysis: Can you link different pieces of information together to see what it means without asking for help?

- *Tip*: Learn how to connect the dots with information. Don't just look at one piece of information that someone gives you. Visualize and imagine other things that could be connected to it.
- *Tip*: Read various ancient proverbs or literature quotes to develop analytical skills that will help you see the metaphor behind each quote.
- *Tip*: Ask other people that you know and trust how they feel about information that you are analyzing. Since you trust them, this will help you become more open minded and see things differently when perspectives are shared with you.

Evaluation: Can you tell if something is real or false, black or white, up or down? Your ability to evaluate situations and people will help you produce better results.

- *Tip*: Trust your instincts. Don't listen to everything that other people say. Take the time to figure things out for yourself and form your own opinions about things.
- *Tip*: Open your mind to consider multiple sides of the story. This will help you evaluate information and see things better.
- *Tip*: Be decisive. You need to be able to make decisions even when you are unsure. Develop the habit of owning your decisions even with limited information.

Clear Communication: Can you clearly explain something to two or three different kinds of people? You may be able to communicate well with your family, friends or co-workers, but being able to communicate just as well with other people that you do not know will give you a big advantage.

- *Tip*: Before you share information with others, study it first. Be clear about it.
- *Tip*: Consider your audience before you explain something. Be intentional about explaining things in a way that other people can relate to.
- *Tip*: Practice explaining the same thing to two different types of people. This will help you learn how to make adjustments to better connect with people.

Self-Regulate: Are you familiar with how certain thoughts affect your behaviors?

- *Tip: When you get results that you do not want, think about what you were thinking and why you were thinking it. Eventually, you will notice patterns. Then you can change your mindset and make adjustments.*
- *Tip: Calm down before you say or do something. Reducing your emotion before you act will keep you from making choices and decisions that you will regret later.*
- *Tip: Practice metacognition by taking time out each day to unplug, relax your mind, and think about the things that you think about. This will help you to focus and think clearly through situations by releasing built up oxygen and glucose in certain parts of your brain.*

SKILL COMES BEFORE FAME

If you stop to think about every major celebrity or mogul in the world, even though they may be famous today, they didn't start there - they ended up their.

Every celebrity or famous person who wasn't born into fame because of who their parents were, had to earn it. And they had to start out somewhere, by developing a SKILL first. Their skills and their gifts are what eventually opened doors for them.

Steve Jobs developed amazing computer skills… first.
Michael Jordan developed great basketball skills… first.
Oprah Winfrey developed great journalism skills… first.
Jay-Z developed great poetry and lyrical skills… first.
Miley Cyrus also developed singing & acting skills… first.

Everyone wants to be millionaires, and everyone wants to be successful. And if that's what you want, then you have every right to have those ambitions if you choose to. But you can't forget this: unless something is just handed to you, or unless you just get lucky, you must get good at something first.

Your gifts and ability will always be the #1 thing that opens doors for you. The most successful people in the world never started at the top, they started at the bottom, where they developed their skills and developed their talent... first.

When I first started cutting hair when I was younger, I was horrible and I gave myself many bad haircuts. But I didn't stop cutting my hair or practicing, and eventually I got better. I became really good at cutting hair, and *everyone else recognized my skills* by paying me good money to cut their hair also.

The same thing happened to me in sports. I practiced my hoop game a lot, and each time I went to the park to play basketball when I was younger, I always got picked to play – even when adults were bigger and stronger than me they still chose me to play on their teams and I never had to sit on the sidelines with other kids my age.

The same thing happened in my professional speaking career. Although I was nervous when I was selected to speak in front of hundreds of my peers at that first student leadership conference, I survived the experience. Afterwards, many people complimented me on my talents and my ability to engage an audience. Even though I had very poor technique and skills as a speaker when I began, I knew I could work on it if I wanted to.

Eventually, I learned something. I learned that when you are good at something and when you have skills – it doesn't matter if you're cutting hair, playing sports, or speaking on stage – everyone else will realize that you are competent or *"good"* at what you do. When you are competent (or when you have skills) in any area and you know what you are doing, your skills will always open doors for you.

If you do manage to survive the many areas of distraction in today's culture and you do end up figuring out what you want to do with your life, you must commit to taking steps to grow your skills in whatever you do, because *your effort will always increase your ability.* Always!

Here is something that you need to do if you want to take your skills to the next level.

Kids and Teenagers need to focus on mastering the basic fundamentals in school and life. The ability to listen, follow directions, and interpret and analyze are basic fundamentals in life. They are called *critical skills* for a reason. They are necessary for a *successful transition* into society.

Young Adults must learn first and foremost the importance of self-reliance, self-care, and personal responsibility. These skills are critical if young adults want to escape the *victim mentality* that causes people to blame others for their mistakes. Understanding personal responsibility will also help cure the largely growing attitude of *entitlement* that is sweeping our country today. Remember what the doctor said to me at the hospital that night, he said, *"If you want it, go get it... and don't expect anyone to give you anything."*

Adults must be intentional about getting better, growing their skills, and *never becoming complacent*. Taking ownership of your personal development, spiritual development, career development, and interpersonal relationship skills all depend on one thing – a committed focus to getting better, every day.

The skills that I just mentioned are the most important things that people need to develop in their MINDSET before they make it to the next level. I have also realized that every person has different skills, but the problem is that most people may not be able to recognize the skills they have or how to grow them. Everyone has a skill. Some people are so talented that they have many skills. I have realized that there are really 3 major *types of skills* that most people use to open doors for themselves. The first one is…

Building Skills - Building skills allow people to build things for others. This is a real blue-collar type of skill that architects, engineers, and general contractors have. These skills allow people to work with their hands. This is a great skill to have because building skills will always be needed by everyone in our society - no matter what. And, every person has the ability to get really good and grow their building skills simply by using these skills everyday. The more they build with their hands, the more they open doors and create opportunities for themselves by getting better and growing their skills. The second skill is…

Service Skills - Service skills allow people to meet the needs that others have around them. Anyone can have these type of skills. Service skills allow people to help anyone with any needs that they have. Doctors, plumbers, teachers, restaurant servers and even athletes and singers provide services that people either want or need. Service skills are great to have because those skills will always be needed. There are so many service-type of jobs in the world, and it's easy to rise to the top and get your skills noticed if you are really good at what you do. Whenever the world is saturated with certain jobs or skills that many people have, it's easy to stand out if you give outstanding service. And the third skill is...

Creative Skills - Creative skills allow people to use their unique talent or ability to add value to others. People with creative skills are usually passionate about something, and they follow their passion to create opportunities for themselves that are much different than the opportunities that building or service skills provide. The world already needs certain building and service skills, but the world doesn't necessarily *need a person's passion*. People with creative skills need to find a way to grab the attention of the people around them if they want others to respect and recognize their talents, and to do that, people with creative skills must become really good and develop *real skills* in the area that they're passionate about. If they do that, *people will pay for their passion*. But if they don't develop *real skills*, people will just think that their passion is just a cute little hobby.

I just named 3 types of skills that most people have. I have realized that rather you're a builder, server or a creator, once you figure out what type of skills you want to have, you have to focus on growing your skills because every successful person in the world had to grind and work hard to get where they are, but first, they had to realize which skills they needed to develop. So it doesn't matter if you're an adult or a teenager, first, you need to realize which type of skills you have, or which type of skills you... want to have. If you want other people to recognize your skills, and if you want people to take you seriously, you must be willing to put in the time to grow your skills.

THE BIGGEST SKILL THAT OPENED DOORS FOR ME

I have always been very resourceful, even as a kid. I learned how to get what I needed, when I needed it. I guess those genes were passed down to me from my great-grandmother, Mama Hattie. I learned that being resourceful will get you places in life, but it will only take you so far. As an adult, I began to have some negative feelings deep inside whenever my resourceful nature kicked in.

For instance, I always wanted to find the cheapest or easiest way to get what I needed, because that's how I always approached things since I was a kid. I always tried to find the *'best deal'* or I always tried to get the *'hook up'* whenever I purchased things.

Well, one of my favorite quotes is, *"When I was a child, I thought like a child. When I became an adult, I thought like an adult."*

I learned to be resourceful when I was a child because I needed to survive. But after I finished college and graduate school, and once I received my bachelor's and master's degrees and started working for Fortune 500 companies, something changed inside of me. I started to reject my resourceful nature, because I realized that I wasn't running from anything anymore and I didn't want to just survive... *I wanted to thrive.* I realized that it wasn't always good for me to try to get the *'hook up'* or the *'best deal'* - sometimes it's better to pay full price for everything you get.

In order to get more out of life and take my life to another level, I had to do the one thing that's important for everyone to do before they transition to the next level: *I had to really be honest with myself* and ask myself some tough questions. Someone once told me, *"AVERAGE people answer questions that other people ask them, but GREAT people answer tough questions that they ask of themselves."*

So I did it, I asked myself a tough question. I asked, "What skills, attitudes, or behaviors do I need to leave behind me if I want to keep growing?" I already knew what part of the answer was. Being resourceful was one of them. Being resourceful and getting things fast and easy was a valuable skill to have when I was young. But as my vision for my life began to unfold in front of me, I realized that if I wanted to take my life to the next level, I needed to get comfortable with really earning my results and not taking any shortcuts – even if it meant taking the long way. Even if it meant giving three times the effort, I needed to earn it. Keep in mind, I had a BIG vision for what I wanted out of life. My vision was to *go to college, get a job, fall in love, keep growing my skills, start a business, start a family, and then... change the world.* That's how BIG my vision was, but first I had to be really honest with myself about how poorly I performed in certain areas of my life if I wanted to move forward.

I have never met a successful husband, father, or business owner that ever told me how *fast or easy* their journey was. So I committed to doing whatever I had to do, no matter how long it took. I stopped looking for the "hook up" from people, and *I stopped looking for short cuts in my process.*

When you commit to doing the things that matter the most to you, you can't take short cuts. *There is no such thing as an Overnight Success when it comes to the areas of life that are the most important.*

Some of the **smartest people** in the world are in prison today because they chose to take shortcuts or because they chose faster ways to get what they wanted. Some of the **nicest people** in the world are also broken-hearted, divorced, and lonely because they chose to take shortcuts in their marriages or in their relationships with their kids. And some of the **best business ideas** never succeed – even some of the most innovative ones – because the business leaders spent all of their time and energy on figuring out ways to do things *cheaper and faster.*

When you're willing to pay the full price to get to the next level, no matter how much it cost, you will motivate yourself in the process by proving to yourself that you are serious about the results that you want to achieve. If you aren't willing to pay full price, that's okay too - it just means that you aren't as serious as your though you were.

I learned that some skills were very beneficial for me to have at an early in life. I also learned that there were parts of my character and personality that I had to be willing to leave behind if I wanted to get to the next level and move forward in my life... and so do you. That's why I always continued to say to myself...

"*Faith, family, focus, fight...*

"*Faith, family, focus, fight...*

"*Faith, family, focus, fight...*

That's all I repeated to myself over and over again to keep my vision alive in my heart.

When you commit to growing your skills and becoming more competent in the areas that matter to you most, you will get better, and if you're consistent, you won't just get better – you will get really, really good. And other people will respect you more and take your skills seriously.

SKILLS CHECKLIST

TAKING YOUR GAME TO ANOTHER LEVEL

- What can you commit to that will increase your skills?
- What innate skills do people recognize in you?
- Analyze your skills. What competencies do you need to fulfill your purpose? What are your best skills?
- Which emotional intelligence skills do you need to implement right away?
- What steps do you need to take to improve upon your weaknesses?
- Do your skills position you as a builder, server or a creator for others?
- What skills are needed to help your team or organization get better results?

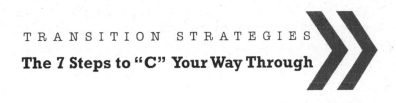
Chapter

11

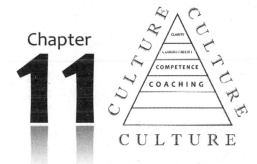

Getting Coached to Run The Plays

When my grandmother raised me at 110 Westlawn Street in Fairmont, WV, she did the best she could to give me everything she had – the rest was up to me. I had to do the best I could with what she gave me, and I came up with all kinds of strategies to be resourceful.

I could tell you about all of the tips, strategies, and techniques that I used to stretch a dollar to its last penny. But there is one technique I used that I've got to tell you about – my red washcloth.

I've had to do my own laundry since I was in my early teenage years. I tried to save a few dollars here and there by keeping my clothes as clean as possible before I needed to wash them. I had one towel and one red washcloth that I used when I showered. I quickly realized that the more I used my towel, the more damp it got and it wouldn't stay clean very long. So I figured out a strategy that would keep my towel fresher… *longer.*

Whenever I finished showering, I would use my red washcloth instead of my towel to dry off with while I was still in the shower. After I squeezed the excess water out of my red washcloth, I would do the same thing all over again - before I stepped out of the shower. Once I got out of the shower, I used my towel to finish drying off. By the time I stepped out of the shower, I had already gotten most of the water off of my body with my red washcloth and my towel didn't get very wet when I used it. This little technique helped my towel stay fresher, *longer*.

Once I realized this little trick, I could go longer periods before I had to do laundry again. This method worked for me for a very long time, even while I was in college. Unfortunately I had no idea that towards the end of my college experience, something would change the way I used my towels and washcloths... forever.

Her name was Lisa. Lisa Gaston. I met her in college, and after we started dating, one of the first things that she noticed was how particular I was about where I hung my towel and my washcloth in my bathroom. Eventually, whenever she was at my apartment, she would place my washcloth and towel in the dirty clothes and then replace them with fresh ones.

Every time she did this, the same thing happened. I would say, *"Who threw my towel and washcloth into the dirty clothes?"* as if I didn't already know who did it.

She would normally respond back with, "Morris Morrison, stop it!"

"Stop what? I just started using those and they were not ready to be thrown into the dirty clothes yet."

In the sweetest voice ever, she would just stand there with her hands on her hips and look at me and say, "Morris Morrison, will you please take a look in your bathroom closet. Do you see how many towels and washcloths you have? You have plenty of clean ones, so stop using the same one over and over again. You are not 13 years old anymore, and it's time for you to grow up."

I guess it's hard to change old habits. But you know what, she was right – it was time.

#TheresAlwaysAGirl!

THE POWER OF FEEDBACK

Everyone needs to hear some feedback every now and then to change their bad habits. That's why coaching is so important. Coaching is the next part of the *7 Steps to "C" Your Way Through,* and it's probably the most important step in the process.

One of the best ways to escape the pull that culture and bad habits can have on your life and one of the best ways to achieve progress is by getting coaching and feedback. Lisa was my girlfriend and she definitely wasn't my coach. But she still gave me feedback that I *needed* to hear. I had old habits that I needed to change and –because she was my girlfriend – Lisa had no problem telling me which habits I needed to work on right away.

In Chapter 10, I talked to you about competency and the importance of growing your skills. Before you commit to taking steps to growing your skills in certain areas, it's a good idea to know which areas you should start with first.

Receiving coaching and feedback will change your life… if you let it. If you are the type of person who thinks that you already know everything, then coaching isn't for you. If you're the type of person that can't take it when someone points out something that you need to do better at, then coaching isn't for you. But if you're the type of person that wants to have an advantage over your biggest competition, then coaching is for you.

Remember, emotional intelligence and self-awareness are two of the biggest strengths that a person can have. Having a high EQ will help you defeat your biggest competition – the person staring back at you in the mirror every day.

Remember Coach Joe Gerarde? He was one of *The Real Heroes* that I introduced you to in Chapter 4. Well one day after basketball practice, Coach Gerarde pointed out something to me that I didn't realize.

He said, "You know what Morris, you always do exactly what I tell you to do and you never give me any back talk. Do realize that?"

I said, "No, not really."

He said, "If you always stay coachable and you keep that attitude throughout life, being coachable will take you places."

Back then, I had no idea what he was talking about because my mindset was, "You are my basketball coach, so I am supposed to listen to you."

But Coach Gerarde noticed something about me. He realized that I didn't always have parents around me when I was younger, so I was very hungry for feedback and coaching.

I was open to hearing what others had to say, even though most kids go through a period in their lives where their parents begin to get on their nerves, so they push back because they want to be independent and they want to think for themselves. But the sooner you begin to seek out advice on how you can get better, the sooner you will have a real advantage over your competition.

Here are a few examples of how coaching and feedback helped me run better plays every day.

MICHAEL BELMEAR

Michael Belmear was the VP of Student Affairs at Fairmont State College when I was a student. He instantly became a mentor for me. I looked up to him more than anyone else in my life, other than my dad Chuck. He was one of the first professional black men that I ever met, and he made a *POWERFUL* difference in many people's lives. He had tremendous leadership influence, and when he walked into a room, his presence alone shifted the entire energy of the place. He always dressed in the best professional attire and everything that he said and did *inspired people* . He was absolutely captivating. And... he had tons of swag – he was just a cool guy that everyone loved.

When I was voted Student Body President, I had to report directly to Michael Belmear. After the election results were finalized, he looked at me and he said, "Morris Morrison... the new Student Body President. So, are you ready for your new job?"

"I think so," I replied.

"What do you mean, you *think* so?"

I said, "Do you know how many great student body presidents have come and gone before me? What if I'm not as good as they were? What if I mess up? What if I can't do the job?"

He just turned towards me and he gave me his famous *Michael Belmear* look. It's the look that he gives people when he either thinks they're crazy or when he has something important to say. He tilted his head and his chin close to his chest, and looked up at me over the top of his glasses as he gave me the most important advice that anyone has ever given me.

"Morris, don't you know that *all unhappiness in life is caused by comparison?"* he said.

I said, "Huh?"

"Morris, don't you ever compare yourself to other people – it's the fastest way to be unhappy with yourself."

That quote – *all unhappiness in life is caused by comparison* – was something that his mother, Mrs. Geraldine Belmear, taught him when he was a kid. Once he shared it with me, that was it. I never worried another day about my job as Student Body President. That advice also helped me deal with a lot of insecurities that I had deep down inside. After that day, I stopped comparing myself to other people.

Michael Belmear invested everything that he could into my development. Some days, the feedback that he gave me was tough to hear. But I needed to hear it. He knew where I came from and he knew what my goals were, so at times he just had to give it to me straight.

My relationship with him positioned me to grow my skills in a major way. After I began the habit of getting coaching and feedback from Michael Belmear, I was able to embrace more critical feedback later down the road from other people. Michael Belmear opened the door for that possibility.

STEPHAN DAVIS

As I walked across campus during my senior year in college, Kim Davis, the Director of the Men's Residence Halls yelled out, "Hey Morris Morrison!" As I got closer, she asked, "What are you going to do after you graduate?"

"I want to work in corporate America. Then eventually, I want to own my own business." And that's how it happened.

Within moments, she said, "If you want to work in corporate America one day, then you need to know my brother."

"Who is your brother?" I asked.

"His name is Steve Davis and he is the Vice President of Human Resources for Equitable Gas in Pittsburgh. If you send me your resume, I will forward it on to him."

Kim Davis had my resume in her e-mail inbox within ten minutes. And within 24 hours, I had a lunch meeting scheduled at Equitable Gas's home office in Pittsburgh the following day.

When the receptionist walked me into Steve Davis's office, he had my resume in one hand and a red ink pen in the other hand. At first glance, I remember thinking, "Wow, other than Linda Morgan's AP English class, I have never seen so much red ink on a piece of paper in my life."

But then I thought to myself, *"There sure is a lot of red ink on my resume. Ohhhh I get it, all of that red ink must be the highlights that he made of all the things that he likes about me!"*

Yeah whatever Morris… keep dreaming.

Our meeting went very well that day. Eventually, I found out that all of the red ink on my resume were things that I needed to change.

At the conclusion of our meeting, Steve Davis said two things to me. First, he committed to offering me a fully paid internship in Equitable's HR Department that summer. And second, he told me that I needed to learn the proper etiquette of how to play the game of golf if I wanted to increase my chances of being successful in corporate America.

My response was predictable.

"Golf? I am not playing golf. I am an athlete… I don't play golf. I have no desire to chase a little white ball around all day at some swanky little country club."

He said, "If you want to take your business career to the next level, you need to at least have a fundamental understanding of the game of golf."

I thought to myself, *"This is one area that I will NOT be coachable in – I am not playing golf."* So I looked at him and said, "Sure, whatever. Thanks anyway!"

I started my first HR internship for Equitable Gas later on that summer, all because of Steve Davis. I had no idea at the time that – just before meeting me – Steve Davis was suffering from the unexpected death of another young professional that he was mentoring. Steve Davis never wanted to experience that type of loss again, so he debated whether or not he wanted to invest in another young person's life *in that type of way* ever again. I also had no idea that Equitable Gas officially canceled their summer internship program *a year before* Steve Davis met me. But for some strange reason, after Steve met with me, he met with Equitable Gas's Senior Vice President and Chief Administrative Officer at the time, Greg Spencer. Steve persuaded Greg Spencer to give him the green light to offer me a fully paid internship, complete with a fully-paid relocation allowance, a very nice summer salary and a weekly housing allowance.

What an opportunity. I felt like I was walking in outer space when I stepped into the corporate environment at Equitable, but eventually, Rob Frankhouser, the HR Manager that I reported directly to, got me up and running!

After I finished my summer internship with Equitable, I started graduate school in the fall to receive my master's degree in HR/Labor-Relations from West Virginia University. I returned the following summer for my second internship with Equitable, and I continued to grow my skills.

USING COACHING TO YOUR ADVANTAGE

Many people do not take advantage of the valuable help that coaches and mentors can provide in their lives. Some people forget how easy it is to just ask someone for help – especially when other people are already experienced in what you are trying to achieve. I never had a problem with this, because after losing my parents as a teen, I was always eager to get input from people who could help me. That's why every time I visited my dad Chuck in prison, he coached me and he gave me advice. But once I left those prison visits, I needed to find other ways of getting *real-time* advice when I needed it most.

I was always open to being coached because I was desperate for it, and *because I was so crusty.* I had many crusty edges and burnt ends that I need to fix in my character, and I wasn't ashamed to admit it.

I continued to use the feedback from my coaches and mentors to get better. I am thankful for them, because trust me, *I had many bad habits and behaviors that I needed to work on* . As a matter of fact, I still do. Even today, I still rely on coaching and feedback. I never make any major choices or decisions without consulting my board of directors (my coaches) first.

Over the years, I continued to grow my relationship with Steve Davis. Eventually, I built up the nerve to ask him why he was so willing to help me when I walked into his office that day, especially after losing another person that he coached – someone that he was very close to. The answer that he gave me was kind of harsh at first, but at least he gave me the truth when I asked him.

He said, "Honestly, at first, the only reason why I agreed to meet you in Pittsburgh was because my sister asked me to. But after I saw how many notes you took during our first meeting, I could tell that you were hungry. I could tell that you had a vision for what you wanted out of life and you wouldn't waste any of my time, so I decided to help you."

Wow.

I am glad that Steve decided to help me because I needed every advantage I could find.

Eventually, Steve Davis and I invented a very simple coaching system that helped me better execute the information, or *run the plays,* that he gave me. Here is what the system looks like - the following list are things that every person needs to do if they want to take advantage of the benefits of having a coach.

1st - Listen - When you talk to another person who has the ability to help you get better, be quiet. There are times in life when you should speak, but this isn't one of them. The only time you should be talking when you are around someone who can help you is when you are asking them a question or answering a question that they ask you. Other than that, shut up.

2nd - Write It Down - Keep an ink pen and at least a small piece of paper folded in your pocket at all times. Yeah I know I know, you're probably thinking, "Why do I need to write things down on a piece of paper when I can just write them on my cell phone?" The problem with that is, it's easy to get distracted by other notifications on your phone if you use it to capture information when you are sitting in front of a coach. Plus, you don't want people to think that you are sending a text message and disrespecting their time, when you really are taking notes. It's not a good idea to potentially disrespect a person who has the ability to help you by making them think that you're just wasting their time.

3rd - Use Evernote - Evernote is a note-taking application for smart phones, computers, and tablets that allows you to keep everything in one place. You can store hand-written notes, digital notes, voice memos, videos, and photos all in one place. Oh by the way… its free! It makes no sense to listen closely (step 1) when someone gives you great advice, and it makes no sense to write it down (step 2) if you can't access the information when you need it most. Every piece of advice that's ever been given to me is in Evernote. Every time I get a great idea, I put it in Evernote. Every speech that I have ever been hired to do for a client, is in Evernote. As a matter of fact, every single word of this book that you are reading right now was written in Evernote. Evernote has changed many people's lives by helping them organize their ideas, and have access to critical information at the right times *when they need it the most*.

4th - Execute - After you've been given the plays to run, run them. Even the best quarterbacks have coaches on the sideline who call the plays for them. A quarterback's job is to trust their coaches and *just run the play*. When women have babies, they do the same thing. Many mothers of newborn babies rely on the advice of experienced mothers around them to help them understand what plays to run when they have a newborn baby. Your ideas, your clarity, and the vision that you have for your life are kind of like a newborn baby. They start as ideas that you first have to incubate, then they start to grow inside of you. Your job is to grow those ideas and to make them better, until one day you can do something with them. So be smart. Use the advice of other experienced people around you to help you succeed and give you advantages over your biggest competition – you.

ALL GREAT PEOPLE HAVE COACHES

Remember when I told you that every successful person started at the bottom by growing their skills - skills that ultimately positioned them for success later in life? Well, the ability to receive coaching and feedback, and then implement what you learn, is a real skill.

Many top performers develop advantages over their competition by simply being coachable.

One day, I was reading through my bible and I noticed that Jesus also said that he had a coach. *He didn't say it in those exact words*, but he did say that "His father was the gardener who cut off all of his branches that did not bear fruit, then he threw them into the fire after he cut them off." Then he said, "The gardener even trims back my branches that *do bear fruit*, so that they could have room to produce more fruit".

When I read that, I thought to myself, "Wow, even Jesus had a coach. He was the most influential people in the history of the world, and in John 15, that was his way of telling us that God the father coached him by destroying unproductive habits that kept him from growing."

It doesn't matter who you are or what your religious background is - *even if you have a different faith beliefs than I do*, don't miss the point that I am trying to share.

Everyone needs a coach and all great people get real coaching and feedback from someone who can help them get better.

EVERYONE NEEDS A COACH

Diamonds always sparkle when you see them on a beautiful necklace or in an engagement ring. But diamonds don't start out that way. After they are found in the earth, diamonds must be cut, shined, and polished to look that way.

People are just like diamonds: someone has to polish us and help us look better, be better, and feel better about ourselves.

People always ask me what the difference is between a coach and a mentor. In my mind, they both do the same thing, but coaches are paid to help you perform or execute.

People have coaches in sports, life, academics, business, and many other endeavors. Coaches come in many shapes and forms. All coaches have the same job though – they help you grow your skills.

Mentors do the same thing that coaches do, but mentors do it for free because many of them just want to give back and help others because they love the satisfaction they get from helping other to shine.

It doesn't matter who you are or how old you are. If you think that you are already good enough and you do not need a coach to help you, then your problems are bigger than you realize.

Everyone needs to get critical feedback if they want to get better, even you! Coaches will help you develop the two specific skills that are desperately needed in the world today – emotional intelligence and critical thinking. That's exactly what coaches can help you do. Having a coach to give you feedback will help you to become more self-aware (emotionally intelligent), and they will also help you to solve your problems more effectively (critical thinking) when you face certain situations.

Either way, when you get feedback from people who can really help you, you will develop better habits that will help you make better decisions.

But, all of this depends on two things: *First, do you have any coaches in your life? And second, are you coachable?*

COACHING CHECKLIST ≫

COACHING AND RUNNING THE PLAYS

- Who gives you feedback about your habits and behaviors in your personal life?
- Who gives you feedback about your performance at work or school?
- How do you normally respond when someone gives you feedback about yourself that you do not agree with?
- Are you a coachable person?
- Do you have a system in place to help you capture, analyze, and execute on the feedback that you receive?
- What areas do you need coaching and feedback to help you get better?

Chapter

12

CULTURE

CLARITY
COMMITMENT
COMPETENCE
COACHING
CONFIDENCE

CULTURE

Your Confidence

Jason Babicka was a tall, overweight, socially awkward software engineer. As a former Penn State graduate, Jason was hired at KCRS just weeks before I started working for them as their HR Manager in Pittsburgh, PA. Jason was a very timid and shy person and whenever he talked, he always did this annoying thing where he cleared his throat. When he did finally speak, he spoke so low that you could barely understand what he was saying at times.

He approached me at work one day and said (as he cleared his throat), "I have started a company golf league. Would you be interested in joining us at our golf outings on Monday evenings?"

I said, "What's with you Pittsburgh guys and golfing? How many times do I need to tell you that I am not playing golf?"

"Okay, I am sorry. It's just that I assumed that you were a pretty good athlete since you played college basketball. I guess I was wrong."

I looked at him and said, "What did you say?"

He said, "I apologize. You probably don't want to embarrass yourself."

And the challenge was on. He knew what he was doing. He said just the right words to spark a fire inside of me, so I agreed to sign up for their golf league.

My mentor Steve Davis was pushing me for years to learn how to play the game of golf. Plus, I figured that as the new company HR Manager, it would be a great way for me to build stronger relationships with the employees that I was hired to partner with.

I was horrible when I first learned how to play golf. Eventually Jason started taking me out once a week to teach me how to play and to help me raise my game. We ended up playing a lot of golf and spending a lot of one-on-one time together. After I made pretty big strides in my game, I was really thankful for Jason's coaching and mentoring.

I told Jason how much I appreciated his help. I knew that my golf game wouldn't have been nearly as good without the time that he invested in me. Eventually, I got pretty good and I really was really thankful for his time. I wanted to find a way to repay him, so I asked him if there was anything that I could do to help him.

He said, "Maybe there is something you can do to help me. Can I take some time to think about it and get back with you?"

"Of course."

A few days later he approached me at work and told me that he had given some thought to my offer to help him. I was very surprised by his response, when he said, "Morris, there are a few things I'd like you to help me with if you could. First of all, I want to increase my social skills. I am not the most socially outgoing person, and I want to be more confident. I figured you could help me with that since you're such a people person."

I said, "Okay, sure. Consider it done."

Then he said, "Also, I want to lose weight. I know that you work out and I figured you could help me with that too."

"No problem."

I thought he was finished, but then he said, "And another thing, I want to grow my software engineering skills at work, so I was wondering if you could help me put together a growth plan to give to my boss and help me find some certification skills that would show a return on investment for the company."

I was thinking to myself, "Okay, he wants me to help him grow his social skills, lose weight and grow his technical skills at work – I got this."

I said, "No problem Jason, consider it done."

He said, "But wait, there's one more thing. I have spent a lot of time with you outside of work, and I know that your faith is the reason why you have such a positive and optimistic mindset, and I want to learn how to be more positive also. I was raised in a Catholic church with my family and I am definitely a believer, but I was wondering if you could help me out with my relationship with God? Would you mind if I attended your church with you sometime?"

After hearing him ask me for four things in a row – losing weight, developing his social skills, increasing his software skills, and improving his relationship with God – I felt like saying to him, "Okay sir, is there anything else? Would you also like fries with that order?"

TRANSFORMATION CAN BE POWERFUL

Over the next couple of years, Jason made a lot of progress. First, he started working out more and exercising. Jason never played sports during his life because he was in the band in middle school and high school. There's nothing wrong with being in the band, but when Jason joined a fitness facility to work out and exercise in, he had no idea what he was doing. But I helped him find his way around the gym just like he helped me find my way around a golf course. Jason immediately began to lose weight and he started feeling much better about himself.

Next, we worked on his speaking ability. We practiced making eye contact, speaking clearly, and being projecting confidence when he did speak. During the process, we realized that there were much larger factors that got in the way of his ability to speak confidently – factors like his weight, the way that he dressed, and how he looked. So we started to work on those things too.

The workouts in the gym took care of his weight issue. Then he finally found the confidence to get rid of the *thick eye glasses* that he had been wearing for almost ten years. Jason decided to have LASIK surgery and once his surgery was completed, he looked a completely different person.

Next, we needed to do something about Jason's hair. My hair-cutting skills came in handy when I became Jason's barber. We had to give Jason a makeover, because when I first met him, his idea of a haircut was shaving his hair all the way off. So we put a plan together to let Jason's hair grow longer on the top, to eventually give some hair that he could style.

Next was Jason's professional skills at work. He began studying in the evenings to develop his software engineering skills and he gained multiple certifications in his field. The investment into his own professional development really paid off. He started to make a much larger impact on the software development team at KCRS and he almost doubled his salary within two years.

Finally, Jason started to attend Crossroads Church with me. He also joined our Bible study and he slowly started to develop his faith. When I moved away from Pittsburgh, Jason eventually grew his faith so large that he was able to transition from being afraid of speaking to strangers in public to actually leading our Bible study group.

Jason had incredible results in his life and people literally couldn't believe their eyes. When you witness transformation in someone's life, and it happens right in front of you, it's one of the most powerful things you'll ever see.

I watched Jason's weight drop from almost 255lbs to 185lbs.

I watched him go from barely being able to walk at a speed of 3.0 on a treadmill to running in marathon events.

I watched him transition from wearing thick, pop-bottle eyeglasses, to getting LASIK surgery and sporting a Hollywood, celebrity-type of hairstyle.

Jason became more and more confident in everything that he did in his personal, professional, and spiritual life. The joy and happiness that he had was absolutely contagious, and I had a chance to see it happen right before my eyes.

ADDICTED TO REAL RESULTS

I always loved helping people. When I was in high school, the leadership conference that I attended helped me to realize that I had a gift of speaking and inspiring people, and that was a big moment in my life. Seeing Jason's transformation was another powerful moment for me that changed the way I saw myself.

Jason really inspired me to want to see other people take steps to change their lives, just like he did. I couldn't ignore how great it felt to help Jason along in his journey – *I love helping other people win.* I love that feeling.

Deep inside I felt a sense of purpose that I got from helping people, and when you have purpose, the conviction that you feel inside of you will make you want to keep taking action on that purpose to help more people. But conviction isn't enough. It may be enough to start a fire inside of you, but conviction alone isn't enough to keep a fire going.

You need to have conviction *and* confidence if you want to have the courage to pursue a dream that you really love, especially in America where we have been taught to buy-in to dreams that other people expect us to have. When you want to pursue something that's true to who you are, you must have confidence. If you want to build your confidence, you need to do exactly what Jason did – you must be willing to do the work.

DOING THE WORK TO BECOME MORE CONFIDENT

Remember Clyde Randall, the guy that I met in Laguardia Airport? The last thing that you want to do, is end up like he did. He had the life that many people dreamed of having, but he still wasn't happy because everything came so easily to him and he never had to do a lot of work to get where he was in life because everything was always given to him. Well, if you want to take your skills to the next level, and if you aren't scared of doing the type of work that Jason did, here are a few examples of the *work that you can do* to increase your confidence and give yourself the energy that you need to pursue your dream. First, you need to…

Prepare for Your MMT – Your *Morning Mirror Test* is a test that everyone takes each morning when they look at themselves in the mirror each morning. When you see yourself in the mirror, you either like what you see, or you don't. There are no gray areas. You can improve your MMT by doing the following…

Increasing Your Competency (Skills) – When you increase your competency, you grow your skills. Every time you learn something new, you create new neural pathways in your brain. Increasing your skills is the biggest way to feel confident about anything you're doing, because without even realizing it, you will feel more equipped to handle anything that comes your way. Any time you do something for the first time, or whenever you try something new, you will always have a small amount of fear or hesitation. Why? Because those neural pathways haven't been developed in your brain yet. You will feel twice as confident about anything that you do, the second time you do it. Why? Because you'll have the skills and the ability to do it, and, your brain will revisit the same neural pathways that it created the first time. So what's my point? Commit to getting better at everything that you do by growing your skills, and by making a decision to *never stop learning* – because your confidence depends on it.

Stop Comparing Yourself To Others (CYO) – When you *Compare Yourself to Others* it will strip you of your confidence, unless you compare yourself to someone that you respect and someone who you can learn from. Remember, *all unhappiness is caused by comparison*, so make sure that you ONLY compare yourself to others who can help you grow.

Develop Your Speaking Skills – Being able to speak well will dramatically increase your confidence. The more comfortable you are speaking to others, the more opportunities you will create for yourself by understanding how to connect with others. Unless you live on an island by yourself, you will always need the help and support of others to achieve your goals. People who speak well in public – whether they speak to 2 or 2000 people – always leave a good impression on others. Studies show that employees get promoted faster in organizations when they can speak and present well in front of groups. Although there are many tips on HOW to speak better in public, the best tip to help you get better at public speaking is very simple: *just speak to people when you're in public.* The more you speak to people that you don't know, the easier it is to do. Any time you get a chance to volunteer to speak in front of a group at work, at home, at church, or anywhere that you live, work, or play, you should do it. Every time you do, you'll get better. Public speaking is the #1 fear of many people. Therefore, when you find ways to get over your fears and become good at speaking in front of others, your confidence will capture the respect and attention of others, and you will open many doors for yourself.

Talk To Positive People – Every time you talk to a positive person, you feel better about yourself and you feel better about life. If you really need a boost of confidence, talk to someone who can breathe life and energy into your goals, and stay away from negative people as if your life depends on it. One great conversation with the right person can completely change your life and your focus.

Talk About Your Goals – Every time you talk to someone about what you want the most, your vision becomes clearer by reinforcing it in your brain. Whenever you talk about where you are going and what excites you the most, you automatically become more energetic and confident about what lies ahead. Sometimes confidence is as simple as believing something in your mind. The more you talk about what you're most excited about in your life, the more you will stay focused on getting there. Even if you don't know how to get there yet, that's okay. Talking to others about your vision will re-energize you, and that's important because you must have energy behind your thoughts and ideas before you develop the confidence to make them a reality – so talk to people about your goals and where you are going.

Develop Your Belief System – Every action that you take is based on what you believe. If you believe that you're not very good at something, you will never have the confidence to make progress towards that goals. Developing your belief system, such as your faith, can help you stay focused when adversity comes your way. Developing your belief system will give you a big advantage over your circumstances, and it will help you to defeat a negative mindset when you start to feel discouraged. Confident people get discouraged too, but the difference is, confident people have a plan for dealing with discouragement when it comes their way. Remember another important thing about confident people, confident people are not only confident in themselves, they are confident in knowing that life is much bigger than them. Confident people have the courage to make big choices and decisions that most people are scared of making because they know that life isn't always about them. If you want to be average, focus on yourself. If you want to achieve the results that you want to see in your life, be intentional about developing your belief system. It will help you to make more confident decisions.

Get More Exercise – It's no secret that exercise changes the way you look and feel. It's very tough to pass your *Morning Mirror Test* if you don't like the way you look and feel. Exercise also causes your brain to release key neurotransmitters such as serotonin and dopamine that make you feel good by boosting your energy. Confident people feel great about themselves and their abilities. If you don't like what you see when you look in the mirror, you need to try your best to address the issue – because your confidence depends on it.

Eat Better Food - The biggest area of instant gratification and *Overnight Success* is in how we fuel our bodies. Food is being processed today at a much faster rate than ever before, to produce food faster and easier. But the hot dogs that we eat today are NOT the same hot dogs that our parents and grandparents ate because they are overly processed. Eating better food will give you more confidence, so use this rule of thumb: *if you can't tell what ingredients are in the food that you're eating*, and if you can't pronounce the words on the label, don't eat it – it's processed. You need to eat more whole foods like fruits and vegetables. Foods such as fish, eggs, dairy products, broccoli, brussels sprouts, and blueberries are great sources of amino acids that your body needs. Amino acids play a key role in the amount of energy that your body has. When you eat better and you focus on giving your body the nutrients that it needs, you will be healthier and you will feel better about everything else that you do – which will give you more confidence.

Eat Less Processed Sugar – Sugar stimulates the same pleasure centers in the brain as cocaine and heroin. Some studies have shown that some sugars, such as high fructose corn syrup, are more addictive than cocaine. High fructose corn syrup is the main sugar used in sodas, drinks, snacks, and even ketchup. If your daily calories from sugar are more than 10% of your total daily calorie intake, you have a problem. People who take in more than 10% of their daily calories in the form of sugar are twice as likely to die prematurely, or... *before they're supposed to die.* Too much sugar also causes you to become obese, suffer from diabetes, and it even increases your risk of having cancer. The Coca plant that cocaine is made from is safe to consume in its natural state, just like corn is also safe to eat as a vegetable. But when the coca plant or the corn plant are highly refined, they produce cocaine and high fructose corn syrup – both of which can be fatal to your body. When researchers let a group of mice choose between cocaine and sugar, the mice chose the sugar over the cocaine because the sugar was more addicting. If you don't believe me, just Google it for yourself and you will be surprised. My point is simple – if you reduce the amount of processed sugars and high fructose corn syrup that you consume on a daily basis, you will be healthier and you will position yourself to pursue your goals with more confidence.

Get More Sleep – It's real simple: the more sleep you get at night, the better you will perform. Multiple studies have proved that people who get the least amount of sleep at night have the shortest life expectancy. Lack of sleep causes a person to have more fat, feel more hungrier during the day, have less muscle tone, and have higher stress in their lives. Even if you think that you're okay when you only get small amounts of sleep, you're wrong. Getting more sleep will help you look better and feel better about yourself – both of which will help you have higher levels of confidence. If you want to get better sleep at night, try making the temperature in your bedroom a little colder or try eating carbohydrates and proteins before bed. Either one of those will help you sleep better. Either way, you need to do whatever you have to do, and make whatever changes you need to make, to get more sleep, because your life depends on it.

FINAL THOUGHTS ABOUT CONFIDENCE

If you always wonder why some people seem to get better results than others, well, you don't have to wonder anymore because I just gave you eleven reasons why. It's up to you to be just like Jason Babicka and do the work. By doing the work to get better, you will disrupt your previous habits and routines, and you will slowly position yourself to experience the only real form of *Overnight Success* that is possible, by *changing the way you see yourself.*

Confident people trust their own abilities, and when you trust your own abilities, it's easier to follow your own instincts. In chapter 7, when I followed my instincts *(or my "Craig" as I called him)* it led me to listening to country music for the first time in my life. Once that happened, I learned something: *one of the biggest secrets to success* is being willing and open to trying new experiences. And that's exactly what you need to do if you want to really increase your confidence, you must be willing to try new things or to do things differently.

When you increase your confidence, you will increase your ability to trust your own instincts, and you will develop the energy that you need to do the work that it takes, to take your life to the next level.

I have seen many people hesitate when they were forced to make tough decisions because they were either unsure of themselves or unsure of the situation. When you commit to doing the work, just like Jason did, you'll have the confident to trust your own instincts and you'll be able to make the tough decisions that other people would never have the courage to make.

CONFIDENCE CHECKLIST »

INCREASING YOUR CONFIDENCE

- If you could change one thing about yourself, what would it be? Why?
- How would you rate your self-confidence on a scale of 1-10. Why would you rate yourself that way?
- What are you most confident about?
- What are your biggest fears?
- What could you do to overcome your fears to increase your self-confidence?

Chapter

13

Confidence In Action

I always had the vision to be a speaker, author, and consultant. My mentors were more than helpful in making sure that I was exposed to professional experiences that would complement the work that I wanted to do when I started my own company some day.

My mentor Steve Davis pushed me towards the human resources professional, even though I am a naturally extroverted person who would have been better-suited in a sales organization. He told me that a career in HR would give me a chance to really develop competency and skills that would allow me to add greater value to my future clients. So I chose my path in HR.

While working in the human resources field, I attended a business conference at a convention center in downtown Pittsburgh. On the morning of the conference, everyone was talking about the keynote speaker who was about to speak at lunch. I had never heard of Walter Bond before that day. I went to his keynote program at lunch to see what all the hype was about, and when he was finished, my life was never the same.

As I sat there and listened to him speak, I was amazed. I was blown away, because I saw a person standing on stage who was dynamic and who had the audience so engaged that you could hear a pin drop in the room. As I looked at him, I realized that I saw a guy on stage who was living *my dream*.

Walter Bond was a former NBA basketball player and he wasn't a superstar either. No one had ever heard his name or seen his highlights on SportsCenter before. But at $10,000 per speech, he was already making more money in his new career than he ever made playing professional basketball.

After he finished speaking, I knew that I just had to meet him. He had a long line of people wanting to purchase his books and DVDs, so I had to wait a very long time. I waited so long that I had to skip the other afternoon sessions just to meet him.

Two hours later, I was still sitting down at a table next to where he was greeting people at. I wanted to wait for my chance to speak with him privately, without any interruptions.

Finally, after the last person finished talking to him, the event planner approached him and said, "Mr. Bond, your car is downstairs waiting for you. We don't want you to miss your flight out of Pittsburgh."

As he gathered his luggage, I approached him.

"Mr. Bond, sorry to bother you, but would you mind if I walked with you as you head to your car?"

He said, "Sure, I don't mind. Let's go."

"Mr. Bond, you don't know me, but my name is Morris Morrison."

He said, "Your name is Morris Morrison, what kind of name is that?" as he smiled.

I smiled back and said, "Yeah I know, I get that a lot. Mr. Bond, I am a speaker. I speak mainly to youth audiences right now, but my vision is to speak full-time one day to both youth and corporate audiences."

He asked, "Do you have a full-time job right now?"

I said, "Yes, I am an HR Manager for a software company here in Pittsburgh."

"Wow, HR. That's a perfect area of business to work in to help you learn how to run a successful speaking business one day."

I replied, "Thanks, that's what my mentors have told me. Mr. Bond, what you did today is exactly what I want to do for the rest of my life. I have been speaking and working on my skills since I was in high school, but I need to take things to the next level. Would it be okay if I got some advice from you every now and then about what I need to do? Before you answer, I just want to say that I promise not to waste your time, because I know are how busy you are."

Walter Bond just stared at me for a while.

As we continued to walk downstairs to the car that was waiting for him, he looked at me and he said, "You seem like you're pretty clear about what you want. But how do I know that you aren't going to waste my time?"

"Mr. Bond, I will pay my own money to fly to Minneapolis just to have lunch with you - you just tell me when and where."

"Okay, you've got yourself a deal. If you promise not to waste my time, I will help you just like Desi Williamson helped me."

I said, "Who is Desi Williamson?"

"Who is Desi Williamson? Who is Desi Williamson?! Kid, you sure do have a lot to learn."

And that was it. I officially had a new coach and mentor in the professional speaking industry who was willing to show me how to run the plays. From that day on, I slowly started to plan my transition to leave my full-time job in corporate America. I knew that if I wanted to start my own company to pursue my passion full-time, I needed to have a plan.

PLANNING MY TRANSITION

In the fall of 2007 I decided to give myself a deadline. Things really started to come together in my life. I was falling in love with a beautiful girl that I knew I wanted to marry some day, and I could see my future right in front of me. I didn't want the same thing to happen to me that happens to many other people. I did not want to get trapped or *"stuck"* in my own dreams. I knew that once I got married and started a family, I would reduce my chances of being able to walk away from a full-time job to start my own company. So I had to come up with a plan.

In the fall of 2007 I decided to give myself a three-year expiration date in corporate America. After the spring of 2011, I was not going to allow myself to receive a W2 paycheck from a full-time employer. Any money that I made had to come from my own company.

I also knew that I wanted to move to North Carolina where the weather was warmer. When I played pop warner football for the Barrackville Bisons, our team took two trips to McAdenville, North Carolina, to play in the Christmas Town Bowl and I fell in love with the North Carolina when I was a kid.

After I finished my master's degree at West Virginia University, I took a job in BB&T's management development program and I spent even more time in North Carolina at their home office in Winston-Salem. Every time my flight landed in North Carolina, I could see myself living there more and more.

While I still lived in Pennsylvania, the Pittsburgh International Airport lost the bid to secure the US Airways hub in Pittsburgh, so US Air was moving to Charlotte, NC. I knew that if I wanted to be a speaker & consultant and travel the globe one day, I needed to be close to an airport that could provide me with the flights that I needed, and the timing could not have been any better.

One of the biggest pieces of advice that my mentor Steve Davis ever gave me was, "Tell everyone what your dreams are and what you wish to do with your life, because you'll never know who will be able to help you get to the next level." Steve Davis was pretty much on point with all of the guidance and direction that he ever gave me. I am so glad that I actually trusted him, because his words really paid off. Let me give you two examples of how his coaching change my life, big time.

Steve Davis told me that I needed to learn how to play golf if I wanted to succeed in life and business. When Jason Babicka started his golf league at our company and he invited me to play, Steve was very happy that I finally took his advice, even though I wasn't too excited about playing golf. Once I started playing golf, I met another golfer at the driving range one day. His name was DiKarlos Dial.   DiKarlos was a medical student who was finishing up his foot and ankle surgery fellowship at the University of Pittsburgh Medical Center.

DiKarlos and I ended up golfing a lot together during the summer. We had some great conversations and we shared a lot with each other, including our hopes, dreams, and the futures that we wanted to have one day. When Dikarlos signed an offer to accept a job with a medical practice in High

Point, North Carolina at the end of the summer, I said to him, "Well, this won't be the last time we see each other. I will be seeing you in North Carolina soon."

He said, "What are you talking about? Are you moving to North Carolina also?"

"Yep."

"What? When are you moving to North Carolina?"

I said, "I don't know, I have no idea. But you will see me soon."

He said, "I'm confused. How can you tell me that you will see me soon and that you are moving to North Carolina if you have no idea when you're coming? What on earth are you talking about?"

"DiKarlos, I know that I want to move to North Carolina and start my company there one day. So don't be surprised if you get a phone call from me when I am on my way down there."

He said, "Well, that sounds good to me. Maybe we can play a couple of rounds of golf when you come down – and don't hesitate to let me know if I can do anything to help."

I said, "Don't worry, I will take you up on that offer one day."

SEEING IT ALL COME TOGETHER

When I finished my master's degree at West Virginia University, I had several offers from multiple companies. One of the job offers that I received was from Pfizer. Pfizer was the largest, most respected pharmaceutical company in the industry, and it was not easy to get a job with Pfizer because a lot of people wanted to work for them. A Pfizer Vice President once said, "It's easier to get into Harvard Medical School than it is to get a job here at Pfizer, so you should consider it an honor if you are selected to join us."

The fact that I had a previous job offer from Pfizer carried a lot of weight during my transition to North Carolina. When I noticed that Pfizer had a sales position open in High Point, North Carolina, guess who I called?

Yep, you guessed it. I called Dikarlos Dial.

If I would have never listened to Steve Davis, if I never learned how to play the game of golf, and if Jason never started that golf league, I would have never met DiKarlos Dial.

Steve Davis was correct about the advice he shared with me. Learning how to play golf really did help me to grow my career, and he also said, "One of the best things that you can do is *tell people what your goals and dreams are.*"

I was pretty clear with DiKarlos about what my goals were from the first day that we met, and I also told him to expect a call from me one day. He had no idea that he would hear from me just three months after he left Pittsburgh to move to North Carolina.

When I saw the job opening for Pfizer in High Point, North Carolina, I called DiKarlos and I said, "Do you have any Pfizer sales reps that call on your office?"

He said "Yes, but we don't see her very often, but if I see her I will get her contact information for you."

I said, "Can you do me a favor? When you see her tomorrow, will you get her e-mail address and cell phone number for me so that I can reach out to her personally?"

DiKarlos said, "Man, did you hear what I just said. I told you that we don't see her very often."

The very next morning I got a telephone call from Dikarlos Dial.
When I answered the phone, his first words were, "You know what, I can't stand you. You want to guess who the first person was that walked into my office this morning."

I said, "Of course I know who walked into your office this morning - sometimes you just have to have a little faith DiKarlos! Go ahead and tell me, what's her name, e-mail address, and cell phone number?"

He said, "Her name is Carrie Carter and she's expecting your phone call."

I smiled before I got off of the phone with him and I said, "Looks like I will be seeing you sooner than I thought DiKarlos!"

I called Carrie Carter as soon as I hung up with DiKarlos. Immediately I could tell that Carrie had an attitude with me over the phone. She wasn't mean or anything like that. It's just that, when you work for a company like Pfizer, you get many requests from people who want you to *hook them up with a job.*

I realized that the only reason why she took my phone call was because one of her clients asked her to. I knew that I needed to do something to change the tone of the conversation that we were having, so I said, "Listen

Carrie, I did not mean to be disrespectful, but I feel like I need to be direct with you right now. The way I see it, you have one of two choices. You can either choose to help me get a job on your team or you can choose to compete against me if I get a job with one of your competitors in that same territory. We can either make a bunch of money together and have a bunch of fun, or... I can compete against you and eat into your profit margins. Either way, it's your choice!"

There was a long period of silence on the other end of the phone. I had no idea if I had really just put my foot in my mouth. But after what seemed like an eternity, she responded with laughter and said, "You know what, I like you! You're the exact type of person that I like to work with and I will do anything I can to help you!"

I said, "Hey, I'm going to be in town next week and I would love to grab a cup of coffee with you while I'm there."

She said, "I thought you lived in Pittsburgh? You're going to be in North Carolina next week?"

"Yep, I will be in North Carolina for business meetings next week." She had no idea that *she was the business meeting* that I was talking about.

"Sure, I would love to grab a cup of coffee with you."

I immediately called DiKarlos back and I said, "Hey, is it okay if I come to visit you next week? I think I may have a chance to get an interview for that job opening with Carrie's team."

He said, "Of course it's okay, I told you that I've got your back if you ever need anything."

ARRIVING IN NORTH CAROLINA WITH A VISION

In chapter 8 when we talked about the importance of having clarity and knowing what you want, I mentioned that one of the most energetic, positive conversations that you will ever have is when you speak to someone who is clear about what they want - because their energy is contagious. Well, when I showed up in North Carolina the following week, I met Carrie Carter at a Panera Bread restaurant in Greensboro, North Carolina. She brought another Pfizer colleague with her. His name was Jim.

She said, "This is Jim. His partner on his team just took another job somewhere else in the company. That's the reason why the position is currently open. I was hoping that if I introduced the two of you, and if you and Jim hit it off... well, you never know what can happen."

We sat down to have coffee and Jim let me know that he only had about 30 minutes of free time to meet that morning. I knew that 30 minutes was all I needed. As a matter fact, all I needed was ten minutes.

I just needed to have an opportunity to make eye contact with someone on that Pfizer team so that they could see the look of conviction in my eyes and see how serious I was about relocating to the North Carolina market.

Before you know it, 30 minutes turned into 60 minutes, so I reminded them as I pointed at my watch, "Didn't you say that you had to leave after 30 minutes? We have been here for almost an hour. Don't you need to leave?"

They both looked at each other, then Carrie said, "I think we can move some things around today. We're having a good time and we don't want to leave just yet."

When she said that, I knew that I was golden. When she said that, I knew things were looking good in my favor.

After being there for 2 1/2 hours that morning, Jim said, "When do you have to leave North Carolina? Do you think you can stick around long enough to meet with my boss before you leave town?"

When he said that, I definitely knew that I was golden. What Jim did not realize was that I brought one week's worth of clothes with me on that trip, and I planned on not leaving North Carolina until I met the hiring manager for that open position – the hiring manager who just happened to be his boss. But of course, I did not say that to Jim.

I said, "Oh I am sorry, I don't think I am going to be able to stay around to meet your boss, because I have interviews with other pharmaceutical companies that I need to get to.

He had the biggest look of disappointment on his face. Then he said, "Can you give me a few minutes to just call him real quick?"

I said, "I may be able to move some things around if you make a quick phone call to see if he's available right now."

When I said that, Jim immediately jumped up out of his seat and he walked to another area of Panera Bread to make the phone call to his boss.

He came back over to me and he said, "Okay, I got a hold of my boss. He said that he wants to meet you for lunch at the Marriott tomorrow."

And that... was what I came for. That was all I needed.

When Jim said that, Carrie immediately looked at me and she said, "Aww man, I'm kind of sad. Now that I've met you I really want you to be on *my team*.

I said, "What do you mean, *your team?*"

She said, "We have two Pfizer teams here in this territory, and the job opening that you are applying for is not on my team. It's on Jim's team, but I want you to be on *my team!*"

With a big smile on my face, I said "It's alright Carrie, everything will be okay. I'm sure we will be able to work something out!"

I got a phone call from Jim's boss the very next morning. His name was Donnie.

When Donnie called me he said, "I am not sure who you are or what you are trying to pull here, but I need to remind you that this is not how we do things at Pfizer. We have a very specific process that we use to find candidates, and our hiring process can take up to six months to complete. But I will meet you today, only because Jim asked me to. Before we meet, you should know that I have a very busy day and I will not have very much time to meet with you."

I met Donnie at the Marriott for lunch later that day. As soon as he walked in, he sat down at a table and with a slight attitude, he looked at me and he said, "You should know that I have already prepared a final offer to the person who we have chosen to fill this position – you have 30 minutes to tell me why I should even begin to consider you for this job."

After I shook his hand and I said hello, I slid two sheets of paper across the table to him. The first was a copy of the previous offer letter that I had from Pfizer.

I said, "I am very familiar with Pfizer's hiring process."

He said, "You were offered a job with Pfizer, and you turned it down?"

"Things didn't work out the first time around, but now that I have decided which market I would like to transition to, I wanted to at least give you an opportunity to meet me before I took a job with another competitor."

He gave me a strange look as if he wasn't exactly sure what to think. The other sheet of paper that I gave him was a copy of my resume.

When he picked my resume up, he looked it up and down, then he said, "What? You're an Alpha? Jim didn't tell me that you were in Alpha man."

He noticed that I was President of the Rho Tau Chapter of Alpha Phi Alpha Fraternity, Inc. when I was in college. Alpha Phi Alpha was a historically all black male fraternity with previous members such as Dr. Martin Luther King Jr., Frederick Douglas, and many others. I was very surprised that a district manager from Pfizer even knew the significance of it, but when he said, "You're an Alpha," instead saying the full name of my fraternity, I could tell that he was very familiar with it.

With a smile, as he pushed my resume to the side, he looked at me and said, "I know that you may not be able to tell by looking at me, because I may look like just another old white guy, but I want you to know something - I would not be where I am in this company today if it wasn't for two of the strongest leaders that I ever met. Both of them were mentors for me at Pfizer, and they are both *Alpha men*."

When he said *that,* I defiantly knew that I was golden!

As you could imagine, once he said that, the rest of the interview went very, very smoothly. The next thing I knew, four hours had gone by, and Donnie was on the phone with his regional manager in Washington, DC making arrangements to get me to DC the very next morning to compete with their other final candidate in the final round of interviews.

The next day *before the interview*, Donnie called me and said, "I just wanted to congratulate you."

"Congratulate me for what? I haven't even completed the final interview yet?"

"I just wanted to say congratulations because you have already done something that no one has ever done before - you managed to reduce a six month hiring process down to three days. I wouldn't have believed it if I didn't see it for myself. Now go in there and knock this final interview out of the park."

When it was all said and done, I had a brand new job with Pfizer in North Carolina, but it didn't happen the way that I thought it would happen.

Carrie Carter and I both got what we wanted. I got a job in North Carolina, and she was able to get me a job on *her team*.

Carrie's boss, Mike Mosey, made me an offer to join their team before the other team did. And just like that, I began to make preparations to move from Pittsburgh to North Carolina the following month.

GETTING CLOSER TO YOUR PURPOSE

I have never been afraid of making transitions in life. Who knows, maybe it's just in my blood. Maybe it was passed down to me from my great-grandmother Mama Hattie. Maybe it was just my instincts kicking in. Either way, accepting the job offer from Pfizer and moving to North Carolina got me one step closer to my vision.

Pfizer was a dream job for most people. Once I started working for them, it was clear to understand why. Pfizer was consistently honored with many top awards in the sales, marketing, and training development industries. It was one of the best learning and development opportunities of my entire life.

I still kept my vision in the forefront of my mind though. *I gave myself a three-year expiration date* – I was not allowed to accept a paycheck as a full-time employee working for another company after three years of my start date for Pfizer. I had a vision, and I had a sense of urgency because I did not want to get trapped in my own dream once I got married and started a family.

After seeing Jason Babicka have the results that he had in his life, I realized that deep down inside of me I was driven by something deeper – brokenness.

A large part of me was broken - that's just how I was - and I knew that there were many other people that were hurting and broken in this world, just like me and I wanted to help them.

If it weren't for the many people who helped to put me back together and put me on my path, I wouldn't have made it. Instead of visiting my dad in prison, I could have ended up sharing a prison cell with him.

I was convicted and I really did believe that everyone has the power to change their situation if they're willing to do the work. The idea that I could help other people have better lives is what drove me and I knew that I never was created to spend the rest of my life working in corporate America - that just wasn't my calling.

I have had clarity since I was 17 years old about exactly what I wanted to do with my life, but I didn't do it on my own. It was easy for me to be motivated because I had the support of many coaches, teachers, pastors, and mentors who had my back at all times. They helped me to never loose my focus.

Faith, family, focus, fight…
Faith, family, focus, fight…
Faith, family, focus, fight…

When I said goodbye to my grandmother Gwendolyn at Ruby Memorial Hospital, I made many promises to her about what I would do with my life. I promised her that I would graduate from high school. I promised her that I would graduate from college. I promised her that I would try my best to be a good father one day. I promised her that I would try my best to be a good husband one day. I also promised her that I would never sell drugs. Well Grandma, if you're listening right now, I guess I need to say, "I'm sorry."

I guess I ended up selling drugs after all…

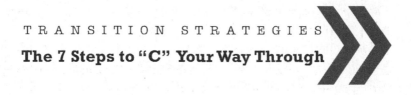

Chapter

14

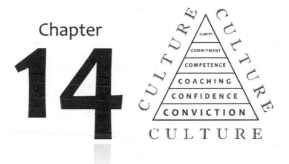

CULTURE

The Power of Conviction

When Ally was a young teenager, her family migrated to the United States from the Philippines in search of a *better life* and a *bigger dream*. Ally's family placed work ethic above everything else.

Ally was very talented, but her biggest passion was doing hair and nails, and she loved the beauty industry. Ally started to develop her passion at an early age, and by her late teenage years, she was already working in beauty spas and nail salons. Over time, she became frustrated with the way that many of the owners ran their businesses.

Ally was a perfectionist and she wasn't afraid of hard work. She knew that she could do a much better job than the other owners that she worked for, so she decided to open up her own nail salon.

For months, Ally met with other salon owners to figure out exactly what she wanted and how to get it. Then she did her research to put a business plan together. Ally developed a very clear vision. But she eventually experienced the problem that keeps many people from starting a business –

she didn't have enough money. She couldn't convince any banks to loan her the money that she needed to open her salon.

After getting rejected by many banks, her instincts started to kick in. Ally did a ton of work to research her ideas and build her plan, and she was not about to throw all of that hard work down the drain. She knew that being a business owner was her destiny.

Ally decided to get even more focused. Instead of bouncing around from bank to bank, she decided to focus all of her energy and attention on one specific bank and one specific banker. His name was Scott Herrington.

Ally was persistent – maybe a little *too persistent* at times – because Scott Herrington asked her not to show up at their bank ever again. Ally kept going back anyway. She showed up at that bank every single day with her business plan in her hand and her vision in her heart. Scott Herrington tried everything to discourage her, including having her escorted out of the building. He even threatened to call the police if she returned.

Ally came back the next day anyway. She walked into Scott Herrington's office, and he said to her, "If you don't leave right now, I'm going to call the police."

Ally just looked at him.

When Scott Herrington picked up the phone, he looked at her and he said, "I'm about to call 911 if you don't leave right now."

As soon as he said that, Ally took two more steps into his office.

He said, "That's it, I'm calling the police."

Scott dialed the first 9. When Ally saw him dial the first number, she pulled out a chair from under the table in his office.

Then Scott dialed the next 1. When he did that, Ally looked directly into his eyes as she sat down in a seat at his table. As soon as Scott saw her sit down, he was angry, but at the same time… he couldn't believe his eyes. He couldn't believe that this girl was willing to go to jail because she believed in her idea *that much.*

Scott Herrington never finished dialing 911 that day. He hung up the phone.

He looked at Ally and said, "How much money will it take to get you to leave my office?"

"$15,000. That's all I need to get my business started."

Scott knew couldn't turn Ally away. He was flat-out… *impressed.*

They completed the paperwork for the loan that day. Once they finalized the terms, Ally left the bank that day with the money that she needed to start her business.

Within three months, Ally returned to the bank and she handed Mr. Herrington a check for $20,000 to pay off her loan.

Scott could not believe that she was paying her loan in full already. When he noticed that she gave him $20,000 he said, "You only owe us $15,000. Why did you give me $20,000?"

Ally said, "I need to expand my business – we are running out of space for our new clients because the business is doing so well. I gave you an extra $5,000 as a down payment for my next loan.

And of course, Ally convinced Scott to give her another loan - this time, for $50,000.

Within the next 24 months, Ally returned with another $100,000 check that she gave to Scott Herrington.

Scott said, "Let me guess, you want to pay your loan off again, and you also want to borrow more money. Is that right?"

Ally just looked at him with a big smile on her face. As Scott smiled back at her, he said "How much this time?"

Ally said, "I want to pay off the $50,000 loan, and I want to put the rest as a down payment towards another $250,000 loan to open a larger beauty salon and spa."

Scott just looked at her. And of course, once he finalized the terms of her loan, Ally left the bank, once again, with the resources that she needed to grow her next big idea.

Ally opened several beauty salons in her market and business was going very well for the new entrepreneur   but she eventually ran into a few problems along the way.

Remember when I said that Ally was a perfectionist? When you call a person a perfectionist, it's another way of saying, "They have a clear vision and a high level of conviction for what they do, and they will never compromise that vision, no matter what."

As Ally grew her beauty salon empire, along the way, she became frustrated with the building management companies that she leased retail space from. So Ally decided that it would be much easier if she just purchased the building for her self. By owning the building, you could control the terms and also lease out the remaining space to other businesses.

Eventually, Ally transitioned from opening beauty salons and spas to also becoming well-versed in commercial real estate.

Today, Ally is a multi-millionaire. She has many commercial real estate properties and beauty salons up and down the East Coast of the United States - all because she had a simple passion for doing hair and fingernails.

THE POWER OF HAVING CONVICTION

The most energizing and inspiring conversation that you will ever have is with a person who is clear about who they are and what they want. Ally followed *The 7 Steps to "C" HER Way Through,* in a perfect manner. Let's look at how she did it.

> *Culture* influenced her work-ethic.
>
> *Clarity* was reflected in her vision to build her salon.
>
> *Commitment* forced her to develop her ideas.
>
> *Competency* helped her to grow business skills.
>
> *Coaching* influenced how she ran her business.
>
> *Confidence* made her walk into that bank.
>
> *Conviction* gave her a seat at the table.

When you are clear about what you want, committed to doing the work, and confident about what you do, it's easier to have conviction for what you do. When you notice that a person is passionate about something, that's another way of saying, "They have conviction."

What Ally did not realize was that Scott Herrington threw her out of his bank on purpose. She didn't realize that Scott threatened to dial 911 just to see how bad she really believed in herself. When she had the confidence to pull a chair out and take a seat at his table, he realized that if she was willing to go to jail for what she believed, then she would have no problems paying back a small business loan.

People will always be willing to invest in you when they see you take initiative to invest in yourself. Even when people tell you "NO", maybe they're not really saying *"NO"* - maybe they're just waiting to see how much conviction you have.

LIVING MY CONVICTIONS - Faith, Family, Focus, Fight

My convictions caused me to pack up and leave Pittsburgh to go to North Carolina and build my dream. Once I got there, I became more and more convicted about something else that I needed to do. My professional goals were all starting to come together, but there was one other goal – *one of my biggest goals*. I wanted to fall in love. I wanted to fall in love and be married to someone who I could share my life with.

When I moved from Pittsburgh to North Carolina, I was still dating Lisa – *the same girl who made me get rid of my red washcloth* – the same girl who consistently threw my towels and washcloths into the dirty clothes, even when I didn't want her to.

Lisa and I made a decision to have a long distance relationship. She was in Pittsburgh and I was moving to North Carolina. The last thing she said to me before I left, was, *"If you like it, then you better put a ring on it."*

I absolutely hated Beyoncé for that one. But I knew that I wanted to propose to Lisa. And I knew *exactly* how I wanted to do it. I had the vision in my heart for a long time.

I wanted our journey together to begin in the same place where my journey began – in New York City. Lisa had been begging me to take her to Rockefeller Center at Christmas time, so it created a perfect way to make my plan happen and I knew that I had to take advantage of the opportunity.

Lisa had no idea that I was going to propose to her (at least that's what I like to tell myself). I told her that we were going to Washington DC for the weekend for a speaking engagement that I had, and I asked her to come along with me so that we could do some sightseeing while we were there.

I drove up from North Carolina to Pittsburgh to pick up Lisa and take her to DC. The night before I got to her house, I stopped in Parkersburg, West Virginia, along the way to speak with her grandfather first. Lisa's father Terry passed away when Lisa was a young teen, so I had to honor and respect her father and her family by asking Lisa's grandfather for permission to have Lisa's hand in marriage.

When I arrived at her grandparent's house, her grandmother greeted me at the door with a really big smile on her face. *She knew exactly why I was there*. When I sat her grandparents down on the couch to speak with them, I began to cry and her grandmother did too. We were crying for the same reason. If they wouldn't have lost their son Terry, I would have had no reason for being there that evening.

It was the toughest conversation I've ever had, but once I finished, they both gave me their blessing, and Lisa's grandmother rushed me to the door with a plate of homemade chocolate chip cookies and a Coca-Cola. As I walked out of the door she said, "It's late, so you're going to need these snacks to give you some energy to make that drive to Pittsburgh. Now please be careful, drive safe, and go get your girl!"

OUR NEW YORK CITY ENGAGEMENT TRIP

When Lisa and I started our trip to New York City the very next morning, it was absolutely the worst traveling conditions that I've ever had in my life. An unexpected snowstorm started to cover the roads. But there was a bigger problem: I had an absolutely jam-packed agenda for the next three days in New York City, and Lisa had no idea about any of it. She thought that we were headed to Washington DC. When she noticed that I wasn't going in the right direction, she began to say, "You are going the wrong way, you are going the wrong way... I'm telling you, you are going the wrong way - this is NOT how you get to Washington, DC!"

I said, "Will you please just sit back and relax. I promise... *I've got this* Lisa and I know what I'm doing. Just sit back, relax and watch some of the DVDs that we brought."

I brought some of our favorite New York City love stories for the drive up – movies like *Serendipity* and *Sleepless in Seattle*. I was dropping all kinds of hints!

Lisa still couldn't relax because the snowstorm was getting worse and there were many traffic accidents around us. She thought that I was the worst boyfriend in the world because I didn't stop and pull over - I just continued straight ahead – because I was focused.

She had no idea that we had to be on the corner of 5th and 57th Avenue in New York City by 3 o'clock that day. We had to be there to get one of the surprises that I planned for her. Lisa absolutely loved the TV show "Sex in the City," and one of my friends arranged for us to do the *Sex in the City*

Tour while we were there. I knew that Lisa was going to love it, but I also knew that we couldn't be late.

Lisa kept saying, "You are going to kill us, you need to pull over. I can't believe you don't care about me, why won't you just pull over? Look at all of these accidents around us. If you don't pull over you are going to kill me."

On our way to New York City that day, we got into one of the worst fights that we'd ever had in our relationship up until that point. She thought that I was trying to kill her, literally.

She had no idea what I had planned, but it was okay. I had absolute clarity and conviction for what was about to happen, so I just took all of her comments, yelling, and arguing on the chin and I let it roll down my back — *even though it was hard to do!*

When we finally got there, I looked up and I pointed at the sign that said, *Welcome to New York City*.

With a big smile on my face I looked up and I said to Lisa, "Hey babe, look at that. We're in New York City!"

She said, "New York City... New York City... I knew you were going the wrong way. Do you know how far away we are from Washington DC?"

I said, "Girl, are you serious? Are you serious right now? Lisa, I was trying to surprise you by taking you to New York City for Christmas!"

"So you mean you lied to me!"

I replied, "Lied to you... Lied to you... I would like to call it a surprise!"

Once our emotions calmed down a bit, we ended up having a great experience. We had dinner at the famous Tavern on the Green before they closed their doors for good. We went to Magnolias Café, one of our favorite cupcake places in the entire world. We even had dessert at the famous Serendipity Restaurant where the movie *Serendipity* was filmed.

We also went to another very special place — the apartment on Madison Avenue that my mother and I lived in when I was first born. That was a very emotional moment for me. As I stood there, looking at the place where I once lived, many thoughts and emotions ran around inside my head. When Lisa leaned over and hugged me, it was exactly what I needed. In my heart, I knew that we were about to live the rest of our lives together, and standing in front of my first home in New York City was exactly what I needed to see to move forward with my life.

The very next night, we were at the ice skating rink in Rockefeller Center. It was a very, very cold December night. It was also the week before Christmas and the place was jam-packed. People were everywhere.

The Christmas tree in Rockefeller Center looked absolutely amazing and the look on Lisa's face was priceless. She turned towards me and she said, "I am freezing, will you please get us some hot chocolate?"

When she said that, I knew that it was time for me to make my move. This was the perfect time. When I went to get the hot chocolate, I recruited some local heroes to come upstairs with me to take a few live photographs of my proposal.

I said to Lisa, "Hey, I met this nice lady downstairs when I went to get your hot chocolate. She's a photographer and she said that she would take our picture underneath the Christmas tree. Do you want to?"

Lisa said, "Of course!"

She had no idea that I took seven cameras with me on the trip. I had each of them stuffed down inside of my winter jacket, along with the box containing the engagement ring.

As soon as we positioned ourselves under the tree, the first lady begin to take photos. Then, all of a sudden the other people popped out with the remaining cameras that I gave them. Lisa said, "Who are all of these people and why are they all taking our picture?"

I said, "I have absolutely no idea!"

"No Morris, really, who are these people?"

"Lisa, I have no idea. Relax, just go with it!"

Now remember, we were standing in the middle of Rockefeller Center in New York City at Christmas time. The place was packed. When everyone noticed all of the cameras taking pictures of us, a crowd started to gather around us. Before I knew it, there were also paparazzi that were standing there taking pictures. Lisa looked at me and she said, "Morris, what is going on?"

When she turned away from me again to look back at the crowd, that's when I made my move. As I got down on one knee, Lisa turned back towards me and she looked down at me on the ground and she said, "Morris what are you doing, and who are all these people?" Then all of a sudden Lisa saw that diamond ring!

As I asked her to marry me, the crowd behind us started to cheer, "Say yes, say yes, say yes, say yes!"

During the commotion of everything, she actually forgot to say yes at first. But as she held the hot chocolate in her hand, I reached up to put the ring on her finger and she said, "Of course, of course... yes I will marry you!"

And that was it.

It was absolutely one of the best days of my life.

~ ~ ~ ~ ~

Before we left New York, I knew that no trip to New York City would be complete without an appearance on "The Today Show." So we showed up early the next day with a big, homemade sign for all of the viewers to see. When Matt Lauer and Ann Curry came outside, Matt Lauer noticed the big West Virginia logo on our poster.

He looked at us and he said, "Hey! Let's gooooo Mountaineers! I love West Virginia, I used to live there!"

After I gave Matt Lauer a big fist pump, I looked at Ann Curry and I said, "Hey Ann look, we just got engaged!" as I pointed at Lisa's hand.

Ann Curry immediately ran over to us and gave Lisa a big hug and she put a perfect ending on an already perfect engagement trip!

Lisa and I were both really happy.

I was excited that I was about to become a married man, but I was even more happy that I didn't have to get angry every time I heard Beyoncé sing, "If you like it then you better put a ring on it, if you like it then you better put a ring on it!"

#TheresAlwaysAGirl

~ ~ ~ ~ ~

As Lisa and I continued to move forward in our relationship, the vision for what I wanted in my life was all starting to come together. My mindset began to shift to a focus on making my transition out of corporate America and into starting my own company. During that time, Lisa and I attended a dinner event in North Carolina one evening at the home of a very wealthy couple. As Lisa and I both networked with people and worked the room, I overheard Lisa say something to one of the gentlemen that bothered me.

The guy said, "So what does your fiancé do?"

Lisa responded, "He works for Pfizer. It's a pharmaceutical company." The guy responded by telling Lisa how great of a company Pfizer was and how big of an opportunity it was for a person to work there.

Later on in the conversation, he said to Lisa, "Yes, that sounds like a great job for your fiancé. I can tell that he really connects well with others and he has so much energy. I bet he really does well in sales for a company like Pfizer!"

Lisa said, "Yep, he sure is a talker and he has the gift of gab. That's why he is also a motivational speaker on the side!"

The guy said, "Yes of course, I can definitely see him doing well at something like that!"

There was something about Lisa's comment to that guy that made me angry inside. After I gave it some thought, I realized exactly what made me so mad. I hated the way I felt when she said, "He is also a motivational speaker… on the side."

On the side? On the side? Why did hearing those words make me so mad? I was mad because those words were true. I was mad because I did not want to be introduced to someone based on my *day job* anymore. I wanted people to see me the way that I saw myself.

I knew that both my passion and my purpose were to be a professional speaker. But I also knew that if I wanted people to see me the way that I saw myself, I needed to do something to take my conviction to the next level – just like Ally did when she refused to leave the bank that day. The difference was, Ally displayed her conviction by *not* being willing to walk away from the bank that day, but I needed to show my conviction by *being willing to walk away*… from my day job.

I knew that I needed to take my vision to the next level. But first, I needed to talk to Lisa. I asked her to only introduce me to others as a professional speaker from that moment on. I no longer wanted to be introduced by what I did in my day job. I didn't ask her to do that for me because of my ego, I asked her to do that because I realize that I needed to do whatever I had to, to motivate *myself* to take the next step in my plan.

At the beginning of this book, I introduced you to a guy that I met in LaGuardia Airport in New York City – Clyde Randall. He taught me that no matter what you do with your life, you can't fool yourself. *You can never fool yourself.*

When I looked at who I really was up until that point in my life, I knew that I had a BIG vision for what I wanted. I also knew that I had prepared to get to that point in my life – I had a master's degree, I had a variety of experiences from human resources to sales, and I was motivated. But I also knew that all of those things *were not enough.* I needed to be willing to fight harder for what I wanted.

Once I started to introduce myself only as a professional speaker, it fueled my mindset and it helped me to fight harder and continue to burn my vision into my head - *and my heart* - and it changed my level of conviction.

Next, I called my professional speaking mentor, Walter Bond. I wanted him to coach me and make me run the plays. I wanted to know exactly what I needed to do next. The first thing that he told me was that I needed to take my professional speaking skills seriously. I needed to partner with a professional organization that could help me with my professional growth, speaking skills, and my ability to run a successful consulting business. He told me that I needed to join the National Speakers Association.

When I first started to attend the NSA meetings, I did not have enough credentials to become a member because I was not a professional speaker yet. But I was allowed to attend the meetings as a guest. Once I fully immersed myself in the professional speaking culture that I wanted to spend the rest of my life in, I started to develop brand new neural pathways in my brain, and I grew my skills as a speaker. I started working on my speaking technique, delivery skills, and my marketing and branding skills so that I could make the transition from corporate America to starting my own company.

Once I took my transition more seriously and I increased my skills, everything changed – *Overnight.* People started to see me the way that I saw myself.

Remember in chapter 11 when I talked about the importance of being competent and having skills? Remember when I said that if you are good, everyone else will know that you're good? Well, I definitely was *NOT* very good, but my skills were growing, and other people noticed them. I began to book more and more paid speaking engagements which gave me the opportunity to make more money, work on my speaking skills, and continue to invest in my vision.

There is nothing more powerful than experiencing progress in your life. Let me repeat that again. *There is nothing more powerful than the feeling of progress.* The only way to achieve real progress in anything that you do is by earning it. No other person can earn it for you.

Every time you make progress in something, your brain releases dopamine that make you feel good – but there are no shortcuts to achieving progress. That's why, in my opinion, so many people are addicted to using drugs. People use drugs for the same reasons. By using drugs and increasing certain chemicals in their brain, it makes them feel good. Well you know what? I guess I am an addict too, because I am addicted to the feeling of progress and what it does in my life.

I believe that people would use less drugs if they could replace the feelings that drugs give them with the feelings that you get when you work hard, stay on your grind, and become convicted about something. If more people did what they loved everyday, they wouldn't need to use drugs at all - unless of course, they are prescribed *Pfizer pharmaceutical drugs* - *h*ey, I still need to see growth in my Pfizer stock portfolio!

LIVING MY CONVICTION - IN WALKS ANOTHER HERO

One day, someone shared a picture of me on social media. It was a picture of me when I was about eight years old, holding a microphone in my hand and speaking in front of a large audience.

The photo had several likes and comments underneath it. Many of the comments said things like, *"You see, it's been inside of him since he was a child. He's always had this gift since day one."*

I had never seen that picture before. When you see a photograph of yourself that you never even knew existed – and in the photograph you are doing the actual thing that you have dreamed about doing your entire life – it really messes with your head… in a good way.

I realized that I had God-given talents and abilities inside of me since the day that I was born. That picture fueled my desire to speak even more, and it crushed any fears that I had about walking away from my full-time job to follow my dreams because it reassured me that my gifts were always inside of me and all I needed to do was trust them, and use them.

A lady named Jenise reached out to me and she said something to me about the photo that caught me off guard. She said, "*You know what your problem is?*"

I said, "Excuse me?"

She repeated, "*Do you want to know what your problem is?*"

Before I tell you what she said next, let me explain something to you. Whenever someone says to you, "*Do you want to know what your problem is,*" you can guarantee that person is about to tell you.

She said, "Your problem is that you work for that big drug company, and you're addicted to drugs yourself."

I looked at her like she was crazy. I said, "What the heck are you talking about lady, I don't use drugs!"

She said, "Oh yes you do. You're addicted to the worst drug in this country. You're addicted to the drug that keeps more people in this world from being great than anything else."

Just to humor her and play along with whatever she was attempting to do, I said, "Really, I am? Okay, well tell me lady, what drug am I addicted to?"

She said, "You're addicted to the drug that you get high on every two weeks and you know exactly what I'm talking about. You're addicted to that direct deposit paycheck that automatically hits your checking account every two weeks."

"What are you talking about? How am I addicted to direct deposit?"

"Because Morris, you have a gift. Everyone knows that you have a gift and you know it too, and the only thing that's holding you back from using your gift and making a difference the way you were created to, is your fear of walking away from that six-figure salary that you have. The *love of money* always has been the root of all evil and it's causing you to miss out on what you were called to do."

I stood there shocked. I didn't even know how to respond to what she said because she was absolutely right. After I stood there for a moment, I just gave her a big hug and then I thanked her before I walked away.

Do you remember when I stood in the parking lot of Ruby Memorial Hospital on the evening when I said goodbye to my grandmother? Remember when I told you that certain moments in life can produce emotional capital or motivation that will make you *want to do something?*

Well, when that lady said those words to me, she produced some emotional capital inside of me and I heard the Rocky music playing in my head all over again, and you know what happens when you start to dance to music that nobody else hears…

I immediately started my process to transition out of my full-time job and start my own company.

FINAL THOUGHTS ABOUT CONVICTION

When people take bold actions based on conviction, it's inspiring to witness. After hearing about Ally's story of how she followed her love for hair and nails, and seeing where her passion took her, it made me realize that passion, conviction, and purpose will take a person far in life. Around the time that I heard Ally's story, I also met a guy named John Youngblood that was similar to Ally.

John and his wife Anita were well known in the Lake Norman community. John Youngblood said something to me that made a significant difference in the mindset that I had as I prepared to transition out of corporate America. At the time that Lisa and I met him, John was already a very, very successful business owner in the Charlotte area.

When John was in his early twenties, he also had a very tough decision to make. John worked for a large manufacturing company and he made great money for a guy his age. Most people would have given their right hand to have his job. But John had an idea to start his own company, and he was passionate about his idea, so he went to talk to his father to tell him what he was thinking about doing.

John wasn't sure if his father would support his dreams of leaving his job, especially since John had a wife and two young children at home. John's father responded in a way that completely surprised him.

His father said, "Go ahead and give it a shot. Give yourself a couple of years and try it out. If it doesn't work out, you can always get another job!"

At the time that John shared this story with me, we were sitting in his home – one of the most beautiful homes in the whole Lake Norman community. As John told me that story, we were looking out at the lake, through a big window in his living room. Then John turned to me and he said, "Morris, give it a shot, take a chance. If it doesn't work out you can always get another job."

GOODBYE CORPORATE AMERICA - HELLO WORLD

When I started my job with Pfizer on March 31st, 2008, I gave myself a three year time limit before I needed to leave and start my own company. After being inspired by the convictions of other entrepreneurs around me, I realized that I had everything that I needed to make my transition. I had my health, my energy, my faith, and the love of a beautiful woman beside me, and I was clear about what I needed to do.

My last day working in corporate America was March 18th, 2011. I was able to beat stick to the original deadline that I gave myself by just 13 days.

As I stood at the storage unit where I turned in my laptop, company identification and the rest of my work equipment, as I began to walk away from the building, a guy stopped me and said, "Hey man, this might sound weird, and I don't always say things like this, and I realize that I don't even know who you are and I will probably never see you again, but I just want you to know that you have a great presence and great energy about you and I can tell that something big is about to happen for you."

He had no idea how perfect his timing was.

He had no idea how much confirmation that I got from his words

As I stood there looking at him, his words were like a lightening bolt straight to my heart – I knew that I was about to walk into my destiny.

As I shook his hand, I thanked him politely. Then I turned to walk out of the door, ready to take my best shot.

It took me forever to get to that moment.

I dreamed of starting my company for years.

It took longer than I thought it would, but I was willing to wait for it because I knew that I had one shot to do it right, and I was never tempted by making fast money or getting fast results. Even when drug dealers were flashing their money and new cars around me as a kid, I always knew deep down inside that there is no such thing as an *Overnight Success* – at least not in the areas of life that matter most. No matter how much you play the lottery or how many *get-rich-quick* schemes you come up with, there is nothing more powerful than the feeling that you get when you take ownership and responsibility of going after what matters most to you. ***When*** *you do see your dream come alive right in front of you*, it's one of the most powerful feelings in the world.

There is only one real form of *Overnight Success* - it's the success that happens inside of your heart when you *change the way you see yourself* and your purpose. And that's what having conviction will do for you, it will cause you to see yourself, and your entire life, differently. And it will give you the courage to do things that would normally scare other people to death, things like *walking away from a high-paying job* just to do what you love.

When you have conviction in your heart, you passion will overpower any fears or roadblocks that try to stand in your way - no matter how bad they are.

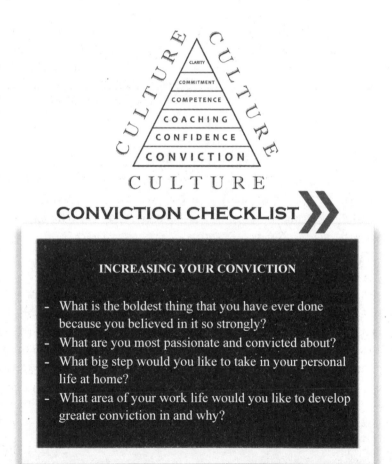

CONVICTION CHECKLIST »

INCREASING YOUR CONVICTION

- What is the boldest thing that you have ever done because you believed in it so strongly?
- What are you most passionate and convicted about?
- What big step would you like to take in your personal life at home?
- What area of your work life would you like to develop greater conviction in and why?

Chapter

15

The Bonus "C"

When Lisa and I began to plan our wedding day, it was a great time in our lives. She moved to North Carolina and successfully transitioned jobs, and my speaking business was gaining more and more momentum.

Life was good.

As I sat outside washing my car one day, I received a text message on my cell phone. The message was sent directly to my cell phone from my website.

Whenever someone left a message on my website's guestbook, the messages automatically came to my phone first before they were approved.

The message said, "You may not know me and you may not know who we are, but I just wanted you to know that we have been looking for you for a long time. We want you to know that we love you very much and we are very proud of all your success and your accomplishments."

Once I saw the name of the person who sent the message, I got butterflies in my stomach.

The message was sent by a girl named Natasha Morrison. As soon as I realized that she had the same last name that I did, my heart started to pound in my chest. I thought to myself, *"Could this be who I think it is?"*

I walked into the house and I held my phone out so that Lisa could see the message. Lisa could tell from the look on my face that something was going on.

In chapter 5, I tried my best to tell you just how much *I hate pretending.*

Back when my grandmother Katherine first told me the news about who my parents really were in New York City, it was very hard for me to walk around and *pretend* like the news didn't rock my world, because it did. Hearing the details straight from her mouth about my mother and father and where I really came from was tough for me to handle.

Well, as I stared down at the text message from a girl named Natasha Morrison, something told me that my life was about to be turned upside down once again.

Lisa said, "Who do you think it is?"

I said, "She has my last name. I think this is someone from my mother's family in Tennessee."

Since I was a kid, I knew that my mother was white and my father was black. I was raised in a strong African-American culture in West Virginia, and I was very proud of who I was and where I was from. My family may not have been perfect (whose family is?); but we were very proud of who we were. It was very surreal for me when I realized that this could potentially be a white person from the white side of my family reaching out to me for the first time that I could remember.

The government has a special place in the race section of most applications today for children who are from mixed-race backgrounds. They typically call those kids *biracial*. Well, that's not what I called myself. I saw myself the same way the rest of my family saw themselves – black – because that is what I experienced in my life.

I have a better way of describing my perspective. Don Cheadle is a very dark skinned, African-American actor in Hollywood. Don Cheadle along with other black celebrities such as Chris rock participated in a DNA program that traced the genealogy of many African-Americans to see where they came from.

When Chris Rock and Don Cheadle found out that they both had high amounts of European (or white) blood in their DNA, the interviewer, Henry Louis-Gates, asked Don Cheadle how he felt knowing that he had mixed races as a part of his ancestry. Don Cheadle responded, saying, "I may have white blood inside of me, but I believe *you are what you have to defend*. And if you are a man of color or a black man, you will always be measured by the color of your skin. It doesn't matter how you identify yourself, that's how everyone else will see you."

Don Cheadle described how I felt perfectly. Throughout my life I have experienced what it was like to be followed around when I shopped at stores just because someone thought that I was going to steal something. I have also been racially profiled in a variety of other circumstances and situations. Even though I never let anyone else determine who I was or what my character was going to be, society still had its own way of telling me how black I was. Throughout my entire life, no one ever came up to me and said, "Oops, I am sorry, I thought that you were another white guy that I know - sorry to bother you."

I never had my identity mistaken as being a that of a white man – I never experienced that. But I have been treated differently because I was black.

I just want you to understand *how I feel about who I am*. Understanding that will help you appreciate how I felt the moment I realized that a white family member contacted me.

After I handed Lisa the phone, and she saw the message from Natasha, she said, "What are you going to do? Are you going to e-mail her back?" I decided to write Natasha Morrison back.

When I emailed her, I also asked her if I could have her phone number so that we could talk directly.

When she responded, she gave me the phone number for the house that she lived in and when I finally decided to call her, things changed for me in a big way.

THE PHONE CALL CHANGED MY LIFE

When I called Natasha on the phone, an older woman answered.

She said, "Hello, hello?"

The old lady's country accent was so thick that I could barely understand what she was saying.

I said, "Hello, hello... Is Natasha there? Can I speak to Natasha Morrison please?"

The old lady on the other end of the phone immediately began to yell, "Tasha, Tasha, Tasha... pick up the telephone!"

When I heard the old lady's loud, country voice yelling on the other end of the phone, I was thinking to myself, "Oh my God, who are these people?"

When Tasha finally got on the phone, the conversation was very tough to follow. I could barely understand what she was saying because of how thick her country accent was.

When you talk to someone live and in person, face-to-face, at least you have a chance to see their mouth move and you can pick up on body language to help you understand what they're saying. But when you can't understand a person over the phone, it makes it very tough to have dialogue back-and-forth. I had to focus very hard to even understand her.

All of a sudden, as I tried to listen to her closely, that little voice inside of me started speaking - you know what voice I'm talking about. It was Craig. My instincts always kick in during moments like that.

Craig said, "Hey. Hey. Hey you."

At first I was thinking to myself, "*Shut up Craig. Leave me alone. I need to focus and listen to this girl so that I can follow what she's saying, and I don't need you distracting me.*"

But Craig would not leave me alone and my instincts kept kicking in.

All of a sudden, Craig said, "*Hey, what are you worried about, her country accent isn't THAT bad. Don't worry, you've got this, because you've been listening to that country music, you can do it! Just pretend that she's singing a country song and you've got this!*"

Craig was right. In the beginning of *The 7 Steps to "C" See Your Way Through* , I talked about the impact that culture can have on us and how it influences the way we think and act. But I also told you about the day that I followed my instincts and started listening to country music – it changed the way I saw a lot of things. But I had no idea that those skills were going to come back and help me later on in a moment like this.

As I listened to Natasha's voice on the other end of the phone, I just pretended that I was listening to a country song, and eventually I started understanding what she was saying a lot better. I just needed to listen to her with my country music ears!

Natasha and I were making a lot of progress in our conversation until Natasha said, "You know, when your mother came home pregnant with a little colored baby, there weren't any colored folks round here back then."

Immediately, I was thinking to myself, "Did she just say what I think she said? Did she just call me colored?"

Then she said, "Heck, as a matter of fact, there still aren't any colored folks 'round here."

I could not believe what I was hearing. I was thinking to myself, "Who still uses the word C word? Did she really just call me *COLORED*?"

I thought that the best way to handle that situation was by changing the subject in the conversation. So I said, "Hey Natasha, can I ask you a question?"

She said, "Sure, you can ask me anything."

"Who was that old lady that answered the phone when I called you just now?"

"Who, Mama?"

"Ohhhh, that's your mother?"

"No Morris, that's *MAMA*!"

"Yes, I heard what you said. You said that she was your mother!"

"No Morris, that's your grandmother. We all call her *MAMA* ."

As soon as she said that, I got butterflies again. I was filled with emotion. I had already lost so many people in my life and the fact that I still had a grandparent, a real, biological grandparent who was still living... just the thought of having a grandparent that was alive really excited me.

I said, "Are you telling me that I have a grandmother who is still alive?"

Natasha said, "Still alive? Still alive? Morris, your grandmother Pauline still mows the grass outside, she still changes the motor oil in the tractor, and she still does all of the grocery shopping. She's as healthy and strong as she can be and she won't even let you help her either!"

Right away, I knew that I wanted to meet my grandmother. I instantly pulled out my laptop to do a Google search to see how far Palmer,

Tennessee, was from where I lived in North Carolina. Palmer, Tennessee was about five hours away.

I said, "Hey Natasha, I'm speaking in Nashville next week. Do you think it would be okay if I came to meet you guys? Do you think it would be okay if I came to meet my grandmother?"

She said, "What do you mean *is it okay?* Of course it's okay! Of course it is. Mama has been praying for this day to come for many years."

As soon as she said that I made up my mind. I was going to meet my white grandmother for the first time.

THE TRIP OF A LIFETIME

I immediately began to prepare for the drive to Tennessee to visit my family. I decided to meet them at my grandmother's house the following Saturday. On the days leading up to my visit, when Natasha and I spoke over the phone she kept saying, "Hey, why don't you come on Friday night instead? Why can't you come on Friday night?"

I realized that I needed to be direct with her.

Deep inside of me, I could not stop thinking about the *colored folks* comment that she had made, and I was a little worried about the situation that I was about to walk into.

So I said, "Natasha, I don't expect you to understand this at all, but... *I am not coming there at nighttime.*"

I stuck to my original plan of arriving there on Saturday afternoon – in the daylight!

Palmer, Tennessee, was a very small town. After doing the research on Google, I realized that the town had less than 1,000 people living there. As we drove up the mountain that leads to Palmer, I stopped at an old gas station and picked up a dozen red roses for my grandmother. As we made our way up the mountain, I had many, many thoughts running through my head. I could not believe that I was about to meet my white family in Tennessee for the first time.

As we drove through the town of Palmer, I seemed like I stood out like a sore thumb. The fact that I was driving a shiny black BMW only made me stand out even more. As I replay the story in my mind, it probably was not a great decision for me to drive that car. I probably should have borrowed a pick-up truck from one of my buddies before I made that trip!

As soon as we got into Palmer, the GPS in my car stopped working and I could not get it to pick up a signal. All of a sudden, I started to panic and I felt my entire body get really warm.

Lisa looked over at me and she said, "Hey, are you okay?"

"Yes... I'm okay."

But I was not okay. I was nervous, especially when I tried to open up Google Maps on my cell phone, only to realize that I didn't have a cellphone signal either.

At that moment I felt like I was about to die.

I thought to myself, "Yep, this is it. This is how I die. I'm in the middle of nowhere and there is no way I will ever get out of here."

As I started to panic, in the back of my mind I started hearing banjos playing. Then I started to think to myself, "What if something happens to us? What if I need to call someone?" I was already nervous about the trip itself, but now I had no GPS signal and no cell phone signal.

Lisa said, "Hey, are you sure you're okay?"

This time I didn't even respond to her because I was scared and very nervous and I was too busy trying to remember some of the directions to my grandmothers house. As we drove around, we passed a small cemetery. I thought to myself, "Could that be the cemetery where my mother was buried at?" I had always dreamed about the day that I would have a chance to visit her grave site.

As we continued to drive, I turned down an old gravel road that took me in the direction of my grandmother's house. As we got near the end of the road, I felt like we were getting close to where the directions were supposed to lead me to. I was still unsure, so I started driving really close to the mailboxes of the houses. And that's when I saw it. That's when the gravity of the moment really hit me. On the mailbox by the road in BIG letters, I saw the name *MORRISON*.

There are many memories that I have from that trip, but seeing my last name on that mailbox was one of the biggest moments for me.

As I glanced up at the house that was sitting on the hill, I saw the double-wide trailer sitting there with broken down cars and equipment in the yard. When I tell you that it was country, I mean it was *country*.

I could not believe that I was looking at my grandmother's little old country house! As I pulled up into the driveway and got closer to her house, I stopped. All of a sudden, I started to get really nervous. Then my instincts took over. I put the car in reverse and started to back all the way back out of the driveway. Lisa looked at me and said, "What's wrong? What are you doing?"

I looked at Lisa and I said, "Relax, I've got this."

I backed the car back down into the street and I started to do that little three-point-turn-around that they teach you in driver's education class. After I turned the car around, I started to back my car up the driveway with the front of my car facing the street.

As I continued backing up the driveway, Lisa looked at me and said, "Why are you backing up the driveway? What are you doing?"

I knew exactly what I was doing. I was nervous and my survival instincts were kicking in. I looked at Lisa and I said, "Hey, I am backing up the driveway so that the car is facing out, towards the road, just in case something happens and we need to get out of here *fast*."

Did I mention that I was nervous?

When I opened up my car door, the house was behind me. I reached into the backseat to grab the dozen roses that I had purchased for my grandmother. As I slowly turned towards my grandmother's house, my 70 year-old grandma was coming down the stairs towards me.

As soon as we stood there face-to-face, we began to hug and embrace each other, and neither one of us wanted to let go.

Ever since that day, many people have asked me what that moment was like. And even though I can never find the words to describe how I really felt deep down inside, the best way for me to describe it is, *"There's no mistaking the feeling that you have when you are hugging the lady, who gave birth to the woman, that gave birth to you. It is an absolutely unmistakable feeling."*

There was an instant connection. The last time my grandmother Pauline had interacted with anyone who was that close to my mother was on the day of my mother's funeral when they buried her. Now, almost 28 years later, I stood in her driveway with my arms wrapped around her and it was very emotional for both of us.

We had a great visit with my grandmother that day. It was great to meet other cousins and family members too. It was even more amazing to see all the photos of all of my white family members that were on my grandmother's living room wall.

Before I left my grandmother's house, she asked me to sit down at the table. When I sat down, she said, "I have a couple of things that I think you need to see." As soon as she said that, I had a feeling that things were about to get really... *REAL*.

First, she began to pull out photographs of me from when I was a child. She had my fourth grade basketball picture, my fifth grade school picture, and my junior high football and basketball pictures. I was amazed because I had no idea that she had any information about me.

I said, "Grandma, where did you get this stuff from? How did you get all of this?"

That's when my grandmother Pauline slid an envelope to me across the table.

Before the envelope reached my hands, I automatically recognized the handwriting on the outside of the envelope.

Let me ask you a question. Do you think you would be able to recognize the handwriting of your mother, father, grandparent, or any adult figure who was responsible for raising you when you were a child? Yeah, I thought so. Most people can, and I recognized the handwriting right away – the envelope was from my grandmother Gwendolyn who lived in Fairmont, West Virginia.

When I opened up the envelope in front of me, I realized that it was a letter that my grandmother Gwendolyn had sent to my grandmother Pauline. Those two ladies had been communicating with each other throughout the years and I had no knowledge of it whatsoever.

In the letter that I opened, Gwendolyn wrote,

"Hi Pauline, I apologize for not reaching out to you sooner. I know that you miss your grandson a lot. I just wanted to send you a letter to let you know that little Morris is okay and he is growing up to be a big boy. He is a handful to deal with and he is very ornery, but I keep him straight. I don't have very much extra money to go around these days ever since my husband died. My kids just don't seem to understand that I cannot help them and give them money like I used to, but they still ask me anyway and I still give them what I can. That's why you haven't heard from me in a while - my phone at the house got

cut off because I didn't have the money to pay the bill. But I wanted to let you know that Morris is doing really well in school, and I was able to give him a great Christmas this year. We got him a brand new bicycle and many other toys that big boys dream of. Well, I have to get ready to go now, but I promise not to take too long before you hear from me again. Love, Gwendolyn."

Just looking at my grandmother Gwendolyn's handwriting made me cry. I really missed her. Seeing her handwriting took me right back to the night at the hospital when I said goodbye to her.

Reading what she written in the letter made me realize just how much she sacrificed to give me a life. When she mentioned that Christmas and the bicycle that she had gotten me, I remembered that it was one of the best Christmases I ever had. That was the only Christmas that my grandmother asked me to write out a list to tell Santa what I wanted for Christmas. And that year, I got every single thing that I asked for. To this day, I have no idea where she got the money or how she was able to make it happen, but she did.

After I finished reading the letter and after I finished wiping the tears away from my eyes, I looked up at my grandmother Pauline with a look of absolute amazement on my face.

I said, "Grandma, you mean to tell me that you and Gwendolyn were communicating with each other all of those years?"

My Grandmother Pauline just looked at me with a slight smile on her face. And she didn't ever answer me. She didn't have to. The look on her face the only answer that I needed to see.

I guess there were many things that I never knew about my life.

"Grandma, why did no one tell me about you before?"

She said, "When you were young, you knew about me. As you got older, Gwendolyn chose to handle your situation the best way she knew how. But don't you worry yourself with all of that. The only thing that you need to understand is that many sacrifices were made just so you could have the life that you've got, and you will never understand all of the sacrifices that people made for you."

After my grandmother shared that with me, she said, "There is something else that I think you need to see."

A part of me was thinking, *"Great, what could she possibly have to show me this time?"*

My grandmother showed me a black treasure trunk.

She said, "When your mother died, this trunk was shipped here, along with your mother's body when she was transported back from New York City. It has some of her personal things inside of it."

A part of me was paralyzed. I absolutely could not believe my eyes.

As I began to look through the trunk of my mother's things, I was amazed by everything that I saw – no matter how big or small it was.

As I looked at documents and paperwork that belonged to my mom, I realized that up until that moment, I never knew what my mother's handwriting looked like. Just to see a piece of paper that she actually wrote on made me feel connected to her.

I was even able to read my mother's daily planner that she had written in up until she died.

There are many details about my life and my mother that my grandmother Pauline shared with me. As I began to connect the dots with what I was previously told about who my mother was, it was clear for me to see that my white family in Tennessee didn't know everything about my mother that I knew. My grandma Katherine, the one who lived in New York City at the time, gave me a different description of who my mother was and how she acted when she was in New York City.

I wasn't exactly sure if my grandmother Pauline knew much about that part of my mothers life. And my grandmother Pauline wasn't the only one that may not have known everything.

After visiting Tennessee, although I was glad to finally meet my white family in Tennessee, the visit caused me to leave with many questions in my mind about who my mother really was, how she lived her life, and even questions about *how* she really died.

As I prepared to leave my grandmother's house, we stood outside in the driveway. After Grandma Pauline hugged me, she looked into my eyes and said, "Don't ever forget what I told you. Don't ever forget that sacrifices were made for you – sacrifices that you'll never really know – just to give you the life that you have today. So don't you waste it. And another thing, you may think that you're a big shot motivational speaker, but you better not ever forget whose last name you have. You better represent my name well in everything that you do, and you better not ever embarrass me, because you are not too big for me to give you a good spanking!"

SURROUNDED BY COMMUNITY

Someone once asked me if listening to country music helped me at all when I made my visit to Tennessee. And the truth is, it did help me. The day that I decided to at least give country music a chance, I opened my mind up to all sorts of possibilities in my life. Country music even made me feel more comfortable when I first spoke to Natasha on the phone. She didn't realize that it helped me, *but I knew it helped me feel more comfortable*, and that's all that matters.

We live in a world today with many different types of cultures and many different types of people. Advancements in technology have enabled us to live in a truly global world. Because of that, we need to have a variety of skills and abilities to help us connect with many different types of people if we want to succeed and make progress in anything that we do.

In chapter 10, you read about the importance of growing your skills. Two of the most important skills discussed were emotional intelligence (EQ) and critical thinking. Well, there is one more area that you need to be intentional about developing if you want to continue to transition well and achieve your goals. You need to develop *cultural intelligence skills*.

Cultural Intelligence, or "CQ" *is your ability to adapt to different situations with people who are different from you*. As the world continues to evolve, each of us may find ourselves in many different types of situations, with people that may have various different types of backgrounds. You will need to develop CQ skills that will allow you to connect to people from different genders, races, generations and cultures if you want to continue to make progress in your goals.

There is absolutely nothing wrong with staying in the same place or doing things the same way that you've always done them throughout your entire life... *if that's how you want to live*. But if you want to get better results, you must be intentional about developing cultural intelligence (CQ) skills that will help you thrive in any situation in today's world.

3 WAYS TO DEVELOP YOUR CQ SKILLS

Embrace New Experiences – Every time you make the effort to experience things that enhance your perspective of others, you will increase your CQ skills. I have always had a variety of people surrounding me – old and young, rich and poor, black and white and everything else in between. As a result, I feel *comfortable* and most important, *I feel confident* no matter where I go or who I am with. In my business, I might be in New York City one day and then North Dakota the next day, so I must be able to understand the dynamics of each place that I go, especially if I want to successfully connect with others. It's simple – embracing opportunities to learn about others will give you a healthier perspective, and it will make you a better person.

Study Other Cultures – People bow when they greet each other in Japan because it's a sign of respect. If you want to bow correctly, you have to learn the basics of when to bow, how to bow, when to smile, and how to be polite. When you learn about other cultures, you won't have to change who you are, but you do have to change how you express certain things to people who are from different cultures than you. A great way to study new cultures is by reading newspapers and books, watching different types of movies, traveling to new places, or simply being friends with people who are different from you.

Learn Other Languages – Your ability to speak another language is the ultimate display courtesy and respect. When you can speak another person language, you will display a high level of cultural intelligence and your effort to learn another language will gain you much respect from people that come from different background than you.

Our world is starving for original people and thinkers who can connect, inspire, and unify people. It doesn't matter who you are or where you're from – increasing your cultural intelligence skills will pay off for you in a big way by helping you to:

- **honor and respect** others
- **relate and connect** to others better
- be more **understanding** of others
- adapt to **diverse situations** better
- show **empathy and compassion** towards others
- be **culturally mindful** in all situations

After I met my grandmother Pauline for the first time, I felt many emotions inside of me. Mostly, I was thankful for the opportunity to connect the dots and get answers to many questions that I had about my life. Most importantly, I am glad that I had the ability to socially and emotionally connect with my white family, even though they were different from me.

The last words that my grandmother Pauline shared with me in her driveway inspired me. When she said, *"Many sacrifices have been made for your life,"* she reminded me that every one of us in this world has the opportunities that we do because we are all standing on the shoulders and sacrifices of others who came before us.

She reminded me that the best way to truly live in a community with each other is by first recognizing that you are a part of a community, and then by recognizing that everything that you are, and every gift that you have, came from a community of many people surrounding you.

Chapter

16

Ready To FIGHT

When Lisa and I got married in North Carolina, about 90 of our closest friends and family members join us on Cliff Champion's boat out in the middle of Lake Norman to celebrate with us. One of the best parts about our wedding day was that I got a chance to dance with my grandmother Pauline on my wedding day after meeting her just 5 months before my wedding!

Pastor Paul Turbedsky from Grace Covenant Church married Lisa and me. Robert Bryan from the *The Great American Family* you met in chapter 1 was the only other person who spoke at our wedding that day. He shared a special blessing for Lisa and me as we began our journey together.

Robert turned to the audience when he was finished and said, "Ladies and gentlemen, today as Morris and Lisa unite to become one family, they are taking their first steps to building a family that will go on to be *world changers.*"

His words were really touching… and *inspiring.*

Lisa and I had a plan for how we wanted our life to go. First, we wanted to get engaged, get married, and then travel and have a bunch of fun for about three or four years while we grew our careers. We wanted to wait at least a few years before we had kids because once the little crumb-snatchers come they change everything. And that was our vision.

Well, we learned very quickly that life doesn't always go how you expect it to.

AN UNEXPECTED CURVE BALL

When the doctor called us into his office, he said, "Oops! Looks like your plan isn't working out the way you wanted it to!"

I said, "What are you talking about doc?"

"Looks like you are having a baby sooner than you thought!"

I was beside myself and I couldn't believe it. I looked at the doctor and I said, "Uhhh? What... How.... When.... wait a minute, what? Pregnant, already? *How?*"

The doctor said, "What do you mean *HOW*? I think you know *HOW* this happened!"

He was right, I knew exactly how it happened, but I just couldn't believe that it was happening already because that wasn't how our plan was supposed to go.

I was so nervous about being a dad that I needed to lighten the mood in the room a little.

I looked up at Lisa and said, "Hold on a minute, how in the world can we be pregnant? *Are you SURE that I am the father?"* She squinted her eyes at me and she mumbled something under her breath that I am glad that I didn't hear. Then I smiled. That's what I do, I use humor to help me through situations.

The doctor said, "Come back next week so we can run more tests and make sure things are progressing well for the baby."

I had a whole week to process what was going on, but I was still in a state of shock. When we arrived at our next appointment, the doctor took things to a whole new level.

He looked up at Lisa and me and said, "Uh ohhhh!"

I said, "What doc? What are you talking about... uh ohhhh?"

He said, "It looks like I was wrong. Looks like you two are going to be having twins!"

I was floored. My body got really warm and I thought that I was going to faint. I was sitting in the back of the room in the corner behind Lisa and the doctors. When the doctor said that we were having twins, Lisa looked up at the doctors and she said, "Will one of you please turn around and tell me what my husband's face looks like right now?"

After the doctor turned around to look at me, he turned back to Lisa and he said, "Your husband is turning white as a ghost!"

I know what you're thinking right now, and yes, you are correct - Chocolate can turn into Vanilla!

I could barely process being a dad, and now this?

Twins?

Twins?

What in the world were we supposed to do with twins?

When we came back the following week for another checkup, the doctor did it to me again. He said, "Uh ohhh."

I said, "What now? What could you possibly have to say now?" He didn't have to say anything, I looked up at the digital screen on the wall and I could see it for myself. I was thinking, *oh no, there's no way in the world. That is not what I think it is.*

I said, "Doc, is that what I think it is? Is that *ANOTHER* baby that I see in there? Please don't tell me that we're having triplets!"

With a smile, he looked at me and said, "I am not quite sure, I can't really tell from this angle." Then he moved things around a little bit to try to get a better view but he still couldn't tell.

He said, "Well either way, we still need to see you two here in the office more regularly than we see single pregnancies because twins run a higher risk. We will be able to see more next week."

I had a whole week to walk around in a daze. I was thinking, "First twins, and now, possibly triplets? Lord, I am going to need you NOW more than ever. What am I possibly supposed to do with twins... or triplets!"

Meanwhile, you should have seen my wife Lisa. One of her biggest dreams in life was to be a mother and she absolutely could not have been happier. She was on cloud nine. She had a permanent smile on her face and life could not have been any better.

The very next week, after the doctor began his examination, as I sat in the corner behind all of the action, I heard the doctor say, "Uh ohhh."

I jumped up and said, "Doc, don't even say what I think you're about to say. If you see another baby in there, you keep it!"

The doctor didn't respond. I could tell by the look on his and his assistant's face that something was wrong. He turned towards Lisa and me and said,

"Mr. and Mrs. Morrison, I am sorry to tell you this. But you have miscarried all of your babies." We were absolutely crushed.

FIGHTING FOR WHAT YOU WANT THE MOST

It was a very tough time for Lisa and me. We had no idea that miscarriages were as common as they are. Studies show that up to 50% of pregnancies end in miscarriage. Up to 80% of miscarriages happen in the first three months of pregnancy. Some miscarriages happen before a woman even knows she's pregnant. We didn't care about all of those numbers though, because that's all they were... numbers. Once it happened to us, miscarriage became real. Feeling what it's like to lose kids was now a reality for us that we had not anticipate experiencing, especially at the beginning of our marriage, at a time when we were supposed to be the happiest. We tried our best to make peace with our situation and we did everything that we could to keep it together during that time.

I read that King Solomon – one of the wisest kings to ever rule – once said that "It's better for a baby to be miscarried than it is for a baby to live in this world."

Well, even though we tried our best to look at the loss of those babies as positively as we could, it crushed us. Lisa began to suffer tremendously from postpartum depression. Within the first six months of our marriage Lisa and I saw our relationship going down the drain. I tried to support her in any way that I knew how, but I quickly realized that a man will never truly know what it's like to lose a baby – not like a woman knows.

Eventually, Lisa and I separated.

After she moved out of our house, the reality of a divorce was the topic of conversation. I thought to myself, "How in the world could my marriage be ending already when it just began?"

The days that followed our separation were rough. I cried as I drove to work every day, I cried during my lunch break, and I cried on the way home.

Even though I had already experienced many challenges and adversity, this was the worst. I had never felt so lonely in my entire life.

And I the last thing that I should have done, was listen to country music during that time. If I would have seen Tim McGraw on the streets somewhere, I probably would have punched him in the face because I had his greatest hits CD in my car and I listened to the same song over and over and over again.

It was a miserable time for me.

When you go your whole entire life without the stability of having parents like I did, it changes you. I didn't realize until I began to lose my marriage just how much I looked forward to creating a family of my own and creating a stable, loving home around me.

When Lisa left, everything changed. I couldn't eat, sleep, or even think straight. All I could do was exercise. Whenever I worked out my mind wasn't focused on anything else. One day while I was working out at the gym, I got a phone call from a number that I did not recognize. Usually I don't answer calls from people that I don't know, but this time I answered it anyway.

"Hello, who is this?"

"Hi Morris, this is Pastor Farrell Lemmings, did I catch you at a good time?"

I said, "Hey Pastor Farrell. Yes, yes you did. I can talk now."

Pastor Farrell was our head pastor at Grace Covenant Church. It's not an everyday occurrence to get a call from your *head pastor,* so I was both excited and anxious about his call. We didn't have a very long conversation that day. Pastor Farrell had heard about what Lisa and I were going through, and he knew that we had separated just months after we were married by Paul Turbedsky, another pastor at his church.

Pastor Farrell just called to let me know that they were all praying for us. He encouraged me to pray and do my best not to give up and his phone call meant the world to me, and it gave me just the encouragement that I needed at that time.

Pastor Farrell's call helped, but it wasn't enough. I still felt broken. Lisa and I were barely speaking to each other over the phone, and her marketing career was busy enough to keep her traveling across the United States and distracted from focusing on us.

I realized that I wasn't experiencing the same feeling inside of my body that she was as a grieving mother, but I was grieving too. Men and women respond differently to situations – especially the loss of a child – and I just wanted us to be there for each other. I felt like we needed to at least be under the same roof together if we wanted to have a chance of making it. But she didn't see things that way. Lisa hated the idea of being in the same room with me. She didn't just hate me; she hated her job, she hated me, and she hated everything about her life. Even though we agreed to get therapy and go to counseling together, it was clear that she did not want to be married to me anymore.

As the weeks went by, I slowly became angrier and angrier... at Lisa. Until one conversation with a former co-worker changed everything.

Remember in chapter 12 when I mentioned how important it was to talk to positive people? Remember when I said that, "One conversation with the right person at the right time can completely change how you see everything."

One of my former colleagues named Kara Nichols tried to get me to understand just how tough it is for women who experience depression. After years of selling pharmaceutical products, Kara was well-versed in the effects that unbalanced chemical levels in the brain can have on a woman.

She looked at me and said, "Morris, your wife is not herself right now. She is in the middle of a storm right now and you can't take any of this personally. Your wife still loves you Morris – you need to believe that. Just give her enough time to get through and everything will be okay."

I was still angry.

I said, "Yeah, I understand all of that. I understand that she might be depressed, but why is she taking it all out on me by leaving me alone? Why can't we fight this together? And why are we headed for a divorce?"

Kara said, "If you don't want that to happen, if you don't want to lose your marriage, then you have to understand the most important thing in a marriage. I have been married for a while and I can tell you that every marriage has challenges. And sometimes when you go through challenges in a marriage, you have to be willing to fight for your marriage when the other person isn't able to fight. *You have to do the fighting for both of you.* Morris, don't give up on your wife - because she isn't able to fight for herself right now, so you have to do the fighting for her."

As soon as she said that, the Rocky music started playing in my head and my whole perspective changed.

Kara was right and I felt like an idiot.

I couldn't believe that I had been so selfish. I couldn't believe that it had taken another woman to get me to understand that my wife was down and out, injured on the sidelines and unable to fight, and she needed me to fight for her. I was already a fighter because I had to fight throughout my entire life, and I was not ready to let anyone, or anything, take my marriage from me.

PUTTING YOUR "FIGHT PLAN" TOGETHER

That phone call from Pastor Farrell, and the message that Kara shared with me, made me want to fight for my marriage again. So I started fighting.

When you're trying to get focused and clear on what you want – especially during tough times in your life – it's important to stay away from people who will discourage you. Instead, you need to spend as much time as possible with people who will reinforce the correct mindset that you need to have.

I knew that I had to be intentional about reminding myself of how good life really is, so I made frequent trips back to West Virginia to see Dorothy Jean Cosby – my Aunt Dot.

My Aunt Dot always seemed to have the best advice. She was a woman of faith and her faith never wavered.

When I went back to see her during my separation from Lisa Aunt Dot said, "Hey Morris, do you remember the time when you were upset after your grandmother Katherine told you all of those things about your parents?"

I said, "Yes Aunt Dot, I remember."

She said, "Do you remember what I told you to do?"

"Yes Aunt Dot, I remember."

When I was 17 years old, I was upset after finding out how my parents had lived their lives in New York City and I was worried about repeating the same cycles in my family and making the same mistakes that they had made. During that time, my Aunt Dot reminded me that God doesn't make any mistakes. She also said that my parents had a chance to live their lives, and I had to make a choice about how I wanted to live mine.

"Morris, God also knew those babies before he put them in Lisa's belly. Those babies are in Heaven now, and they are not in any pain, and they are just fine. And you know what? You and Lisa will be just fine too, so you need to take your butt home and you wait for your wife to come back, and you give her as much time as she needs."

Aunt Dot always knew exactly what to say when I needed to hear it.

Before I left her house, she said, "I was there on the day you got married, and I believed what Robert Bryan said about your family being world changers one day. The question is, *do you believe it?* If you do, don't you let anything or anyone take that away from you."

I left my aunt Dot's house feeling like I had everything that I needed to help me get better. Aunt Dot was right. I knew better and I needed to act like I knew better. She reminded me of what my true role is as a husband: *to die for my wife if I had to, just like Christ did for us.*

~ ~ ~ ~ ~

Eventually, my appetite came back and I was actually able to eat something again. I started to get my focus and my energy back, but I still missed Lisa. As time went by, I continued to come home to an empty house every day.

My dad Chuck was worried about me, and he called me from prison as often as he could to check up on me. He knew that I was hurting, and it crushed him that he couldn't be there for me.

One evening as I sat in the house, I heard a car pull up outside.

When I walked downstairs to open up the door, there she was. My wife Lisa was standing right there.

I just starred at her at first - I couldn't believe she came back.

We had been separated for two months and I wasn't sure how to respond.

We both just stood in the doorway for a few moments.

I thought to myself, "Maybe she's just here to get some more clothes or something, or maybe she didn't expect me to be home right now."

But I was wrong.

Standing in the doorway, Lisa looked at me and said, "I miss my husband. I just really miss my husband."

As Lisa and I stood there in the doorway, we hugged each other and I didn't ever want to let her go ever again. After we walked into the house, we sat down at the table to talk, and Lisa began to tell me how rough the past weeks had been for her and that she was crushed after losing our children.

FAITH, FAMILY, FOCUS, FIGHT

As Lisa and I began to put our relationship together again, it was clear to see that things between us had changed.

One of the biggest changes during that time was her faith. Lisa was mad at God for taking her babies away. She told me that if we were going to work on putting our marriage back together again, I had to understand that she may never have faith again, and I needed to be okay with that if I wanted to love her for who she really was.

At the time, I was okay with that because like Kara Nichols said, "My wife needed me to fight for her because she couldn't fight for herself."

As Lisa and I continued to rebuild our marriage, I never lost sight of my main role as her husband – to love her, support her, and to keep faith in God as the top priority in our family at all times. But I had no idea how to get a her to embrace something that she had already convinced herself was bad. She was still hurting over the loss of our kids. Nevertheless, I was still adamant about positioning our family to grow our faith any way that we could.

During the Christmas season that year, we were leaving town to visit family and we wanted to go to church for a Christmas celebration before we left town. Our schedule did not allow us to go to service at our home church, Grace Covenant.

Elevation Church was a new church in our area that seemed to be getting much attention and many people seemed to really enjoy it, so we looked up the schedule for their Christmas worship experiences and found a time slot that would fit our travel schedule.

When we attended our first worship experience at Elevation, something happened to my wife. A light was turned on and a flip was switched. It was obvious that she had a very positive experience at Elevation. Their music was upbeat, the energy was high, and Pastor Steven Furtick delivered a powerful, inspiring message. I had heard that he was one of the fastest growing pastors in the world, and after seeing him speak *I understood why.*

Over the course of the next year, Lisa and I continued to put the pieces of our marriage back together. We continued going to Grace Covenant, our home church, but we also attended Elevation when we could.

When we attended Elevation's *Code Orange Revival* series, I saw how positive my wife's response was to the type of worship at Elevation and we made the decision to choose Elevation as our permanent home church.

Elevation was in its *Banner Year* campaign to grow the church that year, and Lisa and I had a conversation in our car that changed the direction of our family.

We were so thankful for the change that had happened in our lives and in our marriage over the past year after attending Elevation that we wanted to invest in everything that the church was doing. On the way to church just a week before Christmas, Lisa and I discussed how much we wanted to give to help Elevation expand it's reach, and the idea of investing in the future church that our kids would go to one day was really exciting.

As we drove in the car, we discussed a separate savings account that Lisa and I had for my dad, Chuck. We were saving money to hire a top lawyer that could help us fight my father's case and finally free him from the prison he'd been in for nearly 17 years.

We had thousands of dollars in the account that we had created for him. I looked at Lisa in the car as we drove to church that day and she asked me, *"So how much do you think we should give today."*

I said, "I have prayed and thought a lot about this. I think we have a big chance to grow our faith here. I think we should give money from the account that we saved for my dad's lawyer fees."

She said, "Okay, how much were you thinking?"

I said, "All of it. We should give all of it to the church."

Lisa just looked at me.

Considering how the past year had gone for us, I wasn't too sure where her faith was.

I had no idea how she would respond, but she still reached for the ink pen. Then I handed her the checkbook because I wanted HER to write the check. I wanted her to use her own hands to write the check because I felt like it was important for her to do that to activate her faith.

Sometimes when we participate and we do something ourselves, it connects our hearts, our minds, and our spirits in a powerful way - that's why I wanted her to write the check.

Lisa wrote the check and we cleared out the account. At the church that day, when we dropped the check in the basket, I had three very specific things that were on my heart that I wanted to ask God for. First, I wanted my wife to commit to having a relationship with God. Second, I asked for God to free my father from prison. And third, I asked God to give us another child.

FAITH, FAMILY, FOCUS, FIGHT

The love of money always has been the root of all evil, and it keeps many people from experiencing the best in their lives. I have never had a problem with making money, and I have never had a problem with giving money away, because I truly do believe that the more you give, the more good things will come back to you.

The following week – exactly one week after we wrote that check to give to our church – at the end of the worship experience at Elevation church, I watched my wife Lisa stand up and accept Jesus Christ as her personal savior!

It was the most emotional thing I have ever witnessed in my entire life.

As I looked beside me, my boy Nick and his dad Steve were also standing beside me - both of them got saved with Lisa at the same time. When Pastor Joel Delph jumped down off of the stage to hug us, we just circled up right there as we celebrated!

As we prepared to head to West Virginia for Christmas the next day, we got a phone call that my aunt Dot wasn't feeling very well. I asked Lisa if she would be okay if we changed our Christmas plans that year. I had a bad feeling about Aunt Dot's health and I wasn't too sure if she would make it to see another Christmas. So Lisa and I went to stay with Aunt Dot so that we could wake up with her in her home on Christmas morning.

As Aunt Dot opened her Christmas gifts that we had brought for her, I said, "Aunt Dot, Lisa and I have a very special gift for you today."

She said, "You do?"

I said, "Yep, and you are going to love it. Can you guess what it is?"

As she looked down at Lisa's belly, she said, "I bet I can take a guess what it is - I know exactly what it is. Is it what I think it is?"

I said, "No Aunt Dot, we are *NOT* pregnant yet."

She said, "What do you mean yet?"

On the way up to visit Aunt Dot for Christmas, as Lisa and I drove in the car, Lisa said something that shocked me. As we discussed Aunt Dot's health, we both realized that Aunt Dot wasn't doing too well and that she wasn't going to be around forever. Aunt Dot meant a lot to both of us and we were very close with her. As we drove in the car, my wife Lisa decided to give my Aunt Dot the best Christmas gift that a person could give.

As we drove in the car, Lisa said to me, "I have a great gift idea for Aunt Dot.

"You do? What type of gift are you thinking about getting her?"

"I'm not thinking about a gift that we can *GET* her. I have an idea for a gift that we can *GIVE* her."

"Really? What is it?"

~ ~ ~ ~ ~

The following Christmas morning as we opened up gifts, Aunt Dot tried her best to guess what the gift was. After much guessing and anticipation, we decided to *give Aunt Dot her gift* .

Lisa said, "Aunt Dot you were right, we are not pregnant – yet. But Morris and I both feel like we are going to be blessed with a baby girl by next Christmas and when she comes, we want you to know that we are going to name our first daughter Dorothy Jean Morrison, in honor of you."

Aunt Dot immediately began to cry. We all did.

I said, "Aunt Dot, you know what this means don't you? You have to take care of yourself so that you can meet your namesake when she comes into this world. Okay Aunt Dot?"

As Aunt Dot cried, she said, "That sounds good to me!"

I said, "Aunt Dot, don't you play with me now! You need to do what your doctor says so that you can stay healthy, because we're going to have a daughter one day and you have to be there to meet her, okay?"

Aunt Dot said, "Okay Morris, okay! Now I need to you to call Little Caesars to see if they're open. I have a craving for some pizza!"

I said, "Aunt Dot it's Christmas, we aren't buying you any pizza to eat on Christmas Day." When I said that, she just gave me her usual *Aunt Dot look*, and I just smiled as I took out my cell phone to do exactly what she told me to do - even though I knew that they were closed on Christmas.

Chapter

Ready To DREAM

Two months after spending Christmas with Aunt Dot, we received a phone call that we had been expecting for a long time. We were informed that she had only had a few more days left to live.

When Lisa and I got into the car to drive to West Virginia, we knew that we would be saying goodbye to her.

As soon as we walked into Aunt Dot's hospital room, she was full of energy. It wasn't because we arrived; Aunt Dot was just always full of energy. She was singing and praising and having a great time. After spending the evening with her, before everyone else left, Aunt Dot motioned for my wife Lisa to come over to stand near the side of her bed.

Aunt Dot reached up and hugged Lisa and then she used both of her hands to hold Lisa's face really close to hers. As she held Lisa face and looked into her eyes, Aunt Dot said, "Lisa I just love looking into your eyes. You have the prettiest eyes Lisa."

We knew that Aunt Dot didn't have very long to live, and we all began to tear up. As she continued to hold Lisa's face, Aunt Dot looked into her eyes and said, "Lisa, I just want you to know that she's coming."

Lisa said, "She who?"

"My namesake, that's who. My namesake is coming into this world," Aunt Dot said, as she touched Lisa's belly as if she were already pregnant. Lisa immediately looked up at me. She was wondering what my Aunt Dot was talking about.

Aunt Dot said, "Yep, baby Dorothy Jean Morrison is on her way and you better get ready because she is going to be just like me. She is going to be a handful to deal with, so y'all better be ready!"

Lisa just smiled as Aunt Dot kept her hands on Lisa's stomach.

I planned on staying in the hospital room with Aunt Dot that night. As family members began to leave her room to go home, I walked Lisa downstairs to the car.

As soon as we got out of Aunt Dot's room, Lisa said, "Aunt Dot seems to think that we are pregnant!"

I said, "Who knows. They say that people can see all sorts of things just before they transition to the other side."

PROMISES FULFULLED

Aunt Dot passed away two days later. At her funeral, I was surrounded by Andy Johnson, Germaine Johnson, Josh Cope, and many other friends and family members.

After Aunt Dot's graveside service, I stood there with my boys after everyone else walked to the cars. I looked over to the right and I realized that just a few feet away from Aunt Dot's grave was her sister's grave – my grandmother Gwendolyn. I was glad that I had my boys standing there beside me that day, because saying goodbye to Aunt Dot was tough for me, and looking up and seeing Grandma's grave close to hers made it even tougher.

As I looked over at my grandmother Gwendolyn's grave, I started to think about my dad Chuck. I was going to have to do something that I hated to do – tell him over the phone that we had lost another family member.

When my dad called me the next day, I was nervous about telling him because I didn't want to hurt him. But I didn't have to tell him because he had already heard the news while he was in prison.

I wasn't sure how my dad was going to handle hearing about Aunt Dot's death because we had lost many of our family members while my dad was away in prison, and Aunt Dot was someone that he really looked forward to seeing again if he ever got out. He had already been in prison for almost 18 years for a crime he insisted he didn't commit, and every time a person died in our family, my dad's prison sentence took an even harder toll on him.

After speaking to him about Aunt Dot, I could tell that he wasn't as hurt by the news as I thought he would be - which was odd to me. In the middle of our conversation, he interrupted me and said, "Morris, I have some good news."

Now listen, just in case you have never experienced what it's like to have a family member locked up in prison, you need to know this – whenever someone in prison says to you over the phone, *"I have some good news,"* it usually only means one thing. He confirmed it when he said, "I got a letter from my lawyer today." Then he paused for a minute.

I said, "Okay… are you going to tell me what this letter said?"

He said, "Morris, I think we did it. I think we just had a major breakthrough in my case. I think that Judge Janes is finally going to give me a reconsideration hearing."

Immediately we both started screaming and cheering on the phone. Lisa was standing right beside me and she said, "What? What? Tell me what's going on." I shared the news with Lisa and she and I high-five-ed each other.

After years of fighting the legal system, and after years of trying to get my dad a new trial, we had finally gotten the breakthrough that we had been praying for. If successful, there was a chance that my dad could get his 96 year prison sentence overturned and he could be set free!

We were all excited and nervous at the same time. Even though we were happy at the chance for my dad to come home, we were equally nervous about his ability to transition back into society because 18 years is a long time for a person to be locked up. We also knew that if my dad was released from prison, he would have to live with us because he had nowhere else to go.

While we continued to work with my father's attorney throughout the legal process, something else happened that we were not expecting.

WAS I REALLY DREAMING?

My wife Lisa had recently taken a new job with Chobani Greek Yogurt in its shopper marketing department. Her career was going very well and my company was just starting to get on its feet. Both of us traveled a lot with our jobs, and when we weren't traveling for work, we enjoyed our time together.

I woke up on a Saturday morning in late March with a big smile on my face. I looked at Lisa and I said, "I know that this is going to sound crazy, but you will never believe what I dreamed about last night."

She said, "With you it's hard to tell, anything is possible."

I said, "Lisa I had a dream that I met our daughter – Dorothy Jean.

"What?"

"Yes, she was about two years old and I was walking with her and holding her hand. As we walked together, she kept looking up at me saying, *'Daddy, Daddy, Daddy'* and the dream seemed so real. Can you believe that?"

Lisa looked at me with a slight smile. Although she never really said it to me directly, she was used to hearing about my big ideas all of the time, and she let it go in one ear and out of the other. Even though she didn't say so, I think that the thought of me meeting our future daughter was little too far-fetched for her to even pay attention to. Instead, she just smiled as she looked at me and said, "Okay, that sounds nice honey. Um, anyway... what do you want to eat for breakfast?" And that was that.

On the following Friday night, almost one week after having that dream, we found out that we were pregnant! Now I am not normally the type of husband or person who gets pleasure from being able to say, "I told you so," but I couldn't help saying it to Lisa.

As we celebrated the joy of knowing that we were pregnant, we realized that Aunt Dot was right – the little girl that we were going to name after her was coming into this world.

Baby Dorothy Jean Morrison was on her way. When we first got pregnant, many people asked us if we were going to find out whether we were having a baby boy or a baby girl. Every time someone asked me that, I confidently said, "Nope, we don't have to. Ever since we told Aunt Dot that we wanted to honor her name with this gift, we knew that we were having a baby girl!"

A couple of months later, we finally had the chance to find out if we were *actually* having a boy or a girl. When the doctor gave us the envelope with the answer inside of it, neither one of us took a peek inside. We didn't even break the seal of the envelope. We wanted to share the announcement of little Ms. Dorothy Jean Morrison by having a *gender reveal party* on Lake Norman with many of our closest friends and family.

We took the envelope that our doctor had given us to Sweet Cakes Bakery in Lake Norman. Sweet Cakes was our favorite local cupcake place and they made 80 cupcakes for our party guests. Inside one very large, special cupcake that they had made for Lisa and me to share, they put pink or blue icing on the inside to reveal the gender of the baby.

Bobby and Janet Faulk were clients that I worked with at Keller Williams Realty.. After I began to work with Keller Williams, they quickly became extended family members for us in North Carolina. Bobby and Janet hosted our gender reveal party at their beautiful home in Lake Norman.

As we gathered with our family and friends on that beautiful sunny day in May, many people at the party showed up wearing colors that represented team pink or team blue, depending on what that person thought the sex of our baby was going to be.

As I took a moment to glance at the amazing friends and family members surrounding us, I looked beyond the people to the lake in the background, and the waters of Lake Norman never looked more beautiful.

As we got closer to the big moment, Lisa and I were both anxious to find out what we were having, even though we were already fully convinced that Dorothy Jean – or *"Baby Dori"* as we planned on calling her – was on her way.

As everyone gathered around to cheer us on, Lisa and I both held one hand on each side of the cupcake. As we got into position for the big moment, my boy Reggie yelled out, *"Hey Morris, what if it's a boy? What are you going to name him then?"*

I paused for a moment to think about his question. Then I said, "Reggie, if we have a boy, if we have a boy, then his name will be… his name will be… *Dorothy Jean!"*

And everyone laughed.

As the crowd began the countdown to the big moment, Lisa and I both closed our eyes as we prepared to bite into the cupcake. As soon as we bit into it, we looked down with anticipation and that's when we saw it – we were both amazed and overjoyed when we saw the *PINK* icing oozing out of the side of the cupcake! Then we screamed out, "It's a girl, Baby Dorothy Jean Morrison is on her way!"

And then the crowd went wild (okay, maybe they didn't exactly go wild, but they sure did cheer loud, and deep inside of me, my heart was going wild!) and after that moment, our lives would never be the same.

#TheresAlwaysAGirl

FAITH, FAMILY, FOCUS, FIGHT

As a motivational speaker, I've been blessed with the opportunity to speak in a lot of places. I enjoy what I do so much that sometimes I feel like I am dreaming. Sometimes when I finish speaking to a group, I get the chance to do a live question and answer session with the entire audience. Doing Q&A with audience members is fun, because it's a chance for me to really connect well with audience members after I deliver a speech.

I don't always get to do Q&A sessions, but when I do, it's a really special experience for me because I get to know what people are really thinking and how they really feel in the moment's after my speech.

One of the best questions that anyone had ever asked me kind of sounded like this: "Hey Morris, I have a question. You get to speak at a lot of different places, but is there any speech that stands out to you the most? Where was your favorite speech, and why?"

I automatically knew what was in my heart.

~ ~ ~ ~ ~

As Lisa and I planned for the arrival of Baby Dori, we continued to fight for my Dad's release from prison. Every time we made any type of progress in his case, new problems would come up. After my dad was promised the opportunity for a reconsideration hearing, his heart was crushed once again when he found out that the doors of justice were closed on him once again. At that moment, my dad lost all hope and it was a tough time for all of us.

During that time period, I got an unexpected phone call from the state of West Virginia. They wanted to hire me for a state-level speaking engagement at the state's largest maximum security prison.

Because I have spent much of my life visiting jails and prisons, I have developed a passion for helping inmates. I believe in the power of second chances, and I also believe that some of the brightest people in the world are locked up in prison simply because they made mistakes. So when I agreed to a deal with the state of West Virginia that would allow me to speak at their prison system, I was excited.

Once I got there, I was completely blown away by the level of attentiveness of the inmates. They were all leaning forward in their seats and taking notes when I spoke because they were hungry and they were engaged. I have never had a better speaking engagement in my life, especially when you consider that sitting in front of me were mass-murderers, rapists, drug dealers, and many of what our society considers to be the worst of the worst.

So during the Q&A session when the guy asked me what my all-time favorite speech was, I didn't hesitate to tell him about the speech that I was able to give at the Mount Olive Correctional Center in West Virginia.

Oh yeah, there's one more tiny detail that I forgot to mention. Guess who else was sitting in the front row taking notes that day... Yep, you guessed it – none other than my dad Chuck.

My dad missed out on most of my life. But all of the hurt and pain that I had experienced from not having a dad sitting in the bleachers at my ball games instantly went away.

Even though I had visited with my dad for many years in that prison, this trip was different. My dad had a chance to see me perform as a professional speaker, and it was the greatest feeling in the world.

After I finished speaking, my dad and I were both very emotional. Then, once I arrived back at my home in North Carolina later than evening, my dad called me on the phone. He told me that nobody could stop talking about our story and the life that we had built together.

After that, he was the top dog in the prison – at least for a day or two – and I have never heard my dad sound happier in my life.

Even though we celebrated the chance to be together during my speech, I could tell that my dad's spirit was still broken. The chance of him ever getting out of prison was slowly fading away. He wanted to be home to see the birth of his granddaughter and he wanted to have his life back. Instead, the doors of justice continued to close around him and eventually, a large part of him just gave up.

PREPARING FOR FATHERHOOD

Our doctor asked me, "Morris, when did you say your birthday was again?"

I said, "December 4th."

"Didn't you say that your birthday has been a pretty tough day for you?"

I said, "Yeah, that's the day that my dad Chuck was falsely accused of a crime that he didn't commit and he was given almost 100 years in prison. So yes, my birthdays have been pretty rough since then."

He said, "Well, you better get ready, because your birthday is about to get a lot better. It looks like you may be getting the best present of your life on your birthday this year. Your daughter's due date is December 4th!"

I said, "What? Stop playing with me, stop lying."

"Nope, I am 100% serious with you right now. Just take a look at the screen at the expected delivery date on the bottom."

He was right, I saw it with my own eyes. Lisa and I told Aunt Dot the year before at Christmas that we expected to have a baby girl by next Christmas, but I didn't imagine in a million years that she would come on my birthday!

When we left the office, Lisa and I were both excited. We were very busy preparing for Baby Dori to arrive, even though it was a few months away.

As we planned, I was also busy celebrating the signing of one of my largest clients to date – Microsoft. When Rod Combs hired me to work with their team at an event in Dallas, I was excited beyond belief.

I left the Microsoft event in Dallas to head to Pennsylvania for one more speaking appearance before I headed back home to be with my very pregnant and beautiful wife in North Carolina.

While in Pennsylvania, as I headed to Nemacolin Resort to meet Steve and Trina Cutright for dinner, I was injured in a car accident when a girl hit me from behind as she was texting and driving.

Police estimated her speed to be nearly 65 miles per hour at the moment of impact. She hit me so hard that her car did not come to stop until it was almost 800 feet down the road. Fortunately, just before she hit me, I saw her car approaching very fast behind me when I looked into my rearview mirror. Even though I didn't have enough time to get out of her way, I was able to push myself back against my seat as hard as I could to brace for the impact.

The doctors said that if I hadn't done that, there was a good chance that the whiplash would have broken my neck instantly because of how fast she was traveling.

As I laid there in a bed at Ruby Memorial Hospital after my accident, I realized that I was in the same hospital where I had said goodbye to my Grandmother Gwendolyn. I couldn't help but think about how, if I would have been killed in that accident, I would have never had the chance to fulfill many of the promises that I made to her.

When I thought about how close I had come to never having the opportunity to see baby Dorothy Jean being born, it scared me to death. I was even scared to call my wife Lisa to tell her that I was in an accident, because I didn't want to worry her or send her into premature labor. Unfortunately, social media forced me to inform her, because as soon as they wheeled me into the hospital, people recognized who I was and I worried about someone posting something about my accident on social media before I had a chance to tell my wife Lisa about it. I had to be proactive about the situation, so I posted a photo on social media of me holding a *thumbs up signal* to let my friends and family know that I was alright. It always seemed to work for football players on TV so I decided to give it a shot!

After they released me from the hospital, I realized that I still had a speaking engagement the next day for some kids at a local school, and I didn't want to miss it. Part of me knew that I needed to rest and take it easy, but a larger part of me did not want to miss out on the opportunity to talk to the kids about the dangers of texting and driving. When I began to hear from the doctors about how many accidents they were seeing and how many kids were dying because of texting and driving, I decided to go and do the speech the next day anyway.

Physically, I was in pain and I could barely walk. Even though I had to limp around stage, I don't think I have ever delivered a more passionate message in my life.

Once I left my speech, I knew that I was not well enough to make the six hour drive back to North Carolina. Thankfully, a friend named Brandon Birkshire was willing to drive me all the way home – what a great guy!

When I walked through the door, Lisa and I embraced. Neither of us needed to say a word. As I hugged and kissed my wife, I got down on one knee to hug and kiss Lisa's beautiful belly to say hello to Baby Dori.

The thought that I could have potentially never walked through that door again was something that was on both of our minds as we embraced. Thankfully, neither one of us ever had to experience that.

Chapter

Ready To DANCE

If there's one thing that I've learned about strong, independent women, it's that sometimes they have to do things their own way. My daughter Dorothy Jean Morrison would be no exception.

Although I was very excited about the idea of my daughter being born on my birthday, Baby Dori had other plans.

Lisa began to struggle towards the end of her pregnancy. When the doctor told us during the month of October that we would be giving birth to a premature baby due to complications, we both became concerned. All of a sudden we found ourselves worried that we were going to end up losing another child. But on October 21st, 2013, we gave birth to a healthy, beautiful baby girl.

When Baby Dori came into this world she barely weighed three pounds. Even though we knew that she would have to stay in the NICU for a long time before we could take her home, the toughest part about the whole experience was leaving the hospital and going home without our baby after she was born.

If you have never experienced the passion and dedication of a NICU nurse, then you are truly missing out on one of the greatest, most committed professionals in the world. On one hand, I hope that you NEVER need the help of a NICU nurse, but on the other hand, if you do ever need a NICU nurse, it will change your life because NICU nurses are amazing.

After a month of being in the hospital, Baby Dori still only weighed four 4 pounds, but they finally allowed us to take her home. A few of the NICU nurses that took care of Dori became so attached to her that after she left, they began to show up at our house to help with feedings and diaper changes just to see her. That's how dedicated and committed they are to what they do. One of the nurses happened to be retiring at the same time, so we hired her as our full-time nanny. *Nana Sheila* instantly become a part of our family.

A TOUGH PHONE CONVERSATION

My dad Chuck was excited about the opportunity to become a grandfather. He was not excited about the fact that he was stuck in prison without the chance to see his grandchild being born. Baby Dori came into the world via an emergency C-section, and we did not have time to tell my dad that she was coming. When he happened to call after she was born, he had no idea that we would be telling him over the phone that he was a grandfather. Although my dad was excited to hear about Baby Dori's birth, I could tell that he was still very sad because he couldn't be there.

After Baby Dori was born we found out that the doors of justice had opened up once again for my father. Judge David Janes from Fairmont, West Virginia, decided to give our family the one thing we had been fighting to achieve for nearly 20 years – a chance for my father's prison sentence to be reconsidered in a court of law. Our family was cautious not to get too excited about the chance of him coming home though, because we had already experienced that emotional roller coaster before.

THE PROMISE OF HOPE

My dad's case was a focus of injustice in West Virginia and it garnered interest from many people. Dr. Martin Luther King Jr. once said, *"Injustice anywhere is a threat to justice everywhere,"* and many people quoted that statement when they spoke about my father's case. As a result, the case never died down in the community or in the media.

Eddie White, one of *The Real Heroes* that I spoke about in chapter 4, remained focused on and committed to my father's release from prison. And he wasn't the only one – many other people were too. One journalist in particular, Misty Poe of the *Times West Virginian* newspaper, made it part of her personal mission to highlight the status of my father's case in many of her articles. As a result, she single-handedly ensured that we never lost momentum with my dad's case in the hearts and minds of readers throughout the West Virginia community.

Finally, years of hard work from many courageous people paid off. It was official – Judge David Janes officially granted my father the chance to have a reconsideration hearing, set for April 22, 2014, and we could not have been more excited.

On the day of my father's hearing, I drove from North Carolina to showed up in Fairmont, West Virginia, along with several other family members and friends. When I arrived at the courthouse, the scene was all too familiar for me. As a child, I had sat at my grandmother Gwendolyn's side at that same courthouse during the trials of other family members before they were sent to jail. As I walked up to the 3rd floor where the hearing was being held, I was not prepared for what I was about to see. Once I got to the top of the stairs, I was greeted by a host of friends and family members, many of whom drove hours to be there from different states just to support our family.

During my father's hearing, there were many legal terms used by the prosecution and the defense teams. Most of us in the audience had absolutely *no idea* what was being said. Before we knew it, the judge hit the gavel and the hearing was over. Many of us looked around at each other, clueless as to what the verdict was. We thought to ourselves, *"What did the judge just say? Is Chuck free to go home? Is he coming home with us today? Is he going back to prison? What's going on?"* We had no idea what had just happened. My father's attorney took me out into the hallway to speak with me one-on-one and explain to me what had to happen next. The judge decided to give my father the opportunity that we had been fighting for 20 years – the chance to be a free man. But my dad wasn't able to be released just yet.

The judicial process had to take its course and nothing was guaranteed. Much paperwork had to be filed before my dad could be officially released.

As we all waited outside of the courthouse doors, the police officers walked my father past everyone in shackles, chains, and a prison-issued orange jumpsuit.

As they walked him past all of us standing in the hallway, it was the first time many people had seen him since he had been taken away 20 years before that. Most of the people at his hearing that day had never even met Chuck before, so that was the first time they had ever seen him with their own eyes. Many of them came because they were familiar with his story because of constant news coverage of his case over the years. Many of them simply showed up to show their love and support for a member of their own community who got a raw deal in life. Although many of us were disappointed that my father was not given the opportunity to come home with us that day, one fact still remains – that day went down in history as the day we finally made progress on something that took us 20 years to fight.

To us, it was a victory.

We were happy for my dad, but we still had to wait for the next steps of the judicial process to be completed. But once all of the official paperwork was filed, my dad would finally have the chance to go home to his family. The only problem was, we had no idea just how long that process would take.

FAITH, FAMILY, FOCUS, FIGHT

We had to wait much longer than we expected, *about seven months to be exact*. Eventually, we found out that November 19th would be the official release date for my dad! That would be the day that I could officially show up and wait outside of the prison gates to take my father home from prison – a scene that I'd been dreaming about since I was a teenager. Although the process took much longer than we had anticipated, we benefited from the additional time. The extra time gave Lisa and me an opportunity to prepare for my father's release from prison – the day that he would come to live with us in North Carolina.

Lisa and I were preparing for this day together for over ten years. Throughout that entire time period, we never had a chance to park our cars in our garage because we used that space to store items that my father was going to need when he was released from prison. Everything from furniture to silverware – including pillows, clothes and even Pittsburgh Steelers decorations that every real Steelers fan needed – was all waiting for my dad. For years we never knew exactly when he was coming home, but we never gave up hope that *he was coming home* one day; we wanted to be ready to bless him with whatever he needed, whenever he needed it.

It was actually a good thing that the judge didn't release my dad on April 22nd because that gave Lisa and I more time to prepare. We really wanted to honor my father's presence in our home, so we made many changes as we anticipated his arrival. We even purchased a new home to make room for our *growing family*. There is also one more thing that I did to prepare for my dad's return home. I watched one of my favorite movies of all time, *The Shawshank Redemption*. Even though the main character found his glory by escaping to paradise at the end, the movie also showed interesting parallels of other convicts who did not make the transition out of prison very well.

We didn't want my father to end up like old man Mr. Brooks who's mind was institutionalized from being in prison for many years. The truth was, we had no idea what we would be dealing with when my dad came home. We had no idea who he was after all of those years in prison - I mean we thought we knew who he was, but he didn't even know who he was going to be yet. Either way, it was a risk that we were willing to take and we did everything to make sure we were as ready as possible. We met with counselors and transition specialists whose job was to help families like ours prepare for the arrival of formerly incarcerated inmates like my dad.

TRANSITIONS ARE NEVER EASY

I had many emotions inside of me leading up to the day that I met my dad outside of those prison gates to take him home. There were so many suggestions and recommendations given to us by people that wanted to help. One suggestion in particular really caught me off guard.

Wendy Martin, one of the transition counselors that helped our family to prepare for my dad's arrival, was a Godsend to our family. She helped Lisa and me in a major way by preparing us for the reality of what my dad's transition would really be like. During the final days of our preparation, she gave us some great advice about what to do on the day of my dad's release. She said, "Whatever you do, please do not stop at any fast food restaurants to eat on the way home."

At first I had no idea why she suggested that to us. I thought to myself, " *Of course the man is going to want to eat a really good cheeseburger after 20 years,*" so I was confused by her suggestion.

Then she said, "Unless you want to have an accident in your car on the way home, it's best if you just keep driving and don't stop until you get to your house." Apparently people who have been in prison for 20 years are very sensitive when introducing new food into their digestive systems when they first come home – *who would have known?* Lisa and I both realized there were going to be many other little things just like that which we had never considered, and we knew that we were going to have to be intentional about everything that we did if we wanted my dad to transition well. We were thankful that we had the help and support of professionals who were highly trained to coach us on running the plays that would help us win as a family.

We ran a *Go Fund Me* online fundraising campaign to raise money for my father's transition back home, and many incredible people chose to generously support my dad's release. It was amazing to see.

In the final week leading up to my dad's release, I came home after speaking on the road for a few days. I knew that Lisa and I were about to host a guest in our home for a potentially long period, so I scheduled a surprise babysitter to come to our house so that I could take my beautiful wife out to dinner. I thought that I was surprising Lisa, but she was actually surprising me. When I got home, a house full of people jumped out and yelled, "Surprise!" and they scared me half to death. Members of our Elevation Church e-group surprised us by packing our entire living room full of gifts for my dad, including clothes, shoes, and every supply that a guy could want or need.

After seeing the love and support from so many friends around us, I realized that my family had people who would be there to welcome my dad into a loving community. That meant everything to me. That was the first moment when it really hit me – my dad really was... *coming home,* and the doors of justice were NOT going to close on him this time. That was a very emotional night for me.

THE BIG DAY

For years I pictured in my mind the day when I would finally have the chance to pick my father up from prison. But on the evening of November 18, 2014, the night before my dad's release, I could not sleep. As I tried to fall asleep that night, I found that I was more awake than a kid on Christmas Eve. When I finally did fall asleep, I woke up the next morning singing the words to my favorite song by Notorious B.I.G called *Juicy*. I kept singing the lyrics, *"It was all a dream... It was all a dream... It was all a dream."* But I quickly realized that I was NOT dreaming and today really was... *the day*. I was finally living a dream that had begun in my heart as a kid, a dream that I always knew God would bless our family with... a dream that *I never stopped believing*.

On the way to the prison that morning, I made one phone call. As I drove in the car that morning, all I could think about was how long my dad had really been gone. When I thought about how long 20 years was, I thought about how much of my life my dad had missed out on and how many moments we didn't get to share together. He missed out on our high school state championship basketball game, my high school graduation, my basketball senior night in college, and even my college graduation. When I graduated with my master's degree from West Virginia University, I didn't even go to my own graduation ceremony for the College of Business and Economics because I was tired of attending functions without having parents there.

I started to think about all of the blessings that I had in my life during those 20 years and how many people were there to help me in my father's absence. I began to think about all of the heroes I've mentioned throughout this book – all the teachers, coaches, mentors, and others in the community who were there for me when my parents couldn't be. Specifically, I thought about the men who treated me like a son when my dad couldn't be there. I pulled out my phone because I wanted to make one phone call. I wanted to call Michael Belmear.

Michael Belmear had the biggest impact on me during a time in my life that was a make or break time for my future. In my late teenage years as I transitioned to college, Michael was always there for me no matter what I needed, and I never wanted to disappoint him. He was someone who motivated me because I wanted him to be proud of me. For a young man, it's critical to have that type of influence in your life. When I dialed the number to call him, I wasn't sure if he would be available, but I am glad that he was. When I heard his voice on the other end, it took everything inside of me to hold it all together.

Michael knew that it was a big day for me and my family, and he knew how much we had fought over the years to bring my dad home.

I said, "We did it Michael, we really did it... I can't believe it. I can't believe that I am actually about to pull into this parking lot and my dad is going home with me today."

Michael said, "That's right Morris, this day is finally here. You've done a lot of work to make this day possible."

I said, "Michael, my dad was gone for a very long time and as I pull up to this prison to take him home with me, I realize now, more than ever, just how many people God sent into my life to help me while he was gone. Michael, you were there for me during a period in my life when I needed to have a male role model to look up to the most, and I just wanted to say *thank you* for being a father figure to me when I didn't have one."

"Morris, it's been a joy having you in my life also, and I really appreciate this phone call because this is a big day for you. Thank you for thinking to call me."

After we finished speaking, I ended the phone call and realized that I was also about to also end a major chapter of my life to start a new one. When I pulled my car into the parking lot of the prison on that morning, I could not believe that within a few moments my dad would be sitting right next to me in my passenger seat as we drove home.

I had my car cleaned, detailed and prepared for my dad because I wanted everything to be perfect. Before I walked into the prison, I adjusted the passenger seat to make sure that everything was *JUST RIGHT* for him. Then I realized that I had forgotten to bring *the only thing* that he asked me to bring for the car ride home that day – fresh bottles of water. Dad told me that the one thing that he missed the most after 20 years in prison, was clean, fresh, water to drink!

When I got out of the car to walk across the parking lot, I could tell that I was nervous. Once I walked through the doors of the prison and into the waiting area, I couldn't even sit down because I was too excited.

As I waited for him to come out, there was a large part of me that expected the prison warden to walk out and say something like, "*I'm sorry*

Mr. Morrison, but there's been a mistake. Unfortunately we're not able to let your father go home with you today."

I quickly dismissed those negative thoughts and I turned towards the door that he was supposed to walk through, and that's when I saw it - that's when the prison door's began to open, and everything felt like it was one big blur in my mind. Everything seemed like it was in slow motion, just like it is in the movies during big moments.

When my dad walked out in his khaki-colored, prison-issued clothes, the moment was intense. As soon as I saw him, I ran over to hug him. I hugged him the same way I always hugged him – the same way I used to hug him in the mornings when he dropped me off at school when I was a little kid. I guess some things never change.

After we finished hugging and crying, I handed my dad a garment bag that he took into the bathroom with him to change his clothes. The bag contained a brand new pair of dress shoes, designer jeans, and a nice Banana Republic sweater with a button-up shirt to go underneath it. His attire was completed with a cashmere blazer that Buzz Bizzell had given him personally. When my dad walked into that bathroom to change his clothes, he shut the door behind him.

An audience of people began to gather in the waiting room. We were waiting for the big moment – the *big reveal*, the *transformation*.

As I waited with anticipation outside of the door, I knew that a brand new man was about to emerge from the other side when that door opened. I looked over at the prison guard that was on duty that morning and I said, "Hi sir. Excuse me, can you help me for a moment?"

He said, "Sure. How can I help you?"

I looked over at the bags sitting by the door. The two small bags and one stack of books contained all of my father's personal items that he was allowed to take home with him.

Two bags and one stack of books represented 20 years of his life.

I looked at the prison guard and I said, "Sir, would you mind helping us carry these bags?"

"Sure, no problem, anything to help," he said.

There was a reason why I asked him to do that.

As I spoke with the prison guard, we heard the door handle began to move as my dad opened up the door to walk out.

I wish you could've seen him walk out of that bathroom.

I wish you could have been there to see Mr. Charles Raymond Sanders walk out of that bathroom to embrace his new life. When he walked out of that door, he walked out to his own theme music – music that only he could hear.

You should have seen him. He was just as handsome, energetic, confident, and amazing as he was before he was taken out of my life on December 4th, 1994.

I said, "Wow, look at you. You're looking sharp!"

I turned towards the other people in the room and I said, "And many of you wondered where I get my good looks from?"

Then my dad said, "I feel great... this feels great!"

As we began to walk out of the front door of that prison, my dad reached to grab his bags that were sitting on the ground. As he reached for them, I put my hand out in front of his to keep him from grabbing them.

I said, "Hey Dad, don't worry about the bags, this prison guard is going to carry *your* bags for *you.*"

I wish you could've seen the look on my father's face when I said that to him. After he gave me a smile, we walked out of the door... *together!*

There were cameras present that day as they captured my father's exit from prison after nearly 20 years. He was about to take his first step in 20 years as a free man.

When I gave my iPhone to a lady standing near us to take a video, my dad stared at my iPhone with the craziest look on his face.

I said, "Hey Dad, don't worry it's okay. That's what they call an *iPhone.*"

As the cameras followed us to our car for my dad's last exit from the prison grounds, he looked at me and he said, "Hold on for one second, there's one last thing that I have to do."

I said, "What? I figured you'd want to get in this car and leave as fast as possible."

He said, "I can't, I promised my buddies up there I would do something for them first."

My dad walked out to the middle of the parking lot, then he turned around and looked up at the 5th floor where his friends were. They were standing in the windows as they clapped and cheered for my dad. They were so happy for him.

As my dad began to wave goodbye to them, he looked over at me and he said, "I can't believe I'm about to do this, but I made a promise to them that I would, so I can't let them down."

I looked at my dad and said, "Do what? What are you talking about?"

He said, "I promised them that I would do a *happy dance* in the middle of the parking lot before I said goodbye to them."

As soon as he said that, my dad began to move his arms, legs, and his entire body in a manner that genuinely had me concerned. This dude started to dance and break it down right in the middle of the parking lot.

As his son, I was amazed at how fast it took for my dad to embarrass me *already,* and we weren't even out of the parking lot yet. Oh well, I guess that's just what parents do!

PAPPY'S COMING HOME

During the drive home, my father and I had an amazing conversation. As we reflected on his time in prison, we did the same thing that we always did during my visits over the last 20 years. Each time I visited with my father in prison, he gave me an opportunity to share my dreams and my vision with him. But this time it was different. On our car ride home that day, my dad got a chance to wear the other hat. My dad got a chance to share *his vision* for his life, with me. Of course, his vision would not be complete without mentioning the #1 thing he was looking forward to in the next chapter of his life: his opportunity to be a grandfather and finally meet Baby Dori.

I gave my wife Lisa a phone call from inside of the car just before we pulled into our neighborhood to let her know that we were almost home.

As we drove through the neighborhood, my dad looked at me and said, "Wow son, *you live here?*"

I said, "No Dad, *we live here.*"

He said, "Morris, I am so proud of you and I can't believe that I get to share all of this with you."

He put a smile on my face.

When we arrived at the house, instead of pulling into our driveway with the front of my car facing in, I turned the car around in the middle of the street so that I could back up the driveway. I wanted the house to be behind us so that my dad's big surprise wouldn't be ruined. I didn't want him to see Lisa and Baby Dori when they walked out onto the porch.

I got out of my car and I walked around to open up the door for my dad. As soon as his foot stepped out of the car, we both looked down at the ground. When his foot touched the ground, I just stared at his feet for a second. I couldn't' believe that *my dad* was standing in *my driveway*. I could have stood there in that moment forever, and I am sure that my father could have too. But he couldn't, because the best thing in his *new life* was about to happen.

As my dad slowly turned around towards the house, my wife Lisa was standing there on the porch and she was holding a very special package for my father - his grandchild.

After my dad took his first few steps towards the porch, he had to reach out to hold onto the car as he walked because his knees begin to buckle. The *emotional capital* in that moment was powerful. He finally got his balance and made it onto the porch.

When my dad and Baby Dori made eye contact with each other for the first time ever, it was magical. Baby Dori gave my dad the biggest smile that she could, even though she had no idea who he was.

Up until that moment, they had never met each other before, and we did that for a reason. I never gave up hope that my dad would be coming home one day, and I did not want Baby Dori to meet her Pappy in a prison visitation room.

When Lisa placed Baby Dori into my father's arms, I could have died and gone to heaven in that moment and I would've been perfectly fine with that.

FAITH, FAMILY, FOCUS, FIGHT

Ever since I was a little kid, I fought to free my dad from prison and I dreamed about that day a million times.

One week after my dad came home, we celebrated Thanksgiving with family members and we certainly had much to be thankful for.

A week later, when December 4th came – a day that had brought many mixed emotions for 20 years – I finally had a reason to celebrate my birthday again.

Later that month, I have never had more to be thankful for during a Christmas season and as we celebrated the birthday of Jesus Christ, we made sure to remember that Jesus was the real reason for the season. It was a beautiful season in our lives and we were thankful for everything that God had blessed us with.

After the first month of my dad being home, during the New Year's Eve celebration, I thought long and hard about my dreams. Seeing my dad in our home caused me to learn a big lesson about dreaming. I learned that when you fight for something long enough, if you never forget what you're fighting for, and if you never give up, *no matter what*, you just might have a chance to see your dreams unfold right in front of your eyes. The only difference is, when your dreams do come true, your experience is always better than you ever imagined it could be.

We loved having my dad at home with us and we just wanted to love on him and give him everything he wanted, because he deserved it.

We also wanted to give him a few months to just relax and chill with us as a family before he transitioned to the day-to-day responsibilities of life. So we enjoyed the holiday season and entered the New Year together as a family.

One of my friends and fellow board members at the Lowes YMCA, Greg Law, owns a furniture company in the Lake Norman area. Prior to my dad's release, Greg promised me that he would give my dad his first official job offer when he came home – and he made good on his promise.

My dad started working for Sweet Dreams (a furniture company) in February, just a few months after his release from prison. He began to thrive in his new position, and he immediately started to play an important role on the Sweet Dream's *Dream Team*.

Sam's Club also made my dad a job offer. The Sam's Club and Walmart family have continued to include the hiring of ex-offenders as a part of their mission, giving second chances to many individuals to help them transition back into society when they are released from prison.

My dad had two jobs and he worked every day either for Sam's Club or Sweet Dreams, and life could not have been any *sweeter* for him.

Dad even learned how to drive… *again*. I wish you could have seen him sitting inside of my car when I taught him how to drive. When he sat in the driver's seat, he looked at me and said, *"Where do you put the key in at, and how do I turn this thing on? I feel like I am on an episode of the Jetsons cartoon show."*

We had a great time helping my father transition back into the real world.

After six months of him being home with us, we realized that my father's transition was going much better than what most inmates experience.

My father came home to a warm house, a loving family, positive friends, and a strong support system to help him with his transition back into society. Because of that, my dad was given a chance to thrive right away.

Even though I feel very blessed and fortunate to help my dad pursue his new life, my heart still aches. My heart goes out to the many other prisoners who are released from jail with no place to go. Many of them are released and return to the same environments that sent them to prison in the first place.

Almost 60% of prisoners are arrested and sent back to prison within their first year of being released. Almost 70% of prisoners are arrested within the first three years of being released. And almost 80% of prisoners are arrested and sent back to prison within five years of being released.

Research points to the #1 area that influences whether a person will eventually go back to prison or not: their environment.

My dad has a better chance of *staying free* and never being arrested again than 99% of other inmates that are released from prison, simply because of the environment that he now lives in.

I LOVE TO EAT FISH

A lot of people continued to ask us how long my dad would live with Lisa and me before he moved into his own apartment, and we weren't sure about what that answer should be. We went into the situation without having any expectations. Our main goal was to make sure that my dad transitioned successfully and that his mindset and focus were healthy enough to transition out onto his own.

About six months after his release, my dad was doing really great and his transition was going smoothly. Once he purchased his own vehicle, he slowly began to gain more and more independence. Eventually we realized that there was nothing else that he really needed to do. He was ready to move forward on his own.

When he started to search for an apartment to move into, Lisa and I felt like we were about to send our oldest child off to college or something. We were excited to see him take such a big step, because we knew that having his own place would be a big accomplishment for him. We were also happy to have our house back to ourselves (no offense Dad).

I once heard someone say, *"Fish and family have the same thing in common, they both begin to smell after three days!"* Well, eventually it's easy to get tired of another adult when they stay under the same roof as you for a long period of time - no matter how much you miss them when they're gone.

It's nothing personal, that's just a fact of life.

When my dad finally moved into his own apartment on August 1st, nine months after being released from prison, it was a big day for all of us.

We finally got all of my father's furniture out of the storage unit and moved into his apartment and it was a very surreal moment for all of us.

After moving all weekend long, we finally got everything in place. On Sunday night when we took the last box of food to his house, I stood in the doorway of his apartment before I left. He met me at the door to give me a goodbye hug and placed his hands on my shoulders as he said, "Morris I cannot begin to thank you enough for what you and Lisa have done for me."

I said, "Dad, you did the same thing for me... *remember?*"

He said, "What?"

I reminded him that when Grandma Gwendolyn was hospitalized at Johns Hopkins and I didn't have any place to go, he was the one who took care of me.

I said, "Dad, I have waited for this day for a long time. I have been waiting for a chance to return the favor and do what you did for me."

He said, "Well, I was just doing what anyone else would've done."

I said, "No Dad, not just anyone. It was you. You did that for me – no one else."

As I walked out of the door to leave my dad at his apartment, I realized something – my dad was about to sleep alone...by himself without anyone else around for the first time in over 20 years.

I turned to him and said, "You know Dad, we are just right down the street if you need anything."

As I said that to him, I wish you could've seen the big smile that he had on his face as he took a long glance at his new apartment.

Then he said, "Morris, do you have any idea how long I've been waiting to sleep by myself again! Trust me, I'm okay son. I think I've got it from here!"

"Look at you Dad. I wish you could see the smile on your face right now. I can tell that you are really happy right now. This must feel really good for you."

He said, "Man, you have no idea how long I've waited for this. I have waited many, many years to be free and to finally get my life back."

"Dad I'm happy for you. And I can tell that you're happy right now, and I can tell that you're happy to have your own place to call home again."

"Son you have no idea how happy I am to have my own place."

I said, "It's good to have a house that's yours and a place that belongs to you, huh?"

Dad said, "Yep!"

As I began to walk out the door and down the sidewalk, I said, "Good, that means you won't take any offense to how excited I am to drive down the street to go back to *my house* – a house that we haven't had alone to ourselves in almost nine months, right?"

As he began to close the front door to *his new home*, with a big smile on his face, he looked around at his new apartment, then he smiled again as he looked at me and said, "Nope, I don't take any offense to it at all because I just as excited as you are! Goodnight son, I love you."

Chapter

19

Building Your DREAM

When I was in college, I worked at a telemarketing company to make some extra cash. Kenny Jones is a friend of mine who also worked there with me. On the way home from work one day, as Kenny and I were driving down the road together, one of the front wheels on my car came off.

Thankfully, it happened just before my car merged onto the interstate.

When the front side of my car crashed down onto the ground, Kenny and I both screamed out loud because we had no idea what was going on.

I said, "Kenny, what was that? Did we hit something? Did you see anything?"

He said, "I'm not sure if we hit something or not, but I think that's your front wheel that I see rolling down the road!"

Kenny was right, that was my front wheel rolling down the road!

Thankfully, we were okay.

Kenny and I had to use his mother's car to get back and forth to work for a few days while my car was being repaired. After my car was fixed, Kenny went with me to pick it up at the garage. The total cost for the repairs was close to $400.00. When I pulled out my wallet to pay the man, Kenny put $200.00 on the counter.

I said, "Kenny, what are you doing?"

He said, "I am paying my share."

"Kenny you don't have to do that," I said.

"I know that I don't have to, but I am going to."

I said, "Why?"

Kenny said, "Because, your car got damaged while you were taking *both of us* back and forth to work. So I want to pay my half of it."

I said, "Kenny, you do not have to give me anything."

But he insisted.

I was blown away by Kenny's generosity. I had never experienced anything like that before. Even to this day I have never experienced a more selfless act by anyone. At the same time, it didn't surprise me though, because Kenny was always a very generous person. But Kenny's generosity had nothing to do with the reason *why* he paid half of my bill. He paid half of my bill because he thought that it was just *the right thing to do.*

Kenny Jones has more integrity than any other person that I have met in my entire life, and he learned to live that way from his dad, Kenny Jones Sr., who died when Kenny was just 18 years old. His father always taught him to pay his own way, always work hard, and to always *do the right thing*.

LET'S BUILD SOMETHING

When it comes to doing the right thing, my dad lives by the same philosophy. When my dad came home I was excited to have him back in my life for many reasons. One of the biggest reasons was because my dad has always been great at fixing and building things.

I travel on the road a lot as a professional speaker and my schedule is always busy. When my dad and I want to take time out to connect with each other, we do what most other guys do - *we build stuff.*

Recently, Lisa and I needed a storage shed in our backyard, so my dad and I began to research the project to see exactly what we wanted to build. After we developed our plan and got our ideas approved by our homeowners' association, we started our project.

My dad absolutely loves to build stuff. Me on the other hand - I like to *break stuff,* so it's pretty hilarious to see us working together.

Every time we build things, my dad uses it as an opportunity to teach me new carpentry tips and techniques. Sometimes we joke around and other times we are serious. Every now and then, while we are working I lean over to my dad and say, "You know dad, learning how to build stuff is going to help me to become a better man some day!" Then he'd say something like, "That's right son. *Every man needs to know how to use his tools to build something."*

I said, "When you think about it dad, Jesus was a carpenter too, so these are important skills that I need to learn because you can never go wrong when you learn how to do something that Jesus did."

He said, "Yep son, that's true. Now get out of the way before you cut your hand off with that table saw."

Every time we work on a new project, my dad always says the same thing. *"Son, as long as you take the time to build something the right way, it will last forever."*

Since my dad has been home, he has taught me a lot. And I have learned not to argue with him about many things because he's usually right *most of the time.*

There are two main things that I have learned from working on projects with my dad. *First,* he was right when he said that, *"Every person needs to learn how to use their tools to build something."* And *second,* it doesn't matter what you're building - you could be building a storage shed, a swing set, a career, a marriage or even your dreams - *as long as you build it the right way, it will last forever.*

My dad and my friend Kenny Jones have a lot in common with each other. Kenny paid for half of my car repairs because he thought that it was *the right thing to do* at the time, and my dad believes in *building things the right way.*

Either way, they're both talking about the same thing: having integrity in everything that you build *if you want to build something* that will last forever.

BUILD YOUR LIFE

This book has been something that I have been *building* for many years, and it seems like it took me forever to finish it. One of the reasons why it took me so long was because I never stopped believing that my dad would be freed from prison one day, and I didn't want to release this book until I could celebrate his freedom as a part of the story.

Also, another reason why this book took me a while to complete was because the more I studied the impact that instant gratification has on our lives, the more I realized just how big of an impact technology has on everything that we do. I also discovered something else that was very interesting as I wrote this book - I discovered the power of *The Netflix Effect*. Advancements in technology and the growth of companies like Netflix have changed the way that people watch TV, because streaming TV shows *instantly* to watch TV whenever you want to has changed people in a major way.

Think about it, when you used to watch a TV show in the past, you couldn't just watch the next episode whenever you wanted to. You had to wait to watch it on TV if you wanted to see it.

The Netflix Effect has also changed what it's like when we go to the theatre to watch a movie. The average length of a movie is about two hours long, which means you only have about 120 minutes to emotionally connect with characters and the storyline of a movie. But today, the ability to watch an entire TV series online is changing the way our brains are wired. Today, when you watch your favorite show online, you get 30 to 100 hours of time to connect with characters in a story instead of the normal 30 minutes to two hours that we used to get when we watched a TV show or went to the movies.

I recently watched the TV show *Breaking Bad* on Netflix. Once I started watching it, I couldn't stop. When an episode ended, I couldn't wait to see the next one, and that TV show was all that I could think about. After I finished watching the final episode and the show was finally over, I didn't know what I was going to do with myself because I didn't want the show to end. I was so connected to the storyline and the characters in the show that I actually felt a little depressed when it was over. Guess what? Many other people have experienced those same feelings also.

Hollywood has recognized that *binge-watching* shows is changing the way we consume TV and movies. As a result, many writers in Hollywood have changed the way they write the scripts for each show. Let me give you an example...

A typical evening TV show lasts for about 60 minutes. If you were to sit down to watch a typical crime TV show in the past, the writers would use about 42 minutes to introduce the plot and solve the crime, and they would use the remaining 18 minutes of the show for commercials.

Because of *The Netflix Effect*, Hollywood has changed how they produce TV shows. Instead of using all 42 minutes of a show to solve a crime, they now use about 21 minutes to solve the crime and then they use the other 21 minutes to connect you to the backstory of the characters that are on the show.

Why do they want you to know the backstory of the characters? Because when you know a character's backstory, it helps you to connect and relate to them better. If you feel more connected to a character in a show, you are more likely to *binge-watch* that TV show once it's posted online, and the production companies will make more money. It's pretty simple to understand.

I'm not telling you all of this because I want to change how you watch TV or because I want you to stop binging on TV shows online. I am telling you this because I want you to understand that things are changing around you - fast. I am not mad about it either, because I love binging on my favorite shows. But you must understand how technology is changing your life and how it's impacting everything that you do.

When I realized how much technology is changing how we think and how we act, I changed my whole approach to writing this book. People have always told me that I had a great story and that my story should be written in a book someday, but I never wanted to write a book that was only about me - I don't need that type of attention. I get enough attention from what I do on stage as a motivational speaker.

So what did I do? I learned from the brilliant minds in Hollywood and I tried to write this book just like they write their scripts for TV shows and movies.

I learned something from *The Netflix Effect* and I combined it with what I learned from my great-grandmother, Mama Hattie. Mama Hattie passed down some pretty simple wisdom to everyone in our family about what it takes to run a business. She said that all you needed to do if you wanted to get people to buy what you are selling, is create something that people want, and something that people can't say no to.

Well, once I learned that people were committing so much time to *binge-watching* TV shows just because they were connecting to the backstory of the characters on those shows, it changed everything about how I wrote this book.

That's why this book begins with an introduction that tells you what the book is about, just like they do on TV shows. Then this book goes straight into my story for the first five chapters. After that, I placed *The 7 Steps to "C" Your Way Through,* directly in the middle of the book because the desire for instant gratification was the crime that I attempted to solve with this book. After that, I finished up with the rest of my story to keep you connected to my backstory.

Why am I telling you all of this? I am telling you this because the culture around us makes a difference in everything that we do. In this case, Netflix and other advancements in technology have produced a part of today's culture that impact all of us, and today's culture completely changed how I wrote this book. I wanted to write a book that could help you make progress in whatever you are building in your life, but I also wanted to write a book that you enjoyed reading. So I had to take today's culture into consideration when I wrote this book and I had to *come up with a plan* to write it in a way that connected with today's readers in a relevant way.

I am telling you this because *you also need to come up with a plan* if you want to make progress on your goals. You may be able to *binge-watch* a TV show, *but you can't binge-watch your life*. You can't just press a button to watch the *next episode* or instantly progress to the next chapter of your life, because *real things* never come *real fast*. And if they do, they won't last because there is no such thing as having *Overnight Success* in the areas of life that matter most.

BUILDING IT THE RIGHT WAY

You were designed to work hard and give your best effort. When you work hard *your effort will always increase your ability,* because your brain forms new pathways every time you do something. That's why when things are just *handed to you*, or when you *achieve something easily* without giving a lot of effort, it's difficult to recreate that success again - because you didn't earn it. And remember what Clyde Randall taught us – no matter how successful you are, *you can never fool yourself.*

The 7 Steps to "C" Your Way Through were designed as a blueprint to help you defeat the attraction that we all have to instant results and the idea of *Overnight Success.* The 7 steps were designed to help you experience progress in your life, and if you apply these 7 steps to whatever you are building, and if you remain consistent, these steps will help you to achieve the most powerful form of instant gratification that comes from *changing the way you see yourself.*

The 7 steps below will help you *transition to the next level* of whatever you're building and they will help you to achieve progress in the areas that *matter most to you,* even when the culture around you tries to distract you.

Culture will influence everything that you do if you aren't 100% intentional about how you think, how you act, and who you surround yourself with. You must be open to trying new experiences. When I listened to country music for the first time, it opened my mind. I realized that I liked country music and listening to country music *expanded* my mind and it forced me to try many new experiences. Your ability to be open to new experiences will directly influence your ability to *transition to the next level* in anything that you're building. When you become willing to step outside of culture to try new things, it's the first step in your ability to develop your own vision to build your own American Dream.

Clarity will help you to focus and develop a vision to see where you're going, and vision will help you to defeat the powerful pull that culture has in our lives by keeping you focused on where you're going. Remember, Tom the limo driver said, *"You can never be lost as long as you know where you're going."* The best thing you can do to experience great progress and build something great is to take the time to get focused on where you are going. You owe it to yourself to at least figure that out.

Commitment comes down to one thing - taking action. *You have to fight to keep your vision alive in your heart.* The main thing that will keep you fighting, consistently, is the feeling of progress. You will never make great progress if you are constantly connected to your devices. Practice metacognition by taking time out to unplug each day to think about what you're thinking about. *Take time to put your phone down long enough to visualize what you want, and then pick up your shovel and start digging.* Once you commit to taking action, help will always show up along the way - I promise. That's just how it goes.

Competency comes down to one thing: are you good at something? The most famous people in the world today have made a name for themselves because of one reason: *they had skills in something first*. The world will always make room for you if you have enough focus and dedication to build things the right way by working hard to grow your skills. But being good or having skills at isn't enough - if you want to build something amazing, you must continue to develop your emotional intelligence (EQ) and critical thinking skills. Remember, today's kids need to focus on mastering the fundamentals first, today's teens and young adults need to develop accountability and personal responsibility, and today's adults need to continue to grow all of their skills if they want to defeat the mindset of complacency.

Coaching will help you to grow your skills faster than your competition because coaches and mentors will help you to reduce your mistakes and build things that will last forever. If you want to truly benefit from good coaching, you must develop the most valuable skill that a human being can ever have – the ability to listen. Being able to listen to someone else will take your vision to the next level. *If you become coachable you will run better plays that will help you make greater progress in whatever you are building*.

Confidence isn't just about how you look - confidence comes from your ability to work hard, fight through adversity, and achieve progress no matter what. Nothing will help you to get a better grade on your *Morning Mirror Test* better than the feeling of confidence. If you are smart enough to identify the areas of your life that are crushing your confidence, and if you are courageous enough to do something about it, you will grow your confidence and you will change your life. Confidence will help you to trust your own abilities and you will develop a big advantage in life buy learning how to build things by trusting and following your own instincts.

Conviction will give you the courage to make decisions that would normally scare other people to death. Whether you're starting a new business, interviewing for a job, or asking someone to marry you - if you're willing to commit to the first *6 Steps of How to "C" Your Way Through*, your level of conviction will grow. When you *convince yourself first*, it's much easier to convince *others*. Some people call it *passion*, some people call it *conviction,* but regardless of what you call it, your conviction will make it easier for you to fight for what you're building when things get tough, and having conviction will force you to **remember what you're fighting for** when the culture around becomes a distraction.

Community is the most important step in the process because it reminds you that your life is not always about you. *Community* is the *Bonus C,* because once you start to build something great, you can't forget about the reasons *why* you were able to succeed. *Community* reminds you to remember your team at work, or your team on the field, or your team at home, and community reminds you to give credit for your success to the other people who helped you build your dream. Without them, your progress would never be possible. *Community* also reminds you that your drive and motivation to achieve your goals should never be *solely* based on you. Your motivation to build something great should be based on your purpose – a purpose to use your success to influence the lives of everyone else that you live, work, play, and serve with.

RISING ABOVE CULTURE

The moment that you decide to become intentional about everything that you build, everything around you will change. When you decide to take responsibility for the results in your life, you will grow your skills and you will also change the lives of others around you.

There were times in my life when I had no idea how to make it through some of the challenges that I faced. But I realized that it was okay to feel **hopeless and unsure** at times - because let's face it, *sometimes life is just flat-out hard to deal with.* It's okay to struggle to figure out exactly what your next move should be. But what's not okay, is when you make certain decisions **just because the culture around you expects you to.** You must chose to build *Your Dream,* not someone else's. The moment that you decide to live *Your American Dream*, on your terms, you will immediately rise above the culture around you and you will get *results that you want.*

Throughout my life, I constantly repeated the words, *faith, family, focus and fight,* over and over again because I never wanted to forget what I was fighting for. When I stood in that hospital parking lot on the night that I had to say goodbye to my Grandmother Gwendolyn, it changed how I saw the rest of my life. Even though I was lonely, scared and unsure of what to do next, and even though I though about ending my own life, several heroes stepped into my life to show me that they cared enough about me to hold me accountable for everything that I built.

The biggest thing that impacted my life was the words of that doctor at the hospital when he said, *"You can build any American Dream that you want to as long as you do three things."*

Never become a victim.
Take responsibility for your life.
Never expect anyone to give you anything for free.

Those 3 things changed my life. And today I *get to* live an amazing life that allows me to pursue my dreams, love my family, make a difference in the lives of others, and try my best to honor God in everything that I do. *That's how I choose to live my story.*

Today, when I step on stage to speak I am always the guy with the microphone in the front of the room. When I step off stage, people always say things to me like, "Wow, you have an amazing story, you have such a great *backstory!"* Sometimes it frustrates me when I hear that because I am driven by a purpose that motivates me to help you live *your story*, and I want to help you to believe in your own *backstory*. I don't want you to be so caught up in my story that you miss the biggest part of my message, which is, *everyone has a story*.

My story isn't great, my story is just *different*.

You aren't the only person that needs to realize the power of your own *backstory*. Teams and organizations need to do the same thing because every day, consumers make purchasing decisions based on the story behind certain brands, and organizations that are intentional enough to tell the *backstory* of their brand while they build their products will have a better chance of connecting with consumers in this information age that we live in today.

Customers make purchases at the blink of an eye and consumers buy products based on their instincts, so companies must do a great job of promoting their products while *also telling their backstory* if they want to dominate the market. That's why *The Netflix Effect* has changed how TV shows are being produced today – *because it's all about the backstory.* Writers in Hollywood have already caught on to this secret, but sports teams, corporations, and even families, also need to realize this because your backstory is your *true identity*. You must keep this in mind if you want to build something... *the right way*. It doesn't matter if you are an individual, an organization, a team or even a family, if you embrace your backstory, everyone else will too. But first, you must believe that your story matters.

FINAL THOUGHTS

I have always believed that I was here for a reason. Ever since I was a young kid I've had a vision to help others and I wanted to help people be more positive. Because of that, I am constantly on the lookout for positive story's to share with people - which means that *I am always looking for the best stories around me* every day.

Because I am constantly on the lookout for positive stories around me everyday, my mindset is programmed to only see the *great stories* around me. So what do you think I see everyday? That's right, I only see positive things.

You have probably experienced this in your life too. Have you ever decided to purchase a pair of shoes and then immediately once you purchased them, you began to notice how many people around you had the *same shoes*?

It doesn't just happen with shoes either, it also happens with cars. Every time you purchase a new car, *or even when you start to think about buying a certain car*, almost immediately, you began to see that type of car everywhere that you go. People always wonder why this happens and the reason is simple: once you put something into your mind, that's all you will ever see, because it becomes a part of your mindset.

You will always see whatever you focus on.

If you choose to focus on the good things in life, you will see good things. If choose to focus on negative thoughts, then negativity is all that you will ever see.

The moment that you choose to focus on believing that your *backstory* matters, and the moment that you choose to believe that you are here for a reason, you will start to experience the best form of *Overnight Success* that's possible - you will instantly **change the way you see yourself.**

~ ~ ~ ~ ~

About 1 year after my father was released from prison, his life was going great. One afternoon as I sat in a meeting, I received a text message from my dad that said, *"Morris, I am with my parole officer right now. They may be taking me back to jail. I just took a drug test and the results came back positive for opiates and heroin in my system."*

That's all the text message said. Right away I knew what it meant - my dad was going back to jail... *instantly.* I knew that my dad would be taken back to prison for the remaining 70 plus years of his prison sentence because he violated his parole agreement.

I began to freak out.

When I replied to his text to try to figure out what happened, he did not respond to me.

In my mind, I knew what that meant - he had already gone back to jail.

When I thought about all of the work that we did to free him from prison, I said to myself, *"Why would he do anything to jeopardize his freedom like that? Why would he use drugs?"*

After a few moments, I finally got another text message from him that said, *"I pleaded with the officer and I told him that I did not take any drugs, so he is going to let me sit here for an hour so that I can take another test."*

Within moments after receiving that text message, I received my final text message from him that read, *"I just failed the second drug test. I think they're calling the police to take me back to prison."*

I was crushed.

After a couple of hours went by, I didn't hear from him again and I immediately started to think about his cell phone, his wallet, his truck, his apartment, and all of his things that I would need to take care of because he was gone... *again.*

My whole world was crashing around me again.

I left the meeting that I was in and I drove home to talk to Lisa and break the news to her about my dad. I wasn't sure how I was going to explain thing to her.

As I turned into my neighborhood, I planned on sitting in my driveway to cool-off for a while before I went into my house to tell her the news.

As I began to drive down my street, I couldn't believe what I saw in front of my house - it was my dad's pickup truck. My dad was at my house!

I parked my car as fast as I could and I ran into the house. After I ran through the door, I saw my dad sitting on the living room floor playing with Baby Dori. I was so excited to see him, but I was also angry at the same time. I had to leave the room just to calm down for a minute before I could talk to him.

When I walked back in I said, "Dad, what happened? Why didn't you text me back? I thought that they took you back to jail!"

He said, "Oh, I am sorry. I just came straight to your house when I left and I didn't think to look at my phone again. I figured I'd see you when I got here."

I said, "Dad, that was *3 hours ago*, I have been worried sick about you. I thought they took you back to jail! And why did you fail your drug screen anyway - I *KNOW* you aren't using drugs are you? Dad, what's going on?"

He said, "Morris, are you serious! Of course I am not using drugs. I wouldn't do anything to jeopardize my freedom like that!"

I looked at him like he was crazy because I still didn't understand why he failed two drug tests. I gave him a weird look that made it clear to him that I needed some type of explanation. So he looked at me and he said, "You know that poppy seed bread that Lisa gave me the other day?"

I said, "Yeah."

He said, "Well, I guess it caused me to have 2 false positives on my drug screen because they thought that I was using heroin or other opiate drugs because poppy seed is what those drugs are made out of."

I said, "Are you serious?"

I couldn't believe what he was telling me. I had heard about plenty of cases in the news where people were sent to prison for having false-positive drug screens.

So I said, "Dad, they are supposed to take you straight to jail if you fail a drug test. Not only did you fail the first one, but you actually failed *two drug screens*, and they let you go? How could that be possible?"

Dad said, "I don't know, I guess God was on my side today. The parole officer said that he actually believed me when I told him that I wasn't using drugs, so he gave me a couple of weeks to let the poppyseed bread get completely out of my system before they test me again."

I said, "What? What? That never happens. I have never heard of a probation officer doing something like that before!"

He said, "I know, me either - I guess I was just pretty blessed today!"

So my dad went back a couple of weeks later to take a *third* drug test, and of course, he passed with flying colors.

I couldn't wait to call Jason Babicka to tell him what happened. Jason was my friend from Pittsburgh who I introduced to you in chapter 12 - he is the amazing guy that lost all of the weight, changed his life, and became a living-legend - yeah... *that guy.* Anyway, every time Jason goes back home to visit his family in Pittsburgh, his dad usually sends me a homemade nut-roll and a poppy seed roll. And they are delicious! Well, my dad ate some of Mr. Babicka's poppy seed roll and that's what caused him to fail his drug test... *twice!*

When I told Jason about what happened to my dad because of the last poppy seed roll that his dad sent to us, Jason and I both laughed about it, even though we both knew that things could have ended up much differently for my father.

After the day was over and I finally connected the dots, I realized something - I realized that the same poppy seed plant that produces heroin, is the same poppy seed plant that almost caused my dad Chuck to be taken away to prison again, and it's the same poppy seed plant that changed the streets of New York with the introduction of Heroin, the same heroin that my biological father Billy sold on the streets of New York when I was born. I couldn't believe that this one little plant was causing so much drama in my life!

When I stepped back to see how ironic the situation was, I called Jason and I said, "Hey, I need to change my order with your dad for your next trip home. Next time, just tell him to send us *two nut-rolls.* He can keep those poppy seeds to himself."

My Mother Darlene

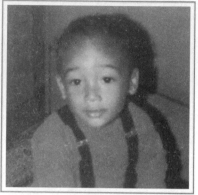

Me As a Baby

My Home In WV

My Angel Gwendolyn

Me and Dad Chuck

Me and Dad Chuck

Speaking Already

Me and Aunt Dot

My Baby Lisa

NYC Engagement

At The Today Show

My Grandma Pauline

Nov. 23, 2006 - 9:00 PM
I had a conversation on the telephone with Morris.

One of the things we talked about is the book he is writing. The book will be his life story. He hopes to go around the places in the world where he can speak about his life. His purpose for doing this is to help someone else realize life is worth living you can make it no matter what the circumstance are. Always put God First! Go Morris Go!

Aunt Dot

Aunt Dot has always supported me. She wrote this letter after I pitched my first book idea to her. It says:

November 23rd, 2006 - 9:00pm

"I had a conversation on the telephone with Morris. One of the things we talked about is the book he is writing. The book will be his life story. He hopes to go around the places in the world where he can speak about his life. His purpose for doing this is to help someone else realize life is worth living & you can make it no matter what the circumstances are. Always put God first! Go Morris Go!" Aunt Dot

With My Mothers Side of The Family

With My Fathers Side of The Family

1st Visit to Mom's Grave

Jason After 1/2 Marathon

My Beautiful Bride

A Very Happy Husband

Grandma's Wedding Dance

AJ, Keenan & Germaine

Stop Texting and Driving!

Speaking at Notre Dame

Speaking at the NBA Rookie Transition Program

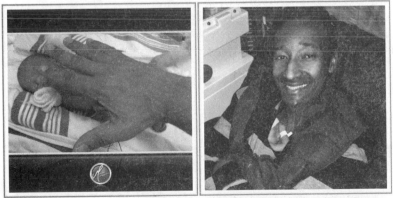

A Very Tiny Baby Dori　　　**Kangaroo Care For The Baby**

Look At Those Cheeks!

Baby Dori Getting Bigger

Pappy's Coming Home

At Elevation Church

A Completed Family

Let's Change The World!

OVERNIGHT SUCCESS »

ACKNOWLEDGEMENTS

Pastor Hershel Walker, Donald Scott, Kenny Jones Sr., Pastor Wesley Dobbs, Larry Mazza, Rich Tribino, Dave Anderson, Walter Bond, Mark Mosley, Horace Tucker, Jeff Allison, Pastor Farrell Lemmings, Pastor Larry Titus, Pastor Steven Furtick, Pastor Joel Delph & Steve Cutright
(In Order Of Appearance)

"Man achieves nothing on his own. Every guy needs many men in his life to show him how to run the plays." #Touchdown

Roberta Moore
"Thank you for loving me and always pushing me to reach for a better life. You are the best #MamaBear that a person could have!"

Andy Johnson
"Men love to fight and boys love to pretend. Thanks for dreaming and pretending with me when we were kids because today we get to live our dreams and fight together as men."

Damian, Germaine, Chad, Gerard and Tyrone
"There's power in numbers. We lifted each other up to be better together than we could've been on our own." #TheCrew

LeAnn Brown
"Thank you for helping to keep the vision for Overnight Success alive in my heart. Your steadfast commitment to believing in this project helped to keep me focused on delivering a message that was true to who I am."

Kenny Jones
"You encouraged and inspired me to produce this book while you were facing some of your biggest challenges. You are a true inspiration."

Josh Cope
"If your salary was based on the way that you impact others, you would be the wealthiest man in the world. You are the greatest encourager that I have ever known. And to think, people always wonder why I am so inspired!"

Horace Tucker
"Your faith in my vision opened doors for me that continue to reap dividends today. Thank you for being such a strong catalyst in helping me to develop my message and for showing me how to do it #TheRightWay!"

Janet Faulk
"Thank you for your continued support of Overnight Success. You never stopped believing in this book and the importance of this story being told. You inspired me to bring this book to life."

Mike Rozgony
"I have never met another person that cares about helping others like you do. It has been amazing to run the plays with you and I am excited about the rest of the story that's yet to come!"

Nick Connor
"Some people have few talents and some have many. You are one of the most talented guys that I've ever met and your commitment to defeating the attraction of Overnight Success will continue to change the world!"

The Allen and Machesky Family
"We never would have thought years ago that our friendship would position us to make such great memories and such an impact in the lives of many families. Thank you for being a part of our family!"

Bryan Edwards
"To one of the brightest minds that I have ever met. Thanks for allowing me to bounce these ideas off of you - you made this book better. You make me... #Better."

Jason Babicka
"The excitement that I have for you simply can not be measured. It has been a pure joy to watch you become a #CultureCrasher and use your testimony to change lives. You are a true inspiration!"

Brad Hibbs Sr., Mo McNeely, Kevin Kucish, Gary Graham and Paul Dumont
"You took an interest in a group of young kids that no one else cared about and you exposed us to a brand new world. What you did for us in Barrackville will never be forgotten!"

Jermaine Davis
"Your wisdom shortened my learning curve and it changed everything about this project! Your coaching single-handedly took this book to a whole new level!""

ALL TYPO'S IN THIS BOOK SIMPLY REFLECT HOW IMPERFECT I AM.

PLEASE BE PATIENT WITH ME AS I CONTINUE TO GROW :)